Resisting State Violence

Resisting State Violence

Radicalism, Gender, and Race in U.S. Culture

Joy James

Foreword by Angela Y. Davis

University of Minnesota Press
Minneapolis
London

Published by the University of Minnesota Press
111 Third Avenue South, Suite 290, Minneapolis, MN 55401–2520
Printed in the United States of America on acid-free paper

Library of Congress Cataloging-in-Publication Data

James, Joy, 1958–
    Resisting state violence : radicalism, gender, and race in U.S.
culture / Joy James ; foreword by Angela Y. Davis.
        p.   cm.
    Includes bibliographical references and index.
    ISBN 0-8166-2812-2 (hc)
    ISBN 0-8166-2813-0 (pb)
    1. Racism—United States.   2. Violence—United States.
3. Minority women—United States—Political activity.   4. Political
culture—United States.   5. United States—Race relations.
I. Title.
E184.A1J27   1996
305.8′00973—dc20   96-19868

The University of Minnesota is an
equal-opportunity educator and employer.

Contents

Part III. Cultural Politics: Black Women and Sexual Violence

Part IV. Teaching, Community, and Political Activism

Foreword
Angela Y. Davis

Recent debates on the role of the public intellectual have not always explored the complex process of linking critical intellectual work with collective organizing practices and consequently do not always reflect an appreciation of the role of the political activist. In this provocative collection of essays on state violence, Joy James foregrounds the work of radical activists during the decade of the 1980s. As an actor herself in the movements she examines, her approach to political activism is one that demands incisive critical analyses, while her intellectual work is deeply informed by questions that insist on radical structural and personal transformation.

These essays serve as a powerful reminder to those who uncritically locate radical activism in the sixties (and sometimes seventies) that the era of Ronald Reagan was not monolithically conservative. James offers us a panoramic view of social movements headquartered in New York during the eighties that addressed local as well as national and international issues. She moves from antiracist organizing to solidarity campaigns with movements in Latin America, the Caribbean, southern Africa, and the Middle East. Her analysis compellingly links multiple forms of state violence—domestic and imperialist—with sexual violence, focusing on the state processes that privatize sexual violence.

Such an acknowledgment of the resistance strategies of the eighties—with all their embedded contradictions—is particularly important in these contemporary times when conservatism has solidified an ideological terrain that renders it more difficult than ever to deploy radical strategies of resistance. At a time when we need to move beyond the black/white paradigm of race relations, beyond masculinist approaches to antiracist activism, and when histories of political activism in the eighties should point the way toward complex and multiple understandings of racism and antiracist activism, racism is narrowly represented as the historical segregation happily overcome with the prodding of civil-rights struggles on the one hand or as a focused assault on black men on the other. Thus, for example, hegemonic representations of affirmative action increasingly define it as a form of reverse discrimination, while such black community organizing efforts as the Nation of Islam's Million Man March tend to place gender hierarchies at the heart of antiracist resistance.

Joy James's analyses emphasize how complex transformative struggles become if we take seriously the challenge to consider how deeply our personal and political lives are shaped by myriad forms of racialist, gendered, and class-inflected violence. At a time when activists and scholars struggle arduously to create models of organizing and research that allow us to hold race, class, gender, and sexuality in creative tension, James's work is a pioneering contribution. Her productive syntheses of vast amounts of material are drawn from contemporary theory, historical literature, current organizing practices, and from her own personal and political history. As she moves from theory to political activism to pedagogy, she is always very much at home, staging bold, often splendidly disrespectful, but always insightful encounters across these borders.

Preface / Reading . . .
Resistance . . .

Written from 1989 to 1995, *Resisting State Violence: Radicalism, Gender, and Race in U.S. Culture* theorizes contemporary politics and activism. Its four parts examine political theory and language, domestic and foreign policies, culture, and education. Part I, "Rage and Resistance Lessons: Political Life and Theory," contains three essays. The Introduction, which describes my use of the terms *radicalism, state,* and *state violence,* provides a brief ethnographic-autobiographical account of political life and lessons among New York City activists in the 1980s. "Erasing the Spectacle of Racialized State Violence," chapter 1, contends that postmodern Foucauldian theories of punishment deflect from the prevalence of racist violence in U.S. policies and progressive resistance to such violence. Its critique of historical lynching and contemporary policing and death-penalty politics traces the trajectory of U.S. political life and racialized violence. Chapter 2, "Radicalizing Language and Law: Genocide, Discrimination, and Human Rights," examines language and human-rights conventions in relation to U.S. policies, arguing that conventional "race" language creates another form of erasure by conceptually severing state racism from genocidal violence.

Part II, "Colonial Hangovers: U.S. Policies at Home and Abroad," begins with chapter 3, "Hunting Prey: The U.S. Invasion of Panama," a critique of the December 1989 bombing of Panama as part of an "antidrug" war. Another American nation with which the United States has had volatile relationships is the topic of the following chapter: "The Color(s) of Eros: Cuba as American Obsession." Chapter 4 contrasts State Department and conservative depictions of Cuba with free-trade advocates', progressive activists', and Havana intellectuals' perspectives on contemporary Cuban society and political, ethnic, and national identities. Concluding Part II, "Border-Crossing Alliances: Japanese and African American Women in the State's Household," chapter 5, speculates on the potential of progressive coalitions of "women of color" to cross ethnic and class divisions and to confront state "colonization" of women.

Dehumanizing representations normalize and rationalize violence in foreign policy. It is important to examine how such representations in national culture pathologize "blackness" and sexuality to portray those most vulnerable to violence as its carriers. Part III, "Cultural Politics: Black Women and Sexual Violence," explores sensationalist depictions of sexual violence and black women. Chapter 6, "Anita Hill, Clarence Thomas, and Gender Abstractions," examines sexual politics in the 1991 Clarence Thomas confirmation hearings. "Symbolic Rage: Prosecutorial Performances and Racialized Representations of Sexual Violence," chapter 7, recounts a family tragedy of domestic and sexual violence subsumed by state ritualized punishment. The ways in which racial politics and state prosecution shape women's coalitions on interracial rape cases is the subject of chapter 8, "Coalition Cross Fire: Antiviolence Organizing and Interracial Rape," which focuses on women's organizing around the 1989 Central Park rape case.

The final part, "Teaching, Community, and Political Activism," analyzes progressive antiracist and antisexist education and activism within a neoconservative climate. Chapter 9, "'Discredited Knowledge' in the Nonfiction of Toni Morrison," investigates the Nobel laureate's views on Africanisms and ancestors and the role of community in antiracist American intellectualism. "Teaching, Intersections, and the Integration of Multiculturalism," chapter 10, advocates an integrative analysis for more comprehensive, critical paradigms and pedagogies in education. Chapter 11, "Gender, Race, and Radicalism: Reading the Autobiographies of Native and African American Women Activists," discusses pedagogy in a comparative study of the life narratives of movement women confronting state oppression and contemporary students reflecting on their relationships to liberation politics.

The conclusion, "United Nations Conventions, Antiracist Feminisms, and Coalition Politics," considers political formations and organizing that emphasize human-rights activism and covenants. It argues for multiracial, international coalitions based on human-rights conventions as indispensable for strategic, progressive interventions against repression and violence.

Acknowledgments

A younger generation of activist-intellectuals—Yifat Susskind, Katarina Gruber, Chris Selig, Cara Page, LaRaye, Ariff Hajee, Shira Katz, Nathan Hale, and Ariana Napier, former University of Massachusetts students, now active in Israel, Palestine, Germany, New York City, and the Bay Area—inspired me to write and teach with some accountability to justice, radicalism, and compassion. Before I, as an academic, encountered their work and that of Mohawk activist-scholar Donna Goodleaf, an older generation of New York activist-intellectuals—such as Women for Racial and Economic Equality organizers Dorothy Burnham and Norma Spector, MADRE's Vivian Stromberg, as well as National Alliance against Racist and Political Repression's Charlene Mitchell—instructed me in political living and long-distance running with their marathon patience and commitments to justice.

Support from academic critics (who have also struggled as progressive activists) enabled me to turn insights gained from intergenerational radicals into a readable text. It was at the suggestion of Janice Raymond that I began this book. Lewis Gordon, Zillah Eisenstein, Elizabeth Hadley Freydberg, and John Ehrenberg offered helpful comments. Angela Davis provided a haven in the hills to complete the manuscript.

This book benefited from the comments of the University of Minnesota Press's anonymous reader and the editorial skills of Louisa Castner. The Department of Ethnic Studies, Karen Moreira, and Evelyn Hu DeHart at the University of Colorado at Boulder also provided important assistance.

Through the difficulties of writing and rewriting, my family's faith—that of my mother Minnie James, aunt Mattie Bailey, and sister Barbara James—along with the spirit-kinship of Madrina, Rick, and Sally MacNichol, sustained me. Sister Patti O'Neal's (1940-1995) public rage against racism and private rage with breast cancer also taught me unforgettable lessons about living and dying with fear and stubborn will.

To these and other friends, human-rights "agitators," constructive critics, and teachers—my thanks.

I

Rage and Resistance Lessons:
Political Life and Theory

Introduction

In his work, *In Theory,* Aijaz Ahmad contends that "debates about culture and literature on the Left no longer presume a labour movement as the ground on which they arise; 'theory' is now seen . . . as a 'conversation' among academic professionals."[1] Indeed, academic debates about culture and politics appear frequently to sever discussions of ethnicity and race, gender, class, and sexuality from the national, ethnic, women's, workers', and gay-liberation movements. Of course, in academe, where self/text preoccupation and individualism may marginalize or psychologize these political struggles, conversation deradicalizes as it inbreeds, while the intellectual-interrogator takes precedence over the activist-intellectual. People who resist impoverishment and violence at times seem discouraged by elite academic discourse, the low threshold of political courage it inspires, as well as its truncated visions of radical change.

Moving beyond introspection or interrogation of texts about violence into conversations that highlight confrontational challenges to violence requires emphasizing the works of peace and justice activists. More than academic texts, the narratives and analyses offered here are influenced by New York City activists, among whom I counted myself, who in the 1980s organized around challenging racism and sexism in U.S. domestic and foreign policies. Rather than being self- or text-referential, the autobiographical political experiences woven into this writing point to the critical thought of radical organizers who differentiated between critique of and confrontation with state violence and who were unsatisfied until the former had moved closer to the latter.

Some postmodern cultural critics are wont to redefine *interrogation of texts* as a form of political activism. Yet even these "left" or "post-left" intellectuals often seem constrained by elite theories that are ill informed about the concrete political battles fought outside of congressional civility. This book departs from such positionings. First, it concurs with Barbara Christian's assertion that theory not rooted in communal practice is elitist.[2] Second, it contends that political or ethical theory that is oblivious to the specificity of people's struggles for dignified existence free of violence, poverty, and domination shows a myopic insularity (rather than universality). *Resisting State Violence* rejects the projection of detached thinking as "subversive"—a projection that obscures the conservative tendencies of elitist theory as well as its creative plasticity in masking acquiescence to hierarchies. Rather, this book "theorizes," to use Christian's verb, the conditions of those most vulnerable to state violence, centering its discussions on radical interventions in U.S. policies, culture, and classroom instruction. Contending that political and ethical reflections on the policies and activism (re)structuring American life dictate a writing unrestricted by the discourse of elitism or an academic carceral (to use a term from Michel Foucault, which I will discuss at length in chapter one), this writing locates resistance in political acts responsive and responding to political crises. On the basis of the specificity of U.S. struggles, questioning the limitations of U.S. democracy, this work theorizes the possibilities of expanding democratic practices by curtailing state abuses, particularly the racialized and sexualized manifestations of violence that victimize "people of color," blacks, women, and the poor.

To emphasize the ways in which individuals and groups in political coalitions and classroom instruction counter state violence, I highlight the work of radicals; consequently, voting patterns, electoral politics, and lobbying receive little attention in this work. That is not to argue that these are inconsequential expressions of U.S. politics. Rather, I contend that these political phenomena have been studied extensively and abundantly elsewhere (including their shifting importance to the majority of U.S. citizens; most Americans—with the exception of the Christian right—fail to vote or lobby consistently). What is rarely reported are political expressions from the margins concerning U.S. policies, and the state violence embedded in those policies.

American political discourse marginalizes critical reviews of radical resistance and state violence. Given the pervasiveness of conservative and liberal ideologies, we rarely consider the democratic means and objectives of radicalism confronting systemic oppression and promoting economic, racial, and sexual justice. In addition, the oxymoron "radical right" obscures the interests that neoconservatives and reactionaries have in state dominance, which is exercised through economic exploitation, police violence, prison executions, military bombings, and covert wars. Authorized or sanctioned by the U.S. government—its agencies and the constituents of state hegemony such as the mainstream media—state violence and coercion remain invisible to most Americans.

Socialist Ralph Miliband's critique of democracy in advanced capitalist societies offers a useful tool for this discussion of state violence.[3] According to Miliband, people in nations such as the United States "live in the shadow of the state," as political actors attempt to influence or represent "the state's power and purpose" in order to obtain its sanction and support (1). We can add that activists also attempt to subvert state practices: radicals challenge its conservative measures while reactionaries undermine its liberal reforms. Despite the state's power, its abilities to reward, and its willingness to penalize (radical) actors, the state "as a subject of political study," as Miliband observes, "has long been very unfashionable" (1). Those who engage in this unfashionable work also study racial and sexual violence to deepen their critical perspectives on coercive state politics. Developing a unifying theory of the state, the most relevant thinkers address economic, racial, and sexual repression in a culture marked by increasing polarizations of wealth and poverty, privilege and disenfranchisement.[4]

Examining power and domination within the U.S. government, culture, and civil society, *Resisting State Violence* describes and analyzes struggles against dehumanizing policies. Referring to Miliband's language about the state system, I investigate repressive elements of the state apparatus, including government(s), military and police, judiciary, and administrative bureaucracy. I explore how the state is racialized and racializes policies and populations to police violence based on nationality, ethnicity, gender, sexuality, and class. Although Miliband distinguishes the state system from the political system of electoral parties and seemingly nonpolitical organizations such as the church, media, corporations, and civic groups, it is not always feasible to maintain a sharp division between the state and civil society, particularly in a racist culture. Without formally sharing in state power, social and ethnic groups can contribute to the erasure or validation of state violence and government misconduct. Frequently in the United States, where racial fears and hostilities are manipulated, state and civil society seem to speak in one voice regarding policing, punishment, and violence as the media, educational institutions, and private citizens are organized to further state hegemony in spite of their autonomy from state apparatuses.

Examining repressive U.S. foreign and domestic policies as well as antiviolence resistance, this work focuses on antiracist and feminist praxis. These arguments and understandings are, of course, like those of every other writer, filtered through the subjective lens of my own political experiences. Unlike the work of every other writer, however, this book is influenced by radical activism that led me to align with politics and people against whom the United States deployed repressive measures.

Political Life Stories

During the 1980s, while pursuing a graduate degree in political philosophy from a conservative Jesuit institution, I lived and worked in an international city; with experiences gained off campus, I supplemented my academic education with lessons in progressive radicalism. The most difficult nonacademic instructions—the hardest to learn, yet easiest, once learned, to remember—were the political lessons about violence destroying or crippling individuals and communities. Cities such as New York can teach a lot about violence, providing information and insights on both violence and resistance that are usually denied or restricted in other parts of the United States. An example is late-night alternative radio, such as the Pacifica station, WBAI, which introduced its listeners to Joanne Grant's work on civil-rights leader Ella Baker; Christopher Simpson's research into U.S. recruitment and employment of Nazis after World War II; and ex-CIA agent John Stockwell's disclosures of CIA-directed death squads and contras in Latin America and southern Africa. Free or donation-only forums in community centers and schools enabled attendees to hear representatives from Palestinian women's groups as well as Noam Chomsky's critique of fascism, state terrorism, and Israel's proxy-state relationship with the U.S. government in the Middle East. Other gatherings allowed interaction with women and activists from Nicaragua and El Salvador. During the height of the U.S.-funded contra war in Nicaragua and the Salvadoran government's use of paramilitary death squads, through the organizing of groups such as MADRE and the Committee in Solidarity with the People of El Salvador (CISPES), concerned U.S. Americans could meet and speak with those directly suffering from and surviving violent repression. Obtaining information on Latin American organizations as well as the Namibian independence movement through the South West African People's Organization (SWAPO), the African National Congress (ANC), or the Palestine Liberation Organization (PLO)—all labeled "terrorist" organizations by the State Department during Ronald Reagan's eight-year presidency—was fairly easy in New York. The contradictory nature of U.S. democracy and national security pursued through violent foreign policies was sobering; the most difficult, nerve-wracking lessons, however, came from studying policies at home. Attempting to respond effectively to local violence, one inevitably faced the blurred yet abrasive distinctions between social work and resistance, survival and freedom, and the contradictions and divisions of the left.

In New York, as in other cities and towns around the country, resistance took place in schools, religious houses, and union halls. American trade unions played a pivotal role in supporting the Coalition of South African Trade Unions during the apartheid regime. The sanctuary movement harbored Salvadorans escaping death squads during the Reagan administration. Progressive churches, whose work is largely overshadowed in the media today by the ascendancy of conservatism, fundamentalism, and the Christian Coalition, were educational and political sites. For instance, more than a few of Brooklyn's churches proved to be houses of radicalism. Park Slope's United Methodist Church turned its pulpit over to Nicaraguan president Daniel Ortega one Sunday in 1987. Several miles away, on Brooklyn's downtown Atlantic Avenue, the Pentecostal House of the Lord Church held SISSA (Sisters in Solidarity with the Sisters of South Africa) meetings. Members of the Pentecostal congregation were also prominent in city demonstrations and acts of civil disobedience, protesting U.S. support of apartheid in South Africa, as well as brutality by the New York

Police Department (NYPD) and "lynch-mob" killings in New York's Howard Beach and Bensonhurst neighborhoods.

Resistance against state violence and control, based on community or political organizing, was not always expressed without contradictions embodying other forms of violence and debasement. For example, the conflicts that erupted in the late 1980s in response to racial attacks on black males in Howard Beach and Bensonhurst both inspired and alienated potential activists. Perhaps the apex of ideal political organizing and coalition building occurred in a multiracial demonstration of ten thousand who gathered at downtown City Hall and Gracie Mansion during the administration of Mayor Edward Koch in response to the Howard Beach beatings of several black men and the killing of a black male youth. (Some argue that Koch's role in racially polarizing the city, one sharply frayed by racist attacks in the mid-to-late 1980s, helped to lead to the election of New York City's first African American mayor, David Dinkins.) The chants and gibes—"Whose streets?! Our streets!" and "No Justice . . . No Peace!"—hurled at police during later street demonstrations, which the NYPD could not always contain, spoke to the resistance embodied in the "Days of Outrage," in which radical antiracists called for a general strike to shut down New York City and paralyze Wall Street, the international financial district. The global strike never sufficiently materialized. In participating in Days of Outrage demonstrations, one realized that the march security guards, despite their macho posturing at times, could not protect individuals from police on horseback who rode on sidewalks in fashionable eastside Manhattan across from the UN to break up peaceful protests. Nor could security members guard against other forms of violence from provocateurs within the demonstration or march. When police began to club peaceful demonstrators attempting to walk across the Brooklyn Bridge during evening rush hour—this obstruction would have had an immense impact, drawing a considerable number of New Yorkers into the contestation over racial equality and safety—demonstrators fought back. Their responses were markedly different from those of protesters beaten when Martin Luther King Jr. tried to lead peaceful marchers across the Edmund Pettus bridge. These unarmed, mostly male marchers at the head of the demonstrators peppered their self-defense with calls of "women and children to the rear." African American women on and near the bridge argued that they could protect themselves and were in no need of such instructions from male demonstrators.

Still, the issue of safety for those engaged in political dissent erupted in other aspects of the Brooklyn Bridge demonstration. During the march to the bridge, a small group of African American male youths menaced male and female protesters, especially female and white marchers, with driving irons. Some saw this harassment of antiracist demonstrators as typifying the violence of alienated young black males. Others, maintaining that it was unlikely that the youths were members of golf clubs, saw them as provocateurs paid by NYPD renegade or rogue cops to destabilize the march. How one read the roles and relationships of provocateurs, police, and protesters shaped one's consciousness about the riskiness of political struggles and the violence arrayed against radical progressives. The coverage of the confrontation at the bridge by local television news and most media commentary did not put these issues in sharp relief or raise ethical questions about how one responds to racist violence, self-defense, and policing to maintain "law and order."

With Noam Chomsky's and Edward Herman's work on manufacturing consent or with common sense and life experiences in mind, progressives considered most media sources not fully reliable in their coverage of racism and antiracist radicalism. Participation in organizing efforts and demonstrations, as well as the city's disturbing volume of diverse, conflicting information, however, encouraged new forms of literacy enabling one to read between the lines. This political literacy meant that engaged readers would often survey the *New York Times*'s coverage of the Days of Outrage or protests over South Africa or Cuba and then discuss and work with organizers around these issues. Such readers routinely traveled in the evening or on weekends uptown to Harlem's Harriet Tubman Public School (such journeys repoliticized Duke Ellington's direction to "Take the A Train") so that local activists would dialogue with representatives of nations debating the levels of repression and resistance in their countries.

The contempt some black women activists expressed for the political speech of those who "only knew what they read in a book" galvanized me to become more than an informed, sophisticated spectator. All my political lessons, even my disagreements and clashes with political organizers, were instructive as I learned to read with specificity through working with or watching the work of the National Alliance against Racist and Political Repression, Women for Racial and Economic Equality, MADRE, Brooklyn Women's Martial Arts, the Black Women's Health Project, the December

12th Movement's Days of Outrage, and the many groups doing solidarity and support work with liberation movements in southern Africa, Latin America, the Caribbean, and Palestine. Sometimes I focused on the work with the transitory attention of a dilettante, sometimes with the staying power of a marathon runner.

Most radical activists read passionately on the run, while organizing and attending political and educational forums and demonstrations, or lobbying for legislation. Waiting for subways, buses, planes, speakers, or cultural workers provided time for reflection. Sometimes the relentless intensity and pervasiveness of violence in governmental policies led to simplistic readings as well as extreme bitterness and isolation. Yet, in general, the radicals I knew transmitted not only political intelligence but also intense feelings, sometimes bigoted and chauvinistic, most times loving and with enormous intelligence and commitment. That intelligence allowed them to understand contradictions and work for coalitions, exhibiting a political acumen often unacknowledged in most mainstream media or academic representations of street radicalism. The immediacy of the political work, particularly work struggling toward saving lives or grieving deaths, meant that one studied nearly every moment. People "read" while marching, standing, or praying at memorials in the mid-1980s for women leaders such as ANC representative Dulce September, who was assassinated by South African paramilitary attachés in Belgium; or for Nicaraguan Sandinista UN representative Nora Astorga, who died from cancer; or at rallies celebrating Nelson Mandela's freedom. Such work meant hours of traveling and watching. Reading often entailed complex contradictions in sites where there were no simple lessons: hundreds standing in black Brooklyn streets in the interracial overflow of mourners at Yusef Hawkins's funeral service following the Bensonhurst "lynching" listened while the church's outdoor speakers piped Nation of Islam's Minister Louis Farrakhan's eulogy whose gentle calls for peace and brotherhood mocked his reputation for fiery, hate-filled oratory.

Economic Violence and Political Conservatism

The June 1995 Supreme Court ruling that Connecticut need not provide for its indigent reflects the "new federalism," as well as the moral and state positioning of the previous and current decades that is marked by punitive discourse and rationalized indifference to the needs of the poor. A decade before the new federalism had caught on, Reaganite politicians authorized the Human Welfare and Social Service Administration to list ketchup as a vegetable in order to cut food assistance to poor mothers on Aid to Families with Dependent Children (AFDC); these same politicians offered the term *benign neglect* (a term coined by Democratic Senator Daniel Moynihan years earlier) to explain how their policies left an estimated thirty-three million people living below the poverty line, millions more on the borderline, and one million homeless during the 1980s. From 1979 to 1984, the percentage of families headed by single women living below the poverty line (set then at $10,609 for a family of four) increased from 34.9 percent to 38.4 percent, with five million additional women pushed into poverty. Demographics showed that 27.9 percent of the households headed by European American women, 52.9 percent of those headed by African American women, and 53.2 percent of those headed by Latinas or Chicanas were impoverished. An advocacy group for poor people, Bread for the World, reported in its 1980s publications that two out of three adults in poverty were women, with women of color twice as likely to be poor than white women; 44.9 percent of African American children compared to 14.7 percent of white children lived in poverty.[5] Such economic and physical violence—African American infants are twice as likely to die in their first year than European American infants; black male teenagers are six times as likely to be murdered than their white counterparts—became defined in the 1980s (through administration pronouncements that homeless people "wanted" to live on the streets, that the poor were "lazy" welfare cheats, and that blacks were violence-prone) as indicative of the deficiencies and deviancy of the poor and people of color, not of the state, its laws, and its lack of implementation of human-rights covenants.

In the past fifteen years, the meteoric ascendancy of ultraconservatives in academe, the media, and the government indicates severe shifts in the U.S. political climate since the 1980 elections. Whether the shifts have been cataclysmic or mere fluctuations depends on how one gauges the stature of ultraconservative intellectuals such as those housed at the think tank, the Heritage Foundation. Considered in the early 1980s to be on the right-wing fringe and a polemical site influential only among the neoconservatives of the Reagan administration, by 1994 the Heritage Foundation had become the designated site of that year's freshmen orientation for the newly Republican-dominated Congress, replacing the historical site of bipartisan orientation, Harvard's Kennedy School of Government, which was considered too liberal and Democratic. The Heritage Foundation, all the while reassuring the public that its orientation was bipartisan, chose as its keynote speaker rightist talk-show pundit Rush Limbaugh.

When the November 1994 elections created the first Republican-dominated Senate and House of Representatives since 1952, the Republican sweep included the rhetoric of a populist pact, an alleged contract to discipline, if not criminalize, immigrants, poor people, blacks, gays and lesbians, and those advocating reproductive rights. The changing political climate has been accompanied by skirmishes in language and imagery: the conservative Contract with America has been renamed by its opponents as the Contract *on* America; liberal-minded critics refer to the prison growth industry and punitive policies for the poor as "drive-by politics"; conservatives dismiss liberal intellectuals and artists as the amoral or immoral "counterculture." Language can be used either to evoke or efface the deteriorating material conditions within the United States. For example, in New York City the number of emergency food providers rose from fifty in 1980 to more than eight hundred in 1994. In November 1994, Mayor Rudolph Giuliani, during the impending Thanksgiving holiday season, admonished churches and private agencies to do more about devastating hunger and malnutrition in the city. Combining chastisement with a performance, the mayor donated two cans of powdered baby formula to kick off a *Daily News* food drive, while cutting emergency food-assistance funds by hundreds of thousands of dollars.[6]

In the preceding decade, despite their diminishing material conditions, many whites, particularly males, voted for candidates who passed policies and legislation benefiting the top 5 percent of the U.S. population. From 1980 to 1990, as documented by the U.S. House Ways and Means Committee's Tax Progressivity and Income Distribution report of March 26, 1990, the pretax income for those in the poorest first decile fell from $5,128 to $4,695 for a loss of 8.4 percent, while rising 3.3 percent in the fifth decile (the lower-middle or working class) from $32,674 to $33,760. The tenth decile gained the most, 37.1 percent; its income rose from $105,611 to $144,832. The wealthiest 5 percent's pretax income increased from $142,133 to $206,162. For the ultrarich, incomes ballooned by 75.5 percent, from $312,816 to $548,969. When these disparate incomes were averaged, everyone seemed to gain 15.5 percent in their income during the previous decade.[7] Within a week of the House Ways and Means report, the *New York Times* reported on March 29, 1990, that economic gains from 1980 to 1989 were tied to property and higher corporate profits: personal savings rates of the net national income declined (8.9 percent to 3.6 percent); average hourly wages decreased (9.84 percent to 9.66 percent), while the percentage of the U.S. population working rose (59.6 percent to 63.3 percent). American families, particularly in the working and lower-middle classes, earned more during the past decade because they worked more: women wage workers were largely responsible for family income gains, as women holding two paying jobs moved from double to triple shifts.

This perception, and reality, of needing to work harder to stay even predictably leads to retrogressive racial and gender politics. Traditionally, for historically privileged sectors in the United States, increasing economic stratification and impoverishment signal a backlash against racial, sexual, and economic progressivism. Eroding standards of living—from 1989 to 1993, the average U.S. household annual income fell 7 percent for a loss of $2,344—promote scapegoating as an outlet for and deflection from declining economic conditions among most voters.[8] The racialized and sexualized scapegoating and resentment are evinced even among the supposedly enlightened classes. In theory, college-educated, middle-class voters are less susceptible to racist demagoguery. In practice, however, this is not always the case: for example, the majority of votes for neo-Nazi David Duke in his 1992 Louisiana gubernatorial bid came from middle-class, not poor, whites.

Playing the Race Card in Electoral War Games

Racialized resentments and fears have also proved politically useful. In his heyday, the late Republican strategist Lee Atwater managed George Bush's 1988 presidential campaign and, observers argue, secured the presidential victory by "playing the race card" through the Willie Horton ad campaign. Atwater informed the Republican party that the "class struggle in the South continues, with the [white] populists serving as the trump card" and that populists incline toward economic liberalism but social conservatism: "When Republicans are successful in getting certain social issues to the forefront, the populist vote is ours."[9] These "certain social issues" focused on criminal violence represented by the black male and welfare abuse represented by the black female. To prove his argument that whites would vote on the basis of social rather than economic issues, Atwater (with Roger Ailes) promoted the Willie Horton ads, which reconstructed Bush's Democratic opponent, Massachusetts governor Michael Dukakis, as "soft on crime"—specifically, in the U.S. lexicon, as soft on the most heinous crimes, namely, black male sexual assaults against white females.[10]

Where criminality is also constructed around "deviant" sexuality, appeals to race prove effective in politics. For example, Bush's Horton tactic—to encourage whites to prioritize social over economic interests—was recycled in 1992 in both David Duke's gubernatorial and Patrick Buchanan's presidential primary races. Marlon Riggs describes Buchanan's use of Riggs's documentary on African American gay men, *Tongues Untied,* as an "ironic reversal of the smear tactic against George Bush himself": Buchanan's controversial campaign ad provided politics with "a new cast of characters to demonize, then scapegoat. The specter of Willie Horton has returned, but this time, at least in Mr. Buchanan's distorted view, he is a leather-clad, bare-chested, sadomasochistic homosexual dancing shamelessly in the street."[11] North Carolina Republican senator Jesse Helms turned federal funding for *Tongues Untied* into the Willie Horton issue of the National Endowment for the Arts, according to Riggs, who argues that it was not only federal funding for cultural work on gay sexuality that was protested but funding for work by and about *black* gay men as well.

Racist as well as homophobic violence and rhetoric were on the rise. In November 1994, Helms, designated but not yet acting chairman of the Foreign Relations Committee told the *Raleigh News and Observer* that the president was so unpopular with military base personnel in North Carolina that "Mr. Clinton had better watch out if he comes down here. He better have a body guard."[12] The senator, who was never censured for his enthusiastic allusion to a presidential assassination, was partly inspired by Clinton's (albeit waffling) support of the rights of gays and lesbians in the military. The increase in hate violence monitored in 1994—homophobic and/or racist and anti-Semitic beatings and killings as well as abortion clinic shootings and executions—conceivably reflected the rise in hate speech and speech advocating violence (Helms's included) that marked the emergence of the new national government.[13] Despite the rather clearly communicated intent of the extreme right, political and news commentators insist that there is little connection between hate speech and murder. Critics have also argued that U.S. citizens are inherently better off than Canadians or Czechs, for example, who are restrained by national antihate speech legislation. Arguments that disavow correlations between hate speech and hate crimes exempt state representatives and the media from responsibility for violence that is in fact patterned after their rhetoric.

There is growing cynicism within mainstream culture about the use of racist rhetoric and stereotypes to fuel white fears of black violence. Even Atwater apologized on his deathbed to Dukakis—but not to African Americans—for the Horton smear campaign. After Susan Smith was indicted for killing her children, whose abduction she initially blamed on a black man, a national weekly ran a cartoon depicting a pinafored Goldilocks confidently informing three frowning bears, who glumly stared at empty porridge bowls, that "a black guy did it." Yet scapegoating and mythologies of black criminality and white victimization continue unabated in national narratives, and Atwater's strategies for the GOP remain fundamentally sound advice for U.S. electoral victories. Such representations allow nonblacks to transcend class differences and interests to form a conservative political bloc. They also work to obscure the specificity of crime, violence, and economic dependency in the United States. In the past decade the largest financial thefts of public monies have been white-collar crimes: inside traders on the stock market, the savings and loan scandals, and exorbitant cost overruns of Pentagon contractors. Most of those receiving public assistance (including so-called corporate welfare) are white. Crime statistics from the FBI report that the majority of cocaine users are white, male suburbanites, while the majority of white assault and rape victims are attacked by other whites. Still, the national icons for welfare cheat, rapist, thief, and murderer as black encourage the acceptance of state violence as state protection.

Racialized narratives constructed around crime, declining national intelligence, and white "victimization" by affirmative action instigated by dark-skinned aggressors—in short, the violent, intellectually unqualified, and morally corrupt who usurp the rights of the law-abiding, moral, and intellectually competent—would be more amusing if such mythmaking were not so widely embraced. *Boston Globe* columnist Derrick Z. Jackson notes that although violent crime is at a record twenty-year low, and although its most likely victims are African American teenagers, the (white) public perceives itself as besieged by black criminals: "In its blazing orange 'Murder' edition . . . *Newsweek*'s graphics department, not to be outdone by *Time*'s blackening of O. J. Simpson's mug shot, displayed the number of homicides in African-American liberation colors."[14] In U.S. visual culture, representations render social violence, particularly sexual violence, as synonymous with blackness. Such images in turn legitimize state violence, for instance, a "war against crime" or the "war on drugs," as necessary. The catch is that these racialized depictions of violence promote racialized responses: in the war on crime, for example, the criminal is embodied in the black.

Sanctioning Violence

Racial and sexual demonizing in the United States usually obscures the fact that violence against women is most often perpetrated by men from their own ethnic group. The state promotes law-and-order campaigns that instruct people, especially women, to acquiesce to state policing efforts, including extralegal or previously illegal police procedures, as the only recourse to countering sexual violence and criminality. The state, therefore, is called on to police angry men who create epidemics of sexual violence (including rape, incest, spousal or partner battery, and murder). Annually, four to six million women are battered by current or former husbands or partners; 52 percent of female murder victims are killed by intimate partners; 23 percent of pregnant women seeking prenatal care have been battered. More African American women "are injured by husbands, lovers, and friends than by car accidents, rapes, and muggings combined," while spousal abuse accounts for 50 percent of African American suicides.[15] According to the Uniform Crime Report (UCR), in 1991 there were 106,593 rapes in the United States: 292 a day, 12 an hour, 1 every 5 minutes; from 1972 to 1991, the numbers of reported rapes increased 128 percent. The National Crime Victimization Survey gives higher statistics than those cited by the UCR: 171,420 reported rapes for 1991 or 469 a day, 19 an hour, 1 every 3.5 minutes. Most rape victims know their assailants. The majority of victims or survivors are youths; the National Women's Study from the Crime Victims Research and Treatment Center in 1992 reports that in 29 percent of forcible rapes the victim is less than eleven years old, and in 32 percent, between the ages of eleven and seventeen. With one in six rapes reported to the police, this study estimates that over a twenty-year period more than twelve million women became rape survivors in a society where only one in one hundred rapists receives more than a one-year prison sentence for his crime. One-fourth of all convicted rapists are released on probation without serving any sentence.[16]

One is hard pressed to know how to discourage and diminish violence in the United States when elected officials condemn it while simultaneously applauding its use by certain sectors of the population. For instance, consider the culture wars. In June 1995, it was considered a bold move when Republican presidential candidate and Senate majority leader Bob Dole denounced a "cultural corporate" industry for extolling and romanticizing violence in Hollywood films and misogyny in gangsta rap. Senator Dole's list of wholesome "family films," however, included *True Lies,* which featured prominent Republican donor Arnold Schwarzenegger's mass killings of "Arab terrorists," and Oscar-winning *Forrest Gump*'s Horatio Alger story of an earnest, IQ-challenged white male in a period film that ridicules Vietnam Veterans against the War, antiwar activists, the Black Panther Party, and Students for a Democratic Society. Dole's criticism was his pledge as a candidate to stem the rise of violence and sexual decadence by demanding the censorship of images and lyrics. Yet at the same time, the presidential contender celebrated violence and sexual decadence in images of state employees: the hero in *True Lies* is a CIA operative who resuscitates his love for his wife by recruiting her as a spy who role-plays as a hooker. In contrast, Dole lambasted Oliver Stone and Quentin Tarantino for productions of violence by nonstate employees or, worse still, violence directed against state employees. (Tarantino's successful *Pulp Fiction* also glamorizes and racializes violence by suggesting that intermingling with blacks increases the possibilities of excitement for whites, and promises opportunities for the expression of white humanity and self-restraint.)[17]

Like the Senate's cultural critics, the courts seem similarly befuddled by society's confluence of rage, violent death, and madness. Consider the cases of a black killer, Colin Ferguson, and a white killer, William Masters. Ferguson was apprehended in the 1993 Long Island Rail Road shooting that left six people dead and nineteen wounded. He left handwritten notes listing the reasons for his assault as "hatred for whites, Asians, Hispanics and 'Uncle Tom blacks.'"[18] The presiding judge allowed Ferguson—who maintained that a white man had committed the shootings after taking the weapon from Ferguson's bag—to represent himself, although a psychiatrist testified at a competency hearing that Ferguson was delusional, paranoid, and mentally incompetent to stand trial. Ferguson had refused an insanity plea and dismissed his counsel, including the late civil-rights attorney and human-rights activist William M. Kunstler, who advocated either an insanity or a "black rage" defense—which in fact were one and the same. The black rage defense was based on the argument that the racial oppression Ferguson experienced as a black Jamaican immigrant to the United States had driven him insane.

The same month of Ferguson's February 17, 1995, conviction in Mineola, New York, William Masters recorded the license plate number of the vehicle of two Chicano youths he had seen spray-painting a highway underpass in Los Angeles. After the youths approached him, he shot both in the back, killing one. Maintaining that he had been threatened for documenting their defacement of public property, referring to the young men using racial slurs, and blaming what he referred to as their "negligent" mothers for the shootings, Masters—who was not licensed to carry a concealed weapon—was released after six hours of police questioning. He was later heralded as a vigilante hero in Simi Valley, the site of the police acquittal in the Rodney King beating case. What is baffling in the constructions of race, criminal violence, and sanity in these two cases is how the state ruled that Masters's act was in self-defense rather than racially insane or illegal, while decreeing that Ferguson's killings and behavior—clinical signs of mental instability—were sane.

Where do we stand amid the contradictory antiviolence stances in the United States? After the April 19, 1995, bombing of the Alfred P. Murrah Federal Building in Oklahoma City, Latino gang members took up collections to help survivors. George Bush publicly gave up his National Rifle Association (NRA) life membership during his May 1995 commencement speech at William and Mary College, denouncing NRA rhetoric that depicted agents from the Bureau of Alcohol, Tobacco, and Firearms as "thugs and stormtroopers." That same month his son, Texas governor George W. Bush, signed legislation that legalized the carrying of concealed weapons.

Just as state responses to criminal—or vigilante—violence foretell arbitrary, almost whimsical standards of antiviolence enforcement, state depictions of terrorism function to absolve the United States of any responsibility for terrorist activities while racializing the domestic and foreign terrorist as black or Arab. Arab American Institute president James Zogby condemned the scapegoating of Arab Americans immediately following the Oklahoma City bombing by citing FBI reports that of the 169 incidents of terrorism within the United States since 1982, three were committed by Arabs and sixteen by Jewish extremists; for Zogby the "cottage industry" of "terrorist specialists" was largely responsible for the racist stereotypes circulating in the media concerning the initial suspects.[19] Yet, the cottage industry of racializing terrorism also used state employees. On a MacNeil/Lehrer NewsHour segment, Senator John Kerry (Dem., Mass.) cited the Black Panthers—not the Weathermen or other white militant leftist or rightist groups that conducted bombing attacks in the 1960s and early 1970s—as the prototype for the Oklahoma City bombing. Senator Kerry's conflation of revolutionary and counterrevolutionary violence, positing that right-wing violence flows from left-wing violence and that only the law-abiding state provides sanctuary, ignores the fact that the Black Panthers were never convicted of the bombings, although criminal charges were made and have been linked to the FBI's harassment of the Black Panthers under COINTELPRO.[20] Revising history seems as prevalent as advocating for the right to violence or the right to bear arms. Armed resistance or revolutionary violence is advanced by those who do not trust the state to wield violence on their behalf or who fear the state's violence against them. What is usually lost in the simplistic dichotomies and conflations of revolutionary and counterrevolutionary violence is how the state might facilitate political violence while criminalizing and condemning it.

Anti-immigrant sentiment feeds violent, international white supremacist movements (the hate movement in Europe sets standards for U.S. adherents to follow). On the Internet one can find recruitment material from white supremacists (as well as snuff pornography). The militia movement is the fastest-growing component of white supremacist groups, with reportedly four times the number of members as the Ku Klux Klan (KKK) and neo-Nazis combined in 1995. At a time when racist organizations and assaults on feminists and civil-rights activists seem to be increasing, the rights of violent groups such as the KKK are reaffirmed by the Supreme Court. Interpreting the Klan cross as an expression of religious speech (many of us are familiar with the cross, particularly a burning one, as representing another form of speech), the Supreme Court ruled on June 29, 1995, that the KKK could not be barred from displaying a large cross alongside a Christmas tree and a menorah in front of the Columbus, Ohio, courthouse. Paradoxically, while enforcing the rights of hate groups known for terrorism, the highest judiciary branch establishes the state as the protector from the violent, the criminal, the terrorist.

Violence is both intoxicating and sobering. In American culture, it often elicits responses of great demonstrative emotion. The national memorial service for the victims of the Oklahoma City bombing, for example, combined state pageantry and patriotism: in its closing moment, in which a black woman gave a rousing rendition of "God Bless America" with an immense U.S. flag in the background, most mourners in the hall stood and wept. But political violence also inspires responses of irrational justification with little or no remorse. For instance, Tom Metzger, a national white supremacist spokesperson, informed the press days after the Oklahoma City bombing that, although the deaths were tragic, the federal government was responsible because it had placed a day-care center in the same building that housed the Federal Bureau of Alcohol, Tobacco, and Firearms and the FBI. In Metzger's mind the government was presumably at fault for placing civilians "in the line of fire" of military targets. In contrast, rather than rationalize the bombing, spokesmen for Indianapolis's Black Panther Militia (unaffiliated with the Black Panther Party) identified a hierarchy of black lives, arguing that for African Americans the deaths of Ethiopians from famine and war should have more significance than Oklahoma City's black victims who worked in a federal building for an oppressive state.[21]

Conclusion

Growing up on army posts with their military memorials and rituals, including the disappearance of fathers for tour duty and training, I was constantly reminded of the use of coercion in policy implementation and patriotic nationalism to provide the glue of civilian acquiescence to state violence in a democracy. Having survived a parent who toured in Korea, the Dominican Republic, and Vietnam—one who returned in altered states, never spoke about his war experiences, and died embittered even after attaining his coveted rank of lieutenant colonel—I listened with particular attentiveness to retired general and chairman of the Joint Chiefs of Staff Colin Powell's September 18, 1995, interview with Terry Gross on National Public Radio's Fresh Air program. Promoting his autobiography and possible presidential bid, Powell parried Gross's probes into his feelings about fighting in Vietnam while blacks in the civil-rights movement fought Bull Connor's water hoses and attack dogs as they tried to desegregate Birmingham, Alabama. Vietnam was a war, Gross reminded Powell, that Martin Luther King Jr. had condemned. The retired general first stated that he considered the war an ill-conceived one against a nationalist rather than a Soviet-backed communist movement (propagandists had portrayed it as the latter); he then talked about coming from a proud line of "buffalo soldiers" and learning to show gratitude to the blacks who served in the U.S. military so that he could benefit from and build on their path-breaking contributions as Americans and men who insisted on racial equality. Although I also appreciate the Tuskegee airmen and other black servicemen and women and come from a (shorter and less illustrious) line of military careerists, Powell's uncritical use of the term *buffalo soldiers*—a term for African American soldiers that comes from the Native Americans who were dispossessed of their lands by the U.S. deployment of cavalry, including these black troops, after the Civil War—leaves me disappointed in what this so-called independent political response offers for democratic, antiviolent societies.

Powell's stance is not surprising, given that career militarists, employed to implement war policies, usually mute or veil their sentiments about the rights of colonized peoples to self-determination and the importance of restricting U.S. violence and domination—if, by chance, they even acknowledge that subaltern peoples have such rights. Occasionally, even militarists, though only a few, boldly denounce U.S. military intervention. In a poster displayed at the UN Church Center, the declarations of marine commander General David M. Shoup made on May 14, 1966—so dissimilar to those of Colin Powell—condemn U.S. aggression:

> I believe that if we had and would keep our dirty, bloody, dollar-soaked fingers out of the business of these nations so full of depressed, exploited people, they will arrive at a solution of their own . . . and if unfortunately their revolution must be of the violent type because the "haves" refuse to share with the "have nots" by any peaceful method, at least what they get will be their own, and not the American style, which they don't want and above all don't want crammed down their throats by Americans.[22]

Thirty years later, there is considerable skepticism, cynicism, and weariness felt about the possibilities of revolution and violent liberation struggles. There is less cynical skepticism and political exhaustion about deescalating violence in U.S. policies.

In our confrontations with violence, survival—staying emotionally, intellectually, and physically alive despite abuse—is a considerable achievement for many. Going beyond mere survival to speculate about liberation, however, *Resisting State Violence* details and expands on progressive radicalism in its discussions of race, sex, class, and violence. The objective of this book has been summed up by one critic's observation: it informs a society in which "most Americans don't have a clue about" the depth and scope of widespread violence, and it moves beyond the headlines of sensationalist crime reports; it is also a "gift back" to those who teach about risk-taking, political thinking and action while exemplifying "sustained resistance"— the ability to struggle for democratic ideals without having interminable battles penetrate one's own core.

Admittedly, there are many forms of resistance to violence; these reflections selectively recall various political experiences with differing emphases. Still, these fragments are useful, for they contextualize and decode political events and ethical responses to violence. And, in so doing, they frame a resistance by critiquing and documenting confrontation. Despite ironic cruelties and contradictions, battles for democratic power create moments of beauty and integrity that coincide with the ugliness of struggle. Reacting to violence in American domestic and foreign policies and cultural practices with more than outrage and despair, we may take heart from Gertrude Stein's observation:

> You always have in your writing the resistance outside of you and inside of you, a shadow upon you, and the thing which you must express. In the beginning of your writing, this struggle is so tremendous that the result is ugly. . . . The person who has made the fight probably makes it seem ugly . . . it is ugly. But the essence of that ugliness is the thing which will always make it beautiful. I myself think it is much more interesting when it seems ugly, because in it you see the element of the fight.[23]

Because so much of what is unpleasant, ugly, and unruly in our lives centers on violence—and its manifestations in poverty, racism, sexism, heterosexism, anti-Semitism, and militarism—the following essays are obviously not pretty musings on resistance. Most radicalism that counters institutionalized poverty, hate crimes, and postcolonial imperialism cannot be pretty or expressed in the niceties of civility; still, courage and integrity in confronting violence frame the ugliness of the battles. To the extent that *Resisting State Violence* goes beyond literary insurgency or rhetorical resistance to bring the element of the fight into our daily lives with the specificity of political struggles around economic, sexual, and racial violence, it offers something of the beauty of resistance.

1 / Erasing the Spectacle
of Racialized State Violence

*Our society is one not of spectacle, but of surveillance. . . . We are neither in
the amphitheatre, nor on the stage, but in the panoptic machine. . . . the pomp
of sovereignty, the necessarily spectacular manifestations of power, were extinguished one by one in the daily exercise of surveillance.*
  —Michel Foucault, *Discipline and Punish: The Birth of the Prison*

Michel Foucault's *Discipline and Punish* offers a body politics of state punishment and prosecution that is considered by some postmodernists to be
a master narrative competent to critique contemporary state policing. Yet
this particular work contributes to the erasure of racist violence. In respect
to U.S. policing and punishment, the metanarrative of *Discipline and Punish* vanquishes historical and contemporary racialized terror, punishments,
and control in the United States; it therefore distorts and obscures violence
in America in general. By examining erasure in body politics, lynching,
and policing; penal executions and torture; and terror in U.S. foreign policy—issues that Foucault overlooks in his discussion of the history of
policing in the United States—we find visceral spectacles of state abuse.

Erasure in Body Politics

Writing about the "disappearance of torture as a public spectacle"—with
no reference to its continuity in European and American colonies where it

was inflicted on indigenous peoples in Africa and the Americas—Foucault weaves a historical perspective that eventually presents the contemporary ("Western") state as a nonpractitioner of torture.[1] His text illustrates how easy it is to erase the specificity of the body and violence while centering discourse on them. Losing sight of the violence practiced by and in the name of the sovereign, who at times was manifested as part of a dominant race, Foucault universalizes the body of the white, propertied male. Much of *Discipline and Punish* depicts the body with no specificity tied to racialized or sexualized punishment. The resulting veneer of bourgeois respectability painted over state repression elides racist violence against black and brown and red bodies.

Foucault states that the "historical moment of the disciplines was the moment when an art of the human body was born" (137). Failing to concretize this "art of the human body," he leaves unaddressed these questions: which body serves as prototype? who bore this representative model or type? Ostensibly talking about the body while ignoring its uniqueness, Foucault explores issues of policing that are restricted to behavior. If one asserts that the "introduction of the 'biographical' is important in the history of penalty. . . . Because it establishes the 'criminal' as existing before the crime and even outside it" (252), one might also note that the biographical is intricately tied to the biological—that is, the "criminal" is identified not only by his or her act but also by his or her appearance.[2] Consider how Foucault's discussion of nonconformity as offense masks the body:

> What is specific to the disciplinary penalty is non-observance, that which does not measure up to the rule, that departs from it. The whole indefinite domain of the non-conforming is punishable: the soldier commits an "offence" whenever he does not reach the level required; a pupil's "offence" is not only a minor infraction, but also an inability to carry out his tasks. (178–79)

Nonobservance and nonconformity are often understood as biologically determined, given that the departure from the norm shows up not only in behavior but visually in terms of physical characteristics that are racialized. Foucault's exclusive focus on actions suggests undifferentiated bodies. Physical appearance, however, can be considered an expression of either conformity or rebellion. Because some bodies fail to conform physiologically, different bodies are expected and are therefore required to behave differently under state or police gaze. Greater obedience is demanded from those whose physical difference marks them as aberrational, offensive, or threatening. Conversely, some bodies appear more docile than others because of their conformity in appearance to idealized models of class, color, and sex; their bodies are allowed greater leeway to be self-policed or policed without physical force. To illustrate: a white male executive in an Armani suit is considered more docile, civilized, and in need of less invasive, coercive policing than a black male youth in a hooded sweatshirt and off-the-hip baggy jeans. (In contrast, white youths who racially cross-dress—with baseball caps turned backwards, "X" t-shirts, low-riding pants—are generally not aggressively targeted by police who distinguish between fashion consumerism and racial membership.) Noting how physique is constructed as a marker for deviancy and criminality, Frantz Fanon writes in "The Negro and Psychopathology" that the "Negro symbolizes the biological danger. . . . To suffer from a phobia of Negroes is to be afraid of the biological."[3] To fear the black is to fear the body; conversely, to revere the black is to idealize the body.

Foucault writes of social fear and policing that are reflected in "binary division and branding," which produces the polarized social entities of the "mad/sane; dangerous/harmless; normal/abnormal"; this "coercive assignment" of labeling, categorizing, and identifying places the individual under "constant surveillance" (199). Foucault, however, makes no mention of sexual and racial binary oppositions to designate social inferiority and deviancy as biologically inscribed on the bodies of nonmales or nonwhites. Therefore, when he reports in *Discipline and Punish* that "the mechanisms of power" are organized "around the abnormal individual, to brand him and to alter him," racial and sexual issues are evaded (199–200). To write that these mechanisms of dominance rely on the panopticism produced by the disciplinary and exclusionary practices for the "arrest of the plague" and the "exile of the leper" (which for Foucault respectively represent the dreams of a "disciplined society" and a "pure community") without considering the role of race in the formation of that disciplined society and pure community is to see the United States through blinders (198). In racialized societies such as the United States, the plague of criminality, deviancy, immorality, and corruption is embodied in the black because both sexual and social pathology are branded by skin color (as well as by gender and sexual orientation). Where the plague and the leper are codified in the black, for instance, the dreams and desires of a society and state will be centered on the control of the black body. Binary oppositions and panopticism will thereby be racialized. In binary opposition, antiblack racism has played a critical, historical role in rationalizing (and inverting) hierarchies of oppressor and oppressed: crazy/sane, dangerous/harmless, and normal/deviant. Foucault ignores this phenomenon, while other theorists such as Frantz Fanon and Sander Gilman explore it.[4] Panopticism and the policing gaze are also informed by racial and sexual bias; the tools for observation and examination that Foucault delineates are constructed within worldviews influenced by racial and sexual mythologies and political ideologies that guide carceral testing. Foucault's *carceral* refers to a network of regimentation and discipline, a prison without walls in turn made up of social networks for surveillance.

Ignoring disenfranchised ethnic minorities policed by both the state and dominant castes, Foucault produces his own binary divisions in *Discipline and Punish*. He reproduces the split between the public and private realms and masks this dualism by obscuring the private realm and the bodies policed there—those of gay men, lesbians, bisexuals, the poor, women, children, and dark-skinned peoples. Their disappearance or theoretical erasure allows the representative body, which Foucault bases on a white male model, to appear as universal. This (mis)measure of man—naturalized and universalized as masculine and European—shapes *Discipline and Punish*'s color- and gender-blind investigations, for instance, Foucault's quintessentially male, military model that is premised on an inequality marked only by rank achieved through individual merit. His assumptions of (false) equality preempt discussions of racial violence.

Historically, discipline and punishment within households and slave quarters and their postindustrial manifestations of domesticated or rebellious children, women, servants, and the incarcerated reveal new dimensions of dominance and terror. Within the private realm or underground economy of prisons or workfare, different forms of punishment with more intensive violence emerge. If the "art of punishing, in the regime of disciplinary power" is designed not to expiate or repress but to "normalize" (182–83), as Foucault argues, then one must recognize that some bodies cannot be normalized no matter how they are disciplined, unless the prevailing social and state structures that figuratively and literally rank bodies disintegrate. Under Nazi Germany, those designated biologically abnormal—the handicapped body, the gay body, the Jewish body, the Gypsy body, the communist or socialist body, and the black body—were to be sterilized, euthanized, or eradicated; considered defective or a subspecies of humans, they could not be normalized under state ideology. The political function of the term *normal* structures hierarchy while masking exclusion through the projection of illusory objective norms. For Foucault, "it was no longer the . . . attack on the common interest, it was the departure from the norm" that constituted threat; the "social enemy was transformed into a deviant, who brought with him the multiple danger of disorder, crime and madness" (299–300). The normalization process is itself constricted and disciplined by the imaginary of the norm—the white, male, propertied heterosexual. Where the criminal or the insane is constructed as belonging to another race, the black criminal or madwoman is doubly offensive, marked by behavior and biology that diverge from the norm. (Although Foucault critiques Césare Manuel de Lombroso's racist criminology, he does not utilize antiracist or critical race theory.)

In this construction of the unspecified body, Foucault is able to sanitize state repression as he argues that manifestations of power or spectacles of violence have been extinguished. In the United States, however, they are held on reserve where the threat and promise of state violence makes surveillance effective. The complexities of the criminalization of dark-skinned people; the destructiveness of gang members who neither perceive themselves nor are portrayed as members of society; the defunding of youth centers (Foucault's "carcerals") for prison construction; and the ethnically and sexually marked bodies for state violence in domestic and foreign policy—none is analyzed by Foucault. One might find that some of us are further from the "perfect camp" in which "all power would be exercised solely through exact observation" and where "each gaze would form a part of the overall functioning of power" than Foucault intimates (171). This "exact observation" is enforced by the threat of violence administered by the state, with poor people and people of color as the most vulnerable targets. The violent state punishments that Foucault generalizes as past phenomena resurface in our postmodern-era policies.

Lynching and Policing

At the beginning of the nineteenth century, we learn from *Discipline and Punish*, with penal reform "the tortured, dismembered, amputated body, symbolically branded on face or shoulder, exposed alive or dead to public view" faded as public spectacle, and with it the "body as the major target of penal repression disappeared" (8). Yet during the nineteenth century, the tortured, amputated body existed, for example, in the frames of Senegalese and enslaved Martinicans under French colonial rule. Even in the post-emancipation era, the brutalized body appears. For instance, in the United States, from the end of the Civil War until the mid-twentieth century, the punished, mangled body was the visceral marker of the ritualized bar-barism of lynching. The convergence of mob and sheriffs oversaw the branded, dismembered black body that symbolized the rage and vindica-tion of a prosecuting crowd and state, so-called redressing white victimiza-tion. In the synonymy of blackness with violence in U.S. society, the specter of lynching appears as the expression of American rage and retri-bution. Ironically, the black, the historical victim of state violence through slavery and Reconstruction with the rise of the Ku Klux Klan and Jim Crow laws, was portrayed as the aggressor. The age of sobriety surround-ing punishment that Foucault claims began around 1830 is belied by the giddy hysteria of lynching that became racialized and increased in number after the Civil War. Curiously and ahistorically, Foucault argues that the "disappearance of punishment as a spectacle" highlighted a shift to a more covert, systemic application of punishment and incarceration, in which the very absence of overt state violence led to a mollification of the mobs and crowds that previously witnessed the spectacles as active audiences: "It was as if the punishment was thought to equal, if not to exceed, in sav-agery the crime itself, to accustom the spectators to a ferocity from which one wished to divert them, to show them the frequency of crime, to make the executioner resemble a criminal, judges murderers, to reverse roles at the last moment, to make the tortured criminal an object of pity or admi-ration" (9). African American lynch victims, however, were rarely trans-formed into objects of pity or admiration in the dominant society, al-though among antilynching advocates they were mourned and eulogized. Rather than the erasure of bodily torture for a carceral of self-policing cit-izens, as Foucault maintains, punitive torture in the United States became inscribed on the black body. Antebellum lynch victims were predomi-nantly white: of the three hundred recorded lynchings between 1840 and 1860, only 10 percent of the victims were African American.[5] In the post-bellum era, when the majority of lynch victims were black, torture, mutilation, dismemberment, and castration, as well as the pickling of body parts as souvenirs, became regular features of lynching.

Lynchings did not disappear as state-sanctioned, mass phenomena until the 1920s and 1930s (the Southern Poverty Law Center's Klanwatch Project documents their continuance in clandestine atrocities). The Commission on Interracial Cooperation's 1933 study of lynching in the 1930s reports what most astute antiracists and black Americans at the time already knew: the death of the victim was not the primary motive in lynching. The prevalence of torture and mutilation established lynching as a terrorist campaign to control an ethnic people subjugated as an inferior race. Lynching was not only a form of punishment (for criminal assaults and theft as well as infractions such as economic competition with whites or simply being in the wrong place at the wrong time) but also a sadistic fixation on the body, focused on the black body, that fueled outrageous retributions. The tortured body as the "major target of penal repression" (Foucault, 8)—executed by self-appointed lawmen and government employees—was often accompanied by the mythology of a predatory, black, male sexual savagery directed against white females.

Black women and girls were also lynched in the postbellum era. Lynching violence, like police brutality, is usually associated with black male victims, for example, the Rodney King beating, which culturally functioned as a visceral spectacle of police racism, punishment, and torture. But men are not the only targets of police discipline. Four years before what became a symbol of police racism and brutality (through channels as diverse as academic texts and urban riots), the Center for Law and Social Justice issued a 1988 report, "Black Women under Siege by New York City Police."[6] Documenting white, male police violence against black women, the center contended that the police and legal system play an instrumental role in repressive violence and that racism often motivates police assaults. The report cites violent actions by white policemen including intentionally driving a patrol car into a woman; beating a woman who had witnessed a police assault on an African American man; spraying mace into the face of a woman whose hands were handcuffed behind her back; and pulling guns on an unarmed woman who, after admitting them into her home, asked why they were there. Few media and government officials focus on such violence, according to the center: "The massive coverage given the Tawana Brawley case has disguised the spate of police and racial attacks on Black women in general . . . . [creating] the view that . . . the deaths of Eleanor Bumpurs and Yvonne Smallwood . . . are usually treated as isolated incidents, rather than as part of an historical and recently increased trend." Tawana Brawley's unsubstantiated accusations against white police and local officials for assault and rape were generally considered to be a hoax, although the African American teenager's charges provided a springboard for her media "handlers," Al Sharpton, Alton Maddox, and Vernon Mason. Eleanor Bumpurs, a sixty-seven-year-old arthritic, obese grandmother, was killed in her apartment in 1984 by shotgun blasts as police attempted to evict her for nonpayment of back rent. Because Bumpurs had brandished a kitchen knife at the white policemen who had broken down her apartment door, the killing was ruled as self-defense. Yvonne Smallwood was an African Caribbean woman beaten to death by police in 1988 after she told the officers issuing a traffic ticket to her black male companion that they should be arresting drug dealers instead. No police were indicted for these or similar deaths in cases such as that of graffiti artist Michael Stewart. The death of women in police custody by means of law enforcement's measures to discipline and punish is an issue rarely raised in feminist explorations of women and violence or masculinist explorations of racism and policing.

Although these particular killings took place outside of public view, local police generally tend to turn surveillance into a spectacle. The use of crowd control and supervision in black areas illustrates this point. The protests in the wake of the police acquittal in the Rodney King beating case (nationwide, the majority of protesters and rioters were nonblack) as well as during the Days of Outrage were not what Foucault had in mind when he wrote that people were "made to accept the power to punish, or quite simply, when punished, tolerate being so" (303). In the mid-1980s, following the civil unrest from the Days of Outrage, New York police officers appeared at Brooklyn's Grand Army Plaza on Labor Day during the Caribbean carnival with a posture of "heavy manners." Floats and steel-drum bands passed street dancers and vendors on Eastern Parkway, accompanied by the drone of police helicopters overhead. Any resident or visiting tourist on the street could look up at the roofs of the Brooklyn apartment houses lining the parade route and see uniformed police, including sharpshooters with the butts of their rifles poised on their hips. The parade was to end officially at a certain hour. In the past, like other parades in the city, the last stragglers and revelers could pack up and depart in a leisurely fashion. That year, however, police rode side by side on horseback, a solid wall of blue-and-white centurions after the last float, sweeping dancers, spectators, and walkers off the parkway.

Not only those under surveillance but the police themselves believe that blacks have not accepted the state's "power to punish" with the tolerance that Foucault imagined. Although Foucault seems to suggest that there is little life outside the carceral, the state disagrees, as evident in its distrust of blacks to regulate themselves and in police reliance on symbolic or real threats to discipline black communities. The state's assumptions are underscored by 1995 polls conducted during the O. J. Simpson trial in which more blacks than whites expressed uncertainty about Simpson's guilt. Moreover, the August and September 1995 news coverage of retired Los Angeles Police Department police detective Mark Fuhrman, who in a taped interview boasted of his hatred for blacks, antiblack harassment, and planting of evidence for indictments, suggested that blacks, as well as others, increasingly distrust the judicial system.

The deadly spectacle of racist police beatings—disciplining poor, feminized, and dark-skinned communities—is overshadowed by more spectacular displays of deadly state force. The 1985 police bombing and incineration of civilians in a black Philadelphia neighborhood provides an illustration that has generated far less attention and social outrage than the Branch Davidian confrontation and deaths in Waco, Texas. The bombing of the headquarters of MOVE, a radical black, back-to-nature organization (with some white members) was supervised by a black former military officer and white police officials and approved by black mayor Wilson Goode, who publicly resolved to end the standoff between police and MOVE members "by any means necessary." In their confrontation with MOVE, police used explosives similar to those deployed in Vietnam; a block of rowhouses was burned down. Eleven people including four children died. Local residents who witnessed the bombing and one of the two survivors give accounts of children who disappeared while fleeing from the back of a burning house surrounded by police. Black residents also offered unsubstantiated reports of police marksmen stationed in the alley shooting survivors and throwing their bodies into the burning house. Conversely, Philadelphia police contend that the parents and caretakers of the children were responsible for their deaths and that police engaged in no criminal activity. Unlike the Branch Davidians (who were implicated in executing adults and children and starting the fire that consumed their Waco compound), those who died in the MOVE bombing did not become martyrs among the extreme right or mainstream America as victims of encroaching federalism and police power; nor were their deaths cited as a motivating factor by extremists in the April 1995 Oklahoma City bombing; and finally, the deaths provoked no public outcry leading to congressional hearings such as those in the case of white separatist Randy Weaver and the deaths of his wife and son during a shootout with Bureau of Alcohol, Tobacco, and Firearm agents. No police were ever indicted or disciplined for the MOVE deaths or destruction of black homes on Osage Avenue in Philadelphia (although a civil suit was settled in June 1996).

Prisons and Penal Executions

Foucault's elision of racial bias in historical lynching and contemporary policing predicts his silence on the racialization of prisons and the death penalty in the United States. For Foucault, during the ancien régime "the infinite segmentation of the body of the regicide" manifested "the strongest power over the body of the greatest criminal, whose total destruction made the crime explode into its truth"(227). That dominating, totalizing power, he argues, appears in contemporary society as "an interrogation without end" or "an investigation that would be extended without limit to a meticulous and ever more analytical observation, a judgement that would at the same time be the constitution of a file that was never closed, the calculated leniency of a penalty that would be interlaced with the ruthless curiosity of an examination" (227). Constant monitoring, bureaucratic documentation and analysis, and interrogation without end are in fact characteristics of American prisons. Yet through its police and penal executions, the United States also enacts violence that is fundamentally different from such ceaseless interrogation. In the bombing of MOVE members in Philadelphia, for instance, interrogation was never intended; rather, the policing objective was the death of the targeted subject(s). In other examples, the FBI-COINTELPRO's harassment and assassination of black and indigenous leaders during the civil-rights, Black Panther, and American Indian movements, including the 1969 shootings of Fred Hampton and Mark Clark by Chicago police and the FBI and the shootings at Wounded

Knee,[7] as well as police killings of nonactivist blacks, Native Americans, and Latinos all indicate levels of violence in U.S. domestic policies (rarely reflected on in academe) that suggest little interest in interrogation.

One may argue, following Foucault, that the "carceral network does not cast the unassimilable into a confused hell; there is no outside. . . . It saves everything, including what it punishes"(301). The U.S. carceral network kills, however, and in its prisons, it kills more blacks than any other ethnic group. American prisons constitute an "outside" in U.S. political life. In fact, our society displays waves of concentric outside circles with increasing distances from bourgeois self-policing. The state routinely polices the unassimilable in the literal hell of lockdown, deprivation tanks, control units, and holes for political prisoners. In *Discipline and Punish* Foucault remains mute about the incarcerated person's vulnerability to police beatings, rape, shock treatments, and death row. Penal incarceration and executions are the state's procedures for discarding the unassimilable into an external inferno of nonexistence. Not everything, nor everyone, is saved.

Foucault's assertion that the end of public executions represents a diminished focus on spectacle and the body fails to consider, as exemplified in death-penalty biases, that bodies matter differently in racialized systems. The value placed on racial, economic, and sexual differences determines the slackening or tightening of the grip on the body. Citing literature on the penitentiary congress to argue that the state "no longer touched the body, or at least as little as possible, and then only to reach something other than the body itself," Foucault also fails to note how essence has been constructed as linked to physical appearance (11). If "something" refers to the soul, then one should consider that in national racist mythology Africans and Native Americans were either presumed to have no soul or one that was debased and in need of conversion and discipline. Foucault's contention that "physical pain, the pain of the body itself, is no longer the constituent element of the penalty. . . . [and that] punishment has become an economy of suspended rights" ignores the fact that not everyone is recognized as a state member with uniformly enforced and equal rights (11).

Superfluous or expendable bodies, institutional inequalities, and racism as components of discipline and punishment in the United States mean that the carceral is customized to fit racialized body politics and that race is a marker for criminality and repression. The Center for the Study of Psychiatry organized a public outcry against the Federal Violence Initiative, which was approved by the National Mental Health Advisory Council and federally funded "to identify at least 100,000 inner city children whose alleged biochemical and genetic defects will make them violent in later life. . . . Treatment will consist of behavior modification in the family, special 'day camps,' and drugs."[8] Currently, legislators are attempting to reinstate funding for this program.

To do a critical reading of Foucault's paradigm, we need only to recall Governor Nelson Rockefeller's use of the New York State militia to suppress the Attica uprising in the early 1970s; Federal Judge B. Parker's ruling in the 1980s that the Lexington Control Unit, which was a behavior-modification prison center for political revolutionaries, must be closed given U.S. government practices to change political views and affiliations through torture; or U.S. prisoners' accounts of brutality and torture in the 1990s. Because Foucault's paradigm normalizes and universalizes prison in one particular form, readers might easily miss or dismiss today's reappearance of other control units, chain gangs for (black) convicts in Alabama (and other states), and popular support for the death penalty.

Behind prison walls, state executions take place as a private spectacle. In theory, the death penalty works to deter potential felons (although no correlation between the death penalty and criminal deterrence has been established); however, in practice state executions function as a punitive spectacle, one shielded from the view of the citizenry but projected into its consciousness. One of the most eloquent writers on the death penalty today is Mumia Abu-Jamal. Considered by many fair-trial advocates to be a falsely accused political prisoner, journalist Abu-Jamal, former Black Panther Party and MOVE member, was sentenced to death for the killing of a Philadelphia policeman. He begins his memoir, *Live from Death Row,* by quoting Albert Camus: "'For there to be equivalence, the death penalty would have to punish a criminal who had warned his victim of the date at which he would inflict a horrible death on him and who, from that moment onward, had confined him at his mercy for months. Such a monster is not encountered in private life.'"[9] When the General Assembly of the Organization of American States discussed a treaty to ban the death penalty in 1987 as an addition to the American Convention on Human Rights, it was noted that two years earlier the European Parliament had adopted a similar treaty and condemned U.S. policy favoring the death penalty. Assembly members noted that the United States seemed committed to the death penalty at a time when other countries were abolishing it. In 1995, in the same month that South Africa outlawed the death penalty, the governor of Pennsylvania signed the execution warrant for Abu-Jamal.

In the United States, where state executions are on the rise, in over twenty-six states persons under age eighteen can be legally executed, according to Amnesty International. The death penalty has been contested in cases of bias in sentencing. Between 1977 and 1986 nearly 90 percent of prisoners executed had been convicted of killing whites, although the number of black victims was approximately equal to that of white victims. In January 1985, in *McClesky v. Kemp,* Warren McClesky, on death row for killing a white Atlanta policeman, argued that his constitutional rights were violated because statistics demonstrated racism in Georgia sentencing. McClesky had first petitioned the United States Court of Appeals for the Eleventh Circuit, claiming that the Georgia death penalty was discriminatory.[10] According to Amnesty International, which reported the McClesky case, in the 1970s Georgia courts were eleven times more likely to sentence to death those convicted of killing whites than those convicted of killing blacks; overall, those who killed European Americans were 20 percent more likely to receive the death penalty than those who killed African Americans; in similar cases, black defendants received the death penalty more often than whites. Ruling against McClesky, the Supreme Court acknowledged that Georgia's death sentencing was racially biased; the majority opinion, however, found the 20 percent disparity to be acceptable, declaring it a "marginal" discrepancy in comparison to past racialized death sentencing. The Court also rejected the appeal on the basis that the plaintiff could not prove that the judge, jury, or prosecutor personally and intentionally acted out of racism. In the absence of such admissions of racism on the part of the penal system, McClesky had no proof that Georgia intended to violate his constitutional rights. Where one cannot prove intent, racist violence is merely a theoretical possibility or improbability on the part of the state. Such improbability was insufficient ground for the court to issue a stay of execution.

Penal institutions are on the outside of U.S. domestic political life, in which the punishing violence inflicted on the incarcerated is rarely considered by the general populace. There are other forms of outside or external infernos. In U.S. foreign policy during the 1980s, the punishment inflicted against people in national independence movements reached a level of terror through U.S. funding of contras in an effort to police by proxy.

Terror in Foreign Policy

In the 1980s, domestic policing and police brutality, including the 1985 MOVE bombing, were upstaged by the grisly spectacle of terrorism in U.S. foreign policy. During this time the deaths of more than 30,000 Nicaraguans and 10,000 Angolans by contras and more than 100,000 Mozambicans by South Africans (linked to CIA funding) represented the use of state terrorism and torture of civilians to destabilize socialist governments and revolutionary struggles. During the Reagan administrations, the tortured, dismembered body routinely appeared as a consequence of Salvadoran and Guatemalan death squads funded by the U.S. Congress or CIA. In El Salvador and Guatemala, torture and terroristic killings were deployed to derail social, political, and guerrilla movements by workers and indigenous peoples. In the contra wars in Nicaragua and Angola, public torture and terrorism were vehicles for challenging the sovereignty of socialist governments. We now know that a U.S. president or commander-in-chief could finance or turn a blind eye to covert support for violence to enforce U.S. hegemony in a certain region. In the post-World War II era, the United States reigned as a global military and economic power; with its status as transnational sovereign, the United States (referring to itself as "America") exerted influence over the Americas, designating Mexico, Central and South America, and the Caribbean as "our backyard."

According to the Washington, D.C.-based Center for Defense Information and *American Defense Monitor,* in 1946 the United States began language and military schools for governments in the Americas. Today, International Military Education and Training (IMET) programs train military leaders and troops, funding the School of the Americas (SOA)—also known as the "low-intensity conflict school"—at Fort Benning, Georgia.[11] Both IMET and SOA taught some of the most notorious dictators and militarists in Latin America and the Caribbean. (After the withdrawal of U.S. occupying forces from Latin American and Caribbean countries, the most professionalized military was left in control.) Rather than policing national borders for outside aggression, SOA graduates policed internal borders, suppressing local, indigenous, or student resistance to state violence and control. Since the 1950s, SOA has trained more than five thousand Salvadoran military personnel, who have been accused of rampant torture and assassinations of civilians, Farabundo Martí Liberación Nacional (FMLN) members, as well as the highly publicized execution of four outspoken Jesuit priests and their housekeeper. Graduates of SOA include some of the region's best-known dictators: Cuba's Fulgencio Batista; the Dominican Republic's Rafael Trujillo; Nicaragua's Anastasio Somoza; its "hall of fame" includes El Salvador's Roberto D'Aubisson, known as an architect of the death squads, and Panama's Manuel Noriega, considered so notorious a drug runner that the U.S. military bombed Panama in 1989 allegedly in order to extradite him for trial in Miami. The school instructed the officers' corps of the Haitian military, which carried out a 1991 military coup against democratically elected president Jean-Bertrand Aristide; in 1994, the United States had to send troops to police its SOA graduates in order to restore Aristide to his presidency (and to stem the immigration of Haitian boat people fleeing torture and execution in their own country).

Mainstream media in the 1980s dubbed Reagan "the Great Communicator" and his successor, George Bush, the advocate for a "kinder, gentler nation"—in his speechwriter Peggy Noonan's words. Leftist progressives derided the violence in their administrations by referring to the presidents as "Ron the Friendly Fascist" and "Dirty Harry" or "Make-My-Day George," respectively. Yet the grim humor of the marginalized left was continuously upstaged by U.S. presidents throughout the 1980s. With what many considered misplaced remorse, Reagan laid wreaths at a cemetery that housed the graves of Nazi stormtroopers at Bitburg. A *New York Times* March 1985 article quoted him as proclaiming that the Nicaraguan "contras are . . . the moral equal of our Founding Fathers"; in a March 6 article, the *Times* reported a senior Reagan administration official's acknowledgment that "the contras have a tendency to kidnap young girls."[12] Several years later in 1987, U.S. media would expose the existence of a CIA torture-instruction manual for the Nicaraguan contras. Further, Bush was implicated in both the Iran-Contra affair and the conflict over Manuel Noriega, for whose country he authorized an invasion to stem cocaine smuggling. Together, the Reagan and Bush administrations engineered the largest peacetime arms buildup in U.S. history, fed the current spiraling deficit, and financed terrorist activities through covert "low-intensity conflict" wars in Africa and Latin America. Tortured and raped by U.S.-funded military death squads in Guatemala, American nun Dianna Ortiz survived with more than a hundred cigarette burns on her body. The Center for Constitutional Rights litigated her case in which a Boston federal judge awarded $47.5 million to Ortiz and eight Guatemalans terrorized by their country's military in the 1980s.[13]

Erasing the spectacle of racialized state violence is simpler if one ignores policy strategies. Instead, one might examine the U.S. government's formation and funding of the Commission on Integrated Long-Term Strategy, which issued a January 1988 report titled *Discriminate Deterrence*.[14] The commission's bipartisan participants included Anne L. Armstrong, Zbigniew Brzezinski, William P. Clark, W. Graham Claytor Jr., Samuel P. Huntington, Henry A. Kissinger, and Albert Wohlstetter. Prior to the disintegration of the Soviet Union, *Discriminate Deterrence* acknowledged that a winnable nuclear war was an unmarketable concept. Although Reagan promoted the image of Russia as an evil empire during his two terms, *Discriminate Deterrence* argued that the East-West conflict must be de-emphasized to allow U.S. conflicts with the Third World to shape policy into the twenty-first century. Former Reagan secretary of state George Shultz remarked in the 1980s that the U.S. had intervened militarily in the Third World more than thirty times since the end of World War II. These interventions included the invasion of Grenada as well as the bombings of Libya and Panama. According to *Discriminate Deterrence*, since World War II, the United States has restricted its military involvement to the Third World. (This policy changed with the conflict in Bosnia in the mid-1990s.) These wars, waged without formal declarations of war, usually reflected U.S. counterrevolutionary ideology and conflicts with (often Soviet-backed) liberation movements in Africa, Asia, Latin America, and the Caribbean. Such wars often targeted civilians, as the United States reserved most of its funding for terroristic activities in Third World countries.

Discriminate Deterrence maintained that to "protect U.S. interests and allies in the Third World, we will need more of a national consensus on both means and ends . . . [including] Security assistance at a higher level and fewer legislative restrictions that inhibit its effectiveness."[15] American economic military assistance flowed to Third World allies that were routinely condemned in the international community for human-rights atrocities—El Salvador, Guatemala, Israel, and the Nicaraguan and Angolan contras. The United States also funded those who most often victimized women, children, and noncombatants, called "soft" targets, in farming cooperatives, schools, day-care centers, and hospitals. Michael Klare satirizes the popularity of warfare by means of contra wars or "low-intensity conflicts" among a U.S. citizenry acquiescent to state violence:

> Low-intensity conflict, by definition, is that amount of murder, mutilation, torture, rape, and savagery that is sustainable without triggering widespread public disapproval at home. Or, to put it another way, LIC is the ultimate in "yuppie" warfare—it allows privileged Americans to go on buying condominiums, wearing chic designer clothes, eating expensive meals at posh restaurants, and generally living in style without risking their own lives, without facing conscription, without paying higher taxes, and, most important, without being overly distracted by grisly scenes on the television set.[16]

By 1988, American-funded contras were responsible for forty-five thousand casualties in Nicaragua. Congress appropriated more than $100 million to the contras in Nicaragua, and millions more were channeled illegally through the CIA and other private operations, as later revealed in the Iran-Contra hearings. In southern Africa, a region far from the United States but one still considered within its sphere of influence, the casualty rates were also high. Repealing the Clark Amendment, which prohibited CIA, covert, and congressional support for UNITA, the Reagan administration channeled $15 million and $27 million, respectively, to UNITA in 1986 and 1987. In Angola, UNITA, headed by Jonas Savimbi, maimed or killed tens of thousands, creating one of the largest amputee populations in the world through its laying of land mines in farm fields, roads, and school yards. Torture, rape, and mutilation used to destabilize socialist governments or movements were routine in these contra wars. In the so-called peace time of the 1980s, Klare argued that "America [was] at war—extensively, aggressively, and with every evidence of continuing such activity"(12), explicating four types of low-intensity conflict:

> (1) *counterinsurgency,* combat against revolutionary guerrillas, as is now being waged in El Salvador and the Philippines; (2) *proinsurgency,* U.S. support for anticommunist insurgents, such as the con-

tras in Nicaragua and UNITA in Angola; (3) *peacetime contingency operations,* police-type actions like the U.S. invasion of Grenada and the April 1986 bombing of Tripoli; and (4) *military "show of force"* threatening military maneuvers of the sort the U.S. is . . . conducting in the Persian Gulf. (12)

The carpet-bombing of Panama and Iraq in the late 1980s and early 1990s was a U.S. military show of force, whose high-tech smart bombs provided a media and patriot spectacle.

In the early 1990s, the well-publicized, if not sensationalist, aspects of U.S. involvement in peacekeeping missions in Somalia and Haiti seem to diverge from policing methods of low-intensity conflicts. Particularly in Haiti, however, which given its status as a former French colony might have been of particular interest to Foucault, destabilization and low-intensity conflicts appear in various forms. For example, in 1987 the CIA financed candidates in Haitian elections, and Aristide's supporters argue that the CIA encouraged the 1991 coup that forced him into exile. This is denied by the U.S. government. The military coup that ousted the democratically elected Aristide, however, was directed by career military officers trained in the United States. Mainstream media venues such as *Time* magazine reported the connections between the U.S. government and terrorist organizations in George Church's 1994 story, "Lying Down with Dogs."[17] This article disclosed that Emmanuel "Toto" Constant, who headed FRAPH (the Front for the Advancement and Progress of Haiti), a terrorist organization succeeding Papa Doc and Baby Doc's Ton-ton macoutes, was on the CIA's and Defense Intelligence Agency's payrolls when he organized FRAPH in 1993. Constant was paid even after acknowledging his connection to FRAPH, which is notorious for maiming pro-democracy advocates with machetes. The U.S. presence in Haiti, ostensibly there to protect people from murder, torture, and rape by the military, police, and paramilitary FRAPH, contradicts the United States' covert funding for Haiti's police and paramilitary. Haitian national Alerte Belance, with the Center for Constitutional Rights, is suing the Haitian paramilitary terrorists who maimed her. In October 1994, National Public Radio described U.S. battalion strikes against FRAPH and attempts to curb FRAPH torture and assassination in order to restore Aristide's presidency; the same segment cited press reports that the CIA had created FRAPH to undermine the pro-democracy movement that elected Aristide.

Conclusion

Mapping the political terrain is an imprecise craft. Boundaries are continuously redrawn through political conflict, compromise, and resignation. Losing one's bearings becomes commonplace when following altered maps with abstractions about policing and policed bodies—abstractions, which in their failure to address the racialization of bodies and punishment, lead to false notions of body politics and repression. To romanticize or falsify the disciplined body, one need only present it as unstructured by race, sex, and class. In contrast, rejecting the illusion of an individual in a casteless society made up of raceless and genderless bodies, one may confront racist and sexist violence in state practices and theories that mask such violence.

The U.S. military's components or counterparts—local police, Texas Rangers, the Immigration and Naturalization Service, the Drug Enforcement Agency, the Federal Bureau of Investigation, and the Central Intelligence Agency—as well as the use of mercenaries and contras speak to a pervasiveness of violence in policing for which *Discipline and Punish* cannot account. One would be hard pressed to rely on Foucault's theorizing to critique the prevalence of racialized state violence, which arguably is the closest form of political terrorism that the United States has demonstrated.

Discipline and Punish offers limited theoretical resources for resistance to U.S. state violence for two reasons. First, Foucault obscures or erases racist violence carried out by the state. Second, his argument that the bureaucratic state and atomized individual supplant the collective community and diminish political resistance through communal power fails to distinguish power from domination, suggesting that only the state is powerful. (Foucault claims that "private individuals" and "the state" have supplanted "the community and public life" as the key elements in social relationships [216].) *Discipline and Punish* posits a Hobbesian view of political society, in which the arrest of the plague or the exclusion of the leper shapes political dreams. Yet this politics of exclusion and arrest signifies not the development but the demise of a political dream based on community. Hannah Arendt argues otherwise. Maintaining that the construction of power stems from communal practice rather than dominance and that community signifies plurality and diversity, Arendt critiques the refusal of nation-states to limit expansionism: "Sovereignty, the ideal of uncompromising self-sufficiency and mastership, is contradictory to the very condition of plurality. . . . [no one] can be sovereign because not one . . . [but many] inhabit the earth."[18] This plurality and power, in fact, are manifested in challenges to the state's refusal to be disciplined by international law and human-rights conventions.

Perhaps because Foucault does not seek or sees little possibility for opposition, *Discipline and Punish* fails to explore resistance to violence. This seems to suggest that only social work is viable within the carceral. Departing from Foucauldian erasures, those who look at political life outside the carceral in order to analyze racialized state violence—at home and abroad—record the largely obscured or denied existence of terror and resistance in the infernos created by U.S. policies.

2 / Radicalizing Language and Law: Genocide, Discrimination, and Human Rights

Antiracism and the Metamorphic Racist

Some civil-rights opponents argue that institutional racism is an anachronism in contemporary America. Others—such as Supreme Court Justice Clarence Thomas, who stated in 1995 that affirmative action was a sin against whites for which black Christians must atone—maintain that racism still exists but believe that programs to redress its manifestations are divisive and abusive to whites. Both groups in the post-civil-rights era contend that whether there is or is not racial discrimination, correcting for it constitutes white victimization.

The 1970s' definitions that distinguished *racism* from *prejudice* in race-relations workshops are obviously considered anachronistic in this anti-civil-rights discourse. A generation ago, Delmo Della-Dora's pamphlet *What Curriculum Leaders Can Do about Racism* argued that racism is the "power to carry out systematic discriminatory practices" through institutions dominated by whites, such as the government, corporations, industry, schools, unions, and churches.[1] Consequently for Della-Dora, in contemporary U.S. society racism is synonymous with white racism. The National Education Association's 1973 *Education and Racism* pamphlet was equally explicit about racial domination in the United States: "Only whites can be racists, since whites dominate and control the institutions that create and enforce American cultural norms and values. . . . blacks and other Third World peoples do not have access to the power to enforce any prejudices they may have, so they cannot, by definition be racists."[2] The rumor passed along with this brochure among United Nations (UN) Church Center seminar planners was that the black woman who author(iz)ed the passages was fired for these assertions. The veracity of the rumor was of less interest than its message: antiracism was no longer a white problem—if it indeed had ever been so—and to assert it as such would be met with considerable opposition and punitive measures.

Antiracist definitions that focus on state dominance, highlighting the institutionalized power of white supremacy, are largely absent from some of the most popular postmodern studies of race, identity, and culture. The rejection of a false equivalence between racism and prejudice has itself been rejected as contemporary speech erases the distinction between the terms *racialized* and *racist*, emphasizing the former. In addition, state abuses overtly shaped by race are mitigated in the aftermath of constitutional amendments guaranteeing rights to all citizens. The disavowal of biological races need not obscure or derail the phenomenon of racism (in other words, racism can exist without races). This disavowal also need not prohibit us from analyzing the relationships of dominance between subjects racialized as white and nonwhite, and the various hierarchies among nonwhites determined by their status vis-à-vis the majority. In a society where texts by whites are considered merely texts and those by "others" are labeled "ethnic texts," race remains an identifying marker as well as an expression of dominance. The realities of racial dominance, though, are often obscured by rhetoric.

Few claim the label of racist as members of a white supremacist or neo-Nazi party. Even David Duke in his gubernatorial campaign continuously stated that he was "not a racist," only a man with the courage to stand up for "white rights and white power" in a country dominated by European Americans. No avowed racist can be found in government, most corporate boardrooms, or academic departments. As racist phenomena disappear by proclamation, exorcised from polite or at least cautious conversation, there is the racist metamorphosis. Now, where one has racism without races, white supremacy without whites, and institutionalized oppression without oppressors, there is no one to hold accountable for justice.

In discourses of denial, dominance reinvents itself. Americans' cultural reluctance to talk about racism, mirrored by an eagerness to talk about race as spectacle, performance, hybridity, or imaginary, suggests a disinterest in discourse on racist U.S. foreign and domestic policies and their relationship to systemic discrimination and genocide. Likewise, to restrict the discourse of race and racism to mere speech, social manners, or the incivility of aberrational minorities or a white fringe ignores the intersections of racist state rhetoric and violence and white-supremacist hate groups. Irrespective of the allegedly disappearing racist and racism in language, law, and society, institutional dominance remains, while white supremacy and its attendants—genocide and fascism—are rendered social fictions.

Racist State Violence and the Genocide Convention

In his 1992 funeral eulogy for Malice Green, a black man beaten to death by Detroit police, Reverend Adams stated that "racism killed Malice Green, and if racism itself is not destroyed, it will destroy our nation. It got Malice Green at night. It will get you in the morning." This eulogy is an unfamiliar refrain to most in the United States. We rarely speak about racist state murders in a language that permits us to understand and mourn our losses. Atrocities can inspire a truth-telling to critique and condemn racist violence. This truth-telling, however, most often happens in eulogies at funerals and memorials. The rest of the time, we usually hear and speak the semi-illiteracy of conventional rhetoric shaping the dominant discourse on race. This semi-illiteracy arises from severing racism from its logical culmination in genocide and from restricting the referent for human atrocities to past holocausts that have been commodified for mass consumption as historical objects and moral reminders. The moral import of racism is virtually meaningless after it has been severed from genocide.

In the midst of denials and obscurantism, some organize to implement international human-rights conventions in the United States. For instance, African and Native American activists have long organized against genocide and human-rights violations in U.S. domestic and foreign policy. In 1951, the African-American-led Civil Rights Congress petitioned the United Nations. With its document *We Charge Genocide: The Crime of*

Government against the Negro People, the congress interpreted and promoted the language of the 1948 UN Convention on Genocide:

> It is sometimes incorrectly thought that genocide means the complete and definitive destruction of a race or people. The Genocide Convention, however, adopted by the General Assembly of the United Nations on December 9, 1948, defines genocide as any killings on the basis of race, or in its specific words, as "killing members of the group." Any intent to destroy, *in whole or in part,* a national, racial, ethnic or religious group is genocide, according to the Convention. Thus, the Convention states, "causing serious bodily or mental harm to members of the group" is genocide as well as "killing members of the group."
>
> We maintain, therefore, that the oppressed Negro citizens of the United States, segregated, discriminated against and long the target of violence, suffer from genocide as the result of the consistent, conscious, unified policies of every branch of government.[3]

Domestic genocidal policies in the U.S. have historically focused on Native and African Americans. Activists and educators have referred to ratified and pending UN human-rights treaties and covenants since their inception. The history of progressive activism around the conventions includes the 1951 appeal to international law by the Civil Rights Congress, which charged the U.S. government with human-rights violations in its petition. The United Nations adopted the Convention on Genocide in 1948, which President Harry Truman signed as a response to Nazi genocidal policies. Because full ratification and enforcement of international treaties would affect U.S. practices, ratified human-rights treaties are often restricted with amendments in order not to alter or constrain U.S. domestic and foreign policies.

According to Francis Boyle, after a thirty-year battle the Senate finally ratified the genocide convention on February 19, 1986, after crippling it with two "reservations," five "understandings," and one "declaration."[4] The convention was adopted by Congress in October 1988; Reagan signed the legislation on November 4, 1988. Congressional fears that indigenous and African Americans would use the convention to bring charges against the United States, led first to obstructions, then to the weakening of the convention before it became a binding treaty. In theory, through this law, genocide, including the inciting of genocide, is deemed a crime in the

United States. If enforced, the convention limits racist free-speech groups as well as the implementation of biased policies, such as those curtailing the sovereignty of Native American nations. The convention also acts as a protector against war crimes and crimes against humanity. In short, the convention provides moral legitimacy for legal resistance to state genocidal policies.

Recently, the International Indian Treaty Council and the Freedom Now Party have used the convention on genocide to petition the UN and educate communities about domestic repression, political prisoners, the disproportionate imprisonment of African, Latin, and Native Americans, and torture in U.S. prisons. Activists and writers also argue for the enforcement of the convention, which prohibits involuntary sterilization of a targeted population under the guise of "population control." Puerto Rican, African, and Native American women have historically been at risk. For example, the U.S. Indian Health Service (IHS) of the Bureau of Indian Affairs has involuntarily sterilized approximately 40 percent of all Native American women, according to Ward Churchill. He also reports that in 1990, the IHS inoculated Inuit children with an HIV-correlated hepatitis-B vaccine banned by the World Health Organization; in 1993, the HIV-correlated hepatitis-A vaccine was tested on Native Americans living on the Northern Plains reservations.[5]

Implemented into law in 1988 with restrictive amendments, the convention on genocide theoretically criminalizes and outlaws such policies that create or incite genocide. In practice, the United States has consistently positioned itself as a state beyond international law rather than an outlaw state; it argues that it has committed no crimes against humanity. Demographic evidence, however, contradicts these claims. For example, African American infant mortality is double that of whites. White life expectancy exceeds that of nonwhites: from 1984 to 1986, the life expectancy for African Americans decreased, from 69.7 to 69.4 years, while the life expectancy for European Americans increased, from 75.3 to 75.4 years; for Native Americans, life expectancy on reservations is forty-five and forty-eight years for men and women, respectively.[6] Neo-Malthusian arguments and political advocates for fewer government programs and less assistance for poorer peoples would cite these discrepancies in longevity as the fault not of government policies but of the individual peoples. Manning

Marable's grim 1983 assessment of the potential impact of state policies on city residents also applies to those who live on reservations:

> The direction of America's political economy and social hierarchy is veering toward a kind of subtle apocalypse which promises to obliterate the lowest stratum of the Black and Latino poor. For the Right *will not be satisfied* with institutionalization of bureaucratic walls that surround and maintain the ghetto. The genocidal logic of the situation could demand, in the not too distant future, the rejection of the ghetto's right to survival in the new capitalist order.[7]

Dismembered language distracts from the impact of racist state policies and the implication of white rights for a dominant ethnic group. Language often mystifies racism to disconnect it from institutional white supremacy and genocide and privatizes it as personal behavior and speech. How we talk about racism, however, determines what we say and do about genocide.

Racist Discourse, White Rights, and White Supremacy

How do you get to be the sort of victor who claims to be the vanquished also?
—Jamaica Kincaid, *Lucy*

Racialized identity and speech are endemic to the United States. Yet a focus on these alone deflects from the political and economic aspects of structural racism and white supremacy. Whether or not anything is publicly said—and no matter how one racially self-identifies—policies perpetuate dominance and genocide. Racism has come to be understood as "a form of discourse . . . that can be effectively blocked by means of linguistic taboos";[8] as racial epithets become taboo, so does antiracist terminology. For instance, the term *race* supplants *racist*; *multiculturalism* and *race relations* supplant *antiracism* in the language of conservatives and progressives alike; reformist policies such as affirmative action are first socially and politically denounced as "quotas" that polarize and handicap a nation; later such policies are legally invalidated, for example, in the 1995 Supreme Court decisions that eviscerated the Voting Rights Act, as well as so-called race-based scholarships and preferential hiring.

The absence of racial epithets notwithstanding, supremacist language and racial mythology inspired the electoral campaigns of neo-Nazi David

Duke and former presidents Ronald Reagan and George Bush. All shared the rhetoric of European neofascist movements, that is, the language of white rights and the redress of white victimization. Neofascists' denunciation of an alleged white victimization, supposedly stemming from "black racism" and equity programs, echoes the language of conservatives, moderates, and progressives alike. White rights and reverse discrimination provide the ideological ground for neoconservatives to advocate and neoliberals to ignore genocidal policies. The ascent from rightist racism to leftist racism is not as steep as we might like to imagine.

For example, in the special issue on whiteness of the liberal national weekly the *Village Voice,* Slavoj Žižek's particular interpretation of Malcolm X allowed him to argue that the idea that whites should accept responsibility for white supremacy is a form of racism: "Only by acknowledging that, ultimately, they can do nothing, that the emancipation of African Americans must be their own deed, only by renouncing the false, self-blame of whites, which conceals its exact opposite, patronizing arrogance, can whites actually do something for African American emancipation."[9] With no one (that is, no one white) held accountable for truly horrific conditions, the overthrow of white supremacy is now a black thing, a struggle for which African Americans become solely responsible. Žižek's argument would move African Americans from a position of structural inferiority to one of equality or superiority, investing them with a special ability—the power to engender social change unilaterally. The consequence of such a Horatio Alger mandate for racial harmony and equality is that genocide becomes reduced to autogenocide.

For the same issue of the *Voice, Tikkun's* editor Michael Lerner (who later coauthored a book on black-Jewish relations with Cornel West) wrote "Jews Are Not White," an essay that is much more circumspect than that of Žižek, but nonetheless one that clearly exculpates the power structure. Without differentiating between Ashkenazic, Sephardic, or Ethiopian Jews, for instance, or referring to the complicity of non-Wasps in white supremacy, Lerner argues that to achieve "the liberatory potential of multiculturalism" we must

> reject the fantasized concept of "whiteness" and instead recognize the complex stories of each cultural tradition, not privileging one group over another. . . . [Today, however, multiculturalism] is merely the

tool of an elite of minority intellectuals seeking to establish themselves inside an intellectual world that has too long excluded them.
And in that context, Jews must respond with an equally determined
insistence that we are not white, and that those who claim we are
and exclude our history and literature from the newly emerging multicultural canon are our oppressors.[10]

Here, few (other than Aryans) qualify as members of a mythic construction of whiteness. (The ironic tragedy is that propagandized claims of
European Jews as deficient in whiteness have fueled and still fuel anti-
Semitic persecution.) White supremacy, however, accommodates non-
Aryan whites in Israel and Palestine, Southern Africa, and throughout
the Americas. Both Žižek's and Lerner's writings are indicative of the
mystification of contemporary racism, institutional anti-Semitism, and
racialized state elites—all of which promotes a conventional language
that with increasing aggressiveness argues for white rights under white
supremacy. The fundamental right of states and whites is to not be held
responsible for racial oppression. The ultimate white right is to claim to
be victimized by those targeted for genocide who engage in resistance
and to seek legal measures through the courts to eviscerate civil-rights
legislation. Instructing us that minorities oppress each other and any
given majority, conventional race language erases the role of state institutions and confuses ignorance and abusive chauvinism with systems of
oppression.

Admittedly, blacks and other marginalized ethnic groups verbally
and physically lash out at whites.[11] That ethnic minorities lack the institutional or state power to dominate majority ethnic groups becomes
irrelevant when racism is crassly reduced to all (real and alleged) ethnic
chauvinism. (Because the chauvinism of people of European descent is
universalized as normative, it does not generally appear to be chauvinistic.) If oppressive state hierarchies are real, the critical distinction between chauvinism and racism must be maintained. Transforming odious
ethnic chauvinism into a colorized version of white supremacy (which
has been the only racialized oppression known in the Americas for half a
millennium) trivializes white supremacy. The different forms of ethnic
pride and revolutionary nationalism among blacks or "people of color"
coexist with but cannot be reduced to the reactionary ideologies of eth-

nic bigots, some of whom receive considerable visibility in the national media and whose own dark-skinned people would be considered by the "ogs"—or original gangstas of racial purity—to head the list for ethnic cleansing.

Colonized groups are granted the equal opportunity of being labeled "ethnic oppressors" or "reverse racists" when a false equality projects illusions of domination that deflect from real structures of oppression.[12] This false illusion of domination, by fictionalizing state racism and complicitous populations, rationalizes an otherwise illogical concept: red, black, brown, or yellow racists or racial oppressors within a white supremacist state. Only when racism is severed from genocide can one argue that oppressed ethnic groups can instigate racist and anti-Semitic policies. Here, dismissing structural critiques promotes debates of ethnic identity and innocence that deflect from struggles against domestic genocide.

If only dominant ethnic groups or states are capable of institutionalizing disenfranchisement and violence, then the difference between fringe black demagogues spouting anti-Semitic epithets and black or white implementors of state policies may be the difference between insulting bigotry and genocide.[13] For example, some Native Americans may espouse bigotry toward African Americans (or black Indians); indigenous Americans, however, have no structural power to inflict policies that reflect these antiblack sentiments. In fact, although also oppressed and stigmatized, African Americans are comparatively more secure economically and more assimilated into the dominant culture. Native American chauvinism against African Americans indicates a subaltern internalization of racial bias—not the appropriation of racial privilege restricted to a white society, which the state has vested with structural dominance and which is in turn invested in the state's racialized authority.

Cynically, the most astute racists make alliances that disregard skin color in order to further racial policies. For instance, in the aftermath of the Oklahoma City bombing, white supremacists rationalizing right-wing violence denounced the two Jewish Supreme Court justices associated with liberal politics but made no mention of the conservative black justice Clarence Thomas, who is noted for his opposition to civil-rights legislation (and whose candidacy to the Court was endorsed by extremists such as David Duke).

Memory and Meaning

The present political chaos is connected with the decay of language.
 —George Orwell, "Politics and the English Language"

However improbable it is to discuss racism meaningfully without referring to genocide, it is equally problematic to speak of the moral opprobrium of genocide without referring to fascism. The meaning of the word *genocide* stems from the tribunals held to address Nazi barbarities during World War II. Constructed as the antithesis to Western democracy and civilization, the concept carries great political and ethical weight and has rarely been used to describe U.S. contexts. The label "fascist" is even more infrequently applied to U.S. policies. Like most governing bodies, the United States denies that its policies are racist, with genocidal or neofascist consequences. State politicians used both terms in interventionist rhetoric, however, to mobilize civilian support. For example, during the bombings of Panama and Iraq, George Bush referred to Manuel Noriega and Saddam Hussein as Hitler-like personae or fascists. The term *fascism* is usually limited to specific historical events in Europe, leaving unexamined the phenomena of fascism and neofascism in state racism. Defining *fascism* as "a system of political, economic, social and cultural organization," Noam Chomsky rejects such conventional restrictions:

> If we want to talk about [fascism] reasonably we have to dissociate it from concentration camps and gas chambers. There was a fascism before there were extermination camps. . . . From a socio-cultural point of view, fascism meant an attack on the ideals of the Enlightenment. . . . on the idea that people had natural rights, that they were fundamentally equal, that it was an infringement of essential human rights if systems of authority subordinated some to others.[14]

Chomsky's argument demystifies fascism as a distant evil, yet it does not acknowledge that Enlightenment ideals of the civilized, rational mind were and are themselves premised on racism. The European Enlightenment's construction of the Western liberal individual as the standard for civilized humanity enabled the reconstruction of those enslaved or colonized by Europeans as essentially inferior. According to Peter Fitzpatrick, this worldview placed and places "the colonized beyond the liberal equation of universal freedom and equality by rendering them in racist terms as qualitatively different. . . . Racism was, in short, basic to the creation of liberalism and the identity of the European."[15] The Enlightenment legacy dulls the recognition of how pervasive racism is, just as the language of denial and rhetorical opposition veils acts of radical resistance to racism.

Given the racialized value of human life as an Enlightenment legacy in Europe and European settler states, humanity (and the abhorrence over its loss) is based on whiteness, as embodied in the European. This argument is not a new one. A UN representative of Bosnia argued in 1993 that Western European and U.S. indifference to the genocide in Bosnia was based on the status of Bosnian Muslims as the "other" Europeans. It is difficult in this context to point to Nazi Germany's genocidal policies as *the* single referent for the memory and meaning of racist atrocities.

Like a catch-22 situation, the more one memorializes genocide in past atrocities, the more opaque the concept may become in contemporary political life. The Holocaust Memorial Museum in Washington, D.C., for instance, has been criticized by a number of writers for its omissions. In her critique of the 1993 dedication of the museum, Alisa Solomon notes the importance of a memorial that documents the historical reality of Nazi Germany's genocidal policies against Jews.[16] In 1993, based on information received from a polling firm, the media reported that an estimated one-fifth of the U.S. population denies this historical reality. Later, the *New York Times* explained that this percentage was significantly overstated because of polling errors based on the phrasing of the questions. Acknowledging the significance of the memorial, Solomon also notes its flaws.

For Solomon, the museum, the state, and corporate donors promote a consciousness in which this tragedy, abstracted from historical and contemporary genocides, is manifested as the only real expression of genocide. It is unlikely that a national poll would be conducted to see what percentage of U.S. citizens believes that indigenous and African holocausts happen(ed) in the Americas. (Given that such a study points to historical and contemporary realities that are minimized or denied in national discourse, such a poll would conceivably produce surprising findings.)

The national museum, dedicated to preventing future holocausts with no mention of American national racism and anti-Semitism, valorizes the U.S. government and ignores its genocidal policies. It calls us to awaken, only to then be anesthetized by the horrors of holocausts as past events, occurring outside this nation, which is now reconstructed as the protector against genocide. As Solomon explains, these contradictions suggest that the spectator was never intended to be an actor:

> [The museum narrative] suggests an outcome that isn't really possible. . . . It strains toward completeness and closure and understanding; these dramatic reassurances are evoked, but never satisfied. Except to the extent that the museum hints at a moral to the story: American democracy. Press materials explain, "the charter of the Museum is to remind visitors of the importance of democratic values and to underscore our national commitment to human-rights." On the way out of the exhibit one practically walks into a wall bearing the seal of the United States. Arched over the eagle and "E Pluribus Unum" are the words "For the dead and the living we must bear witness." (35)

But to what shall we bear witness and how? For Solomon, the Jewish holocaust is presented as "a discourse, a representation forever being deconstructed, a spectacle, an industry" that promises comforting closure to and containment of human barbarism and tragedy: "The Nazis came to power, committed atrocities, and were defeated. The end"(36). In 1995, the *New York Times* reported that the expansion of the museum would include the narratives of contemporaneous European genocides of gays and Gypsies. Information on collaborators, including complicitous states, however, remains problematized by this record of national memory. The collective memory of selective holocausts, remembered in fragmented fashion, reveals the depoliticizing aspects of race language: in other words, the language of the horrified spectator is not necessarily the language of the antiracist activist. Identifying with tragedy (no matter how horrific) by viewing it as a spectacle does not necessarily lead to analysis, moral commitment, or political organizing. Ongoing genocidal practices diminish before the symbolic, as national memory is shaped more by marketing than by regret for racist policies and philosophies that (inevitably) culminate in genocide.

State-constructed memory and meaning obstruct the confrontation of racism as genocide. Calls to consciousness, relying on mystified and Eurocentric constructions of humanity and suffering, are conditioned by the surrealism and hypocrisy of regret. With the loss of European life as the only common and binding referent for such atrocities, no conventional language can denounce the genocide of Native and African Americans as inherently meaningful or morally and politically tragic. Problematizing resistance through this language, Native, African, and European American writers use German Nazism as the recognized referent for the terms *holocaust* and *fascism* to make U.S. genocidal practices meaningful.

Conclusion: Law, Order, and Resistance

First the law dies and then people die.
—1993 sign in Solingen, Germany,
protesting the neo-Nazi arson
murders of five Turkish girls and
women and parliament's amending
of the German constitution to
restrict asylum for foreigners

To prevent chaos, we have law. National laws, however, have the ability to produce their own forms of devastation. American constitutional law sanctioned slavery, broken indigenous treaties, suppression of political dissent, codified sexism and homophobia, and monopolizing capitalism. As an Enlightenment project, constitutional law posits "law's innocence," as law first "marks out the areas" within which racism or sexism are allowed to operate legally and then rationalizes their operation.[17] To consider law not as innocent but as useful to progressive policies requires going beyond the limitations of national law into the potential benefits of international law.

The limitations of constitutional law stem from its malleability by dominant elites and structures that define rights and their enforcement. It is also handicapped by a universalized Western worldview that excludes the contributions to law of traditional, indigenous cosmologies in which community is valued before material profit and individualism. The limitations of U.S. constitutional law also anticipate the frailties of international law. Despite the UN's management by dominant elites and structures, however, the language of its conventions is able to address the dehumanizing aspects of national law. In turn, the obscurantist language that veils or normalizes oppressive policies is called into question.

Political battles have been waged within the United States to mitigate the impact of international law and human-rights covenants on U.S. policies. Francis Boyle reviews how the Constitution's "supremacy clause" renders treaties as part of the "supreme law of the land," superseding national law in conflicts, just as federal law prevails over state or local laws.[18] Article 6 of the Constitution states that "all treaties made, or which shall be made, under the authority of the United States, shall be the supreme law of the land; and the judges in every State shall be bound thereby, anything in the Constitution or laws of any State to the contrary notwithstanding." That treaties are nonbinding unless Congress passes laws for their implementation is a relatively recent byproduct of racist organizing in Congress, according to Boyle, who describes how legislators in the early 1950s sought to obstruct the passage of federal civil-rights laws. These congressional leaders realized that they would also have to block the executive branch from enacting international human-rights treaties that addressed institutional racism. In 1953 legislators in the Eighty-third Congress introduced the Bricker Amendment to the Constitution. The amendment barred the executive branch from negotiating any treaties without elaborate intervention from Congress; if passed, it would have crippled the foreign-policy powers of the executive branch. President Dwight D. Eisenhower's secretary of state, John Foster Dulles, orchestrated a compromise: if the Senate defeated the Bricker Amendment, the executive branch "would not become a party to any human-rights convention or present it as a treaty for consideration by the U.S. Senate."[19] Stemming from that compromise, Boyle explains, arguments arose to counter U.S. ratification of international human-rights treaties, namely, that the Constitution renders such treaties superfluous, for serious human-rights violations do not exist in the United States and, further, that the ratification and enforcement of international human-rights treaties violate states' rights.

These same arguments were used by segregationists to counter federal desegregation laws during the 1950s and 1960s; decades later, conservatives and rightists use these arguments in their advocacy to restrict federal jurisdiction over states and international law's jurisdiction over the federal government. Today, in a so-called new world order (a phrase popularized by George Bush), rightists argue in favor of UN conspiracy theories. Militia extremists insist that the UN plans to invade the United States; using an anti-Semitic tract "The Elders of Zion," they supposedly identify an international cabal dictating U.S. policy. At the same time, institutional politicians such as Senator Jesse Helms assert that the UN is the "nemesis" of the United States.

Law in itself is insufficient to bring about political change. American activists organize for the implementation of international human-rights conventions while working to popularize the language of these conventions. This educational and political strategy resists violent policies by expanding and redefining the conventional concept of rights and entitlements. When the United States signed the UN Charter, it agreed (under Article 55) to uphold "equal rights and self-determination of peoples," "higher standards of living, full employment," and "universal respect for, and observance of human rights and fundamental freedoms for all without distinction as to race, sex, language, or religion." If held accountable to that charter in particular and to international law in general, the United States would be a radically different state, for the charter and other conventions explicitly prohibit state repression, illegal surveillance and imprisonment, police powers such as preventive detention laws (in the 1984 Bail Reform Act), and the criminalization of radical political dissent.

Implementing international law and enforcing human-rights conventions would curtail the rights of individual parties and governments to dominate, exploit, and kill, for instance, if the U.S. government ratifies and implements all of the following: the American Convention on Human Rights; the Universal Bill of Rights; the International Covenant on Civil and Political Rights; and the International Covenant on Economic and Social Rights. American domestic and foreign policy also would be revolutionized by implementation of the International Convention on the Elimination of All Forms of Racial Discrimination, which was submitted to the Senate on February 23, 1978, by President Jimmy Carter; the Convention on the Elimination of All Forms of Discrimination against Women; and the Convention against Torture and Other Cruel, Inhuman or Degrading Treatment or Punishment, which was submitted to the Senate on May 23, 1988, by President Ronald Reagan.

If enforced, the UN's 1949 Geneva Conventions and Nuremberg Principles also would mitigate the barbarism of war. Both outlaw war crimes, crimes against humanity, and crimes against peace; they also mandate that everyone, including military personnel, refrain from such crimes, even if it means disobeying direct orders from superior officers, and they maintain that anyone with knowledge of such crimes who fails to act to prevent them is complicitous. The Nuremberg Principles are contained in the U.S. Army Field Manual, which provided the basis for the prosecution of Lt. William Calley for the My Lai massacre in Vietnam. The principles also cover the wartime treatment of wounded and captured military personnel, civilians, and political prisoners. According to the Geneva Conventions, persons shall not be murdered or exterminated, subjected to torture or to biological experiments, willfully left without medical assistance and care, nor shall conditions exposing them to contagion or infection be created. Although ratifying the Conventions in 1956, Congress has refused to enforce them. This is likely because their implementation would affect low-intensity-conflicts in foreign policies and the treatment of immigrants, political prisoners, and people incarcerated in penal and mental institutions in domestic policies.

II

Colonial Hangovers:
U.S. Policies at Home and Abroad

3 / Hunting Prey:
The U.S. Invasion of Panama

Historically treated as a U.S. possession and private fiefdom, Panama has been invaded on no less than eleven occasions in the twentieth century—five times between 1908 and 1925.[1] Since Panama's nominal independence in 1903, it has functioned as a neocolony of the United States and as a major military base, with the Canal Zone under U.S. jurisdiction.

Panama is a black nation. *Black* as a political rather than racial term denotes the physiognomy of its "colored" citizenry—indigenous, African, and mestizo Panamanians—and their construction as second-class citizens. Of its 2.2 million inhabitants, at the time of the 1989 U.S. invasion around 12 percent were indigenous (Indian), 13 percent African, 65 percent mestizo, 8 percent European or white, and 2 percent other. Although they comprise less than 10 percent of Panama's population, whites own most of the country's land and economic resources. This oligarchy, with its ruling families entrenched and supported by the United States, has dominated Panamanian politics for most of this century. Panama's Guillermo Endara, a corporate lawyer, is one of the by-products of the alliance between Panama's oligarchy and the United States. In the May 1989 elections, his party, the Alianza Democrática Civilista, was financed by the United States at the price of $10 million. The Civilistas were described by nationalist Panamanians, such as Isabel de Del Resonio, a mestiza activist in

El Frente Unido de Mujeres contra la Agresión (FUMCA) who is opposed to U.S. intervention, as "white with money, with cradles of silver. They don't want to see us [black people]."[2]

Color, race, and caste in Panama, although differing from their U.S. counterparts, show some similarities in terms of disenfranchised peoples. A form of apartheid was practiced by the U.S. military in the Canal Zone until the late 1960s. Racism in Panama, dominated by European ruling families and the U.S. military, mirrors the racism in the United States as symbolized by the Whites Only signs, which in past decades were widely visible in the Canal Zone. Panamanian nationalism and resistance have also echoed U.S. civil-rights struggles. In January 1964, for example, major confrontations occurred when Panamanian students attempted to display the Panamanian flag alongside that of the United States outside a high school in the Canal Zone. Residents, accompanied by police, attacked the students. In the days that followed, black students attempting to place national flags in the zone were assaulted and shot by white zone residents. The U.S. military joined the attack as Panamanians fought back: twenty-one people, the overwhelming majority of whom were Panamanian youths, were killed and 450 wounded.

By 1989, white and colored signs were no longer displayed on entrances, swimming pools, or drinking fountains, just as they had disappeared in the United States. But older Panamanians still remembered them in 1989, pointing out to visitors the gates and doorways that displayed the apartheid laws. The extent to which racial codes have changed in Panama largely depends on the wealth of the individual citizen. Isabel de Del Resonio explains: "Before, the [private] schools were all white. Today, if you have money, even if your child is black he can attend."[3] Still, color and race factor into political democracy. In the Canal Zone, black Panamanians still face economic and racial discrimination from the U.S. Southern Command. They also confront discrimination from the present oligarchy.

A War against Drugs?

In September 1994, succeeding Endara, President Ernesto Pérez Balladares pardoned several hundred people associated with the criminal activities of General Noriega. Some media maintained that the election of Balladares was proof that the United States invasion had led to a democratic process.

Others emphasized that the State Department's war on drugs was successful because Noriega is now serving a forty-year prison sentence in the United States. Yet according to Drug Enforcement Administration (DEA) officials, the amount of drug trafficking and money laundering in Panama was indeterminate before the invasion and remains so today. This second objective—to stop the drug flow into the United States—was problematized by the *New York Times* also in October 1994 with another article on Panama's former dictator, "Lawyers for Noriega Say He Was Paid $10 Million to Spy for U.S."[4] Noting that U.S. prosecutors were able to convict Noriega by arguing that his personal wealth stemmed from drug profiteering, the article reported that previously concealed information made public in an appeal brief filed on September 13, 1994, stated that although the CIA admitted to paying "the former Panamanian dictator $160,000 for political favors . . . the defense claims that Noriega was paid more than $10 million for supporting the Nicaraguan contras and the Salvadoran government during its death squad era" (A12). Noriega allegedly received an additional $2 million for caring for the Shah of Iran, who was deposed in 1979. The appeal lawyers accused the trial's presiding judge, Federal District Judge William M. Hoeveler, of undermining the defense by denying Noriega the ability to offer evidence of something other than drug trafficking as the source of his wealth (A12). A year before the invasion, in December 1988, a Senate Foreign Relations Subcommittee report, *Drugs, Law Enforcement and Foreign Policy,* described the employment of Manuel Noriega as "one of the most serious foreign policy failures for the United States."[5]

The invasion of Panama and the seizure of Noriega were carried out under the pretext of the American war, both national and international, against drugs—an interpretation that most media sources to this day relate uncritically. It is worth looking at the nature of that war more closely. Criticisms of the effectiveness of measures to reduce domestic drug consumption, and the militarization of the antidrug campaign were noted in the media. (For example, in domestic financing for the war on drugs, one-third of Bush's funding went to rehabilitation, while two-thirds went to policing.) What is rarely examined, however, is whether the drug war was indeed effective and whether its primary objective was to discourage drug use. At the time of the Panamanian invasion, the United States was attempting to organize the military forces in Peru, Bolivia, and Colombia into an army directed by the United States, ostensibly for drug enforcement. Yet according to senior U.S. officials in Lima, antidrug efforts in central Peru were unsuccessful and winning the drug war in Latin America was not possible. But such criticisms miss the point where these forces are, in fact, used in counterinsurgency wars and in masking low-intensity conflicts.[6] For example, the anticommunist and anti-insurgency nature of the drug wars in the Andean countries has led to attacks on M19 in Colombia and on the Shining Path in Peru, revolutionary groups noted for their armed struggle and their assistance to peasants growing coca leaves. There were also reports that the U.S. military, routing guerrillas who provided protection to peasants from drug lords, allowed the local military to take over this protection.

Under the guise of eradicating drugs, the U.S. government could consolidate political, military, and economic hegemony by destabilizing progressive movements. Government agencies can also seek to profit from or control the informal economy of narcotrafficking, as in the case of Oliver North and the CIA who allegedly channeled cocaine to fund the Nicaraguan contras illegally once Congress had gutted their funding. Further, U.S. state policy may seek to manipulate or capitalize on rather than destroy the drug trade, despite public policy statements. A May 23, 1995, report on National Public Radio described how Mexico became the largest conduit for cocaine into the United States from Colombia, with its 1994 drug trade valued at $30 billion. Attempting to pass the North American Free Trade Agreement (NAFTA) and seeking to increase the congressional comfort level with Mexico, the Clinton administration downplayed the drug trade and any related stories in the press that would problematize passing a trade treaty with Mexico.

American media sources play a significant role in shaping popular perceptions of the war on drugs, the legitimacy of invasions, and the nature of heroic militarism. Drug trafficking is a multinational corporate business, run by corporate leaders, cartels, bank launderers, people who own private fleets, and police who monitor traffic and enforcement. Yet these affluent and powerful leaders are rarely perceived as culpable, even with sporadic press accounts such as a November 21, 1994, article in the *New York Times;* in it, Allen Myerson reported that American Express Bank International agreed to pay a $32 million fine for laundering money for Mexico's largest drug cartel and channeling Colombian cocaine into the United States.[7]

Mass-media representations of drug users and pushers as overwhelmingly black, Latino, or Chicano racialize the war on drugs and the policing of it inside and outside U.S. borders. Although a considerable portion of drug-trade profits accrue to wealthy companies such as American Express (or "shadow" government agencies such as the CIA), there is little insight into the covert nature of the drug trade, criminality, and profiteering.[8]

Attempts to reestablish U.S. control over Panama can be traced back almost a quarter of a century to Richard Nixon's 1971 declaration that the war on drugs was a national emergency. Nixon named Manuel Noriega, then head of Panamanian security, as instrumental in the drug trade. In May 1971, John Ingersoll, director of the Bureau of Narcotics and Dangerous Drugs, drafted a plan, which broached assassination, for worldwide clandestine law enforcement. The alleged White House plan to assassinate both Noriega and nationalist Panamanian head of state General Omar Torrijos Herrera was quashed; by then, the Watergate scandal had begun to break. But the rhetoric of the Nixon administration was to be invoked nearly two decades later in the Bush administration's rationalizations for Operation Just Cause, the State Department code name for the invasion of Panama.

The rationale for the Panama invasion—as a law-enforcement response to drug trafficking—was necessary for mobilizing congressional and popular support, and as such it should be closely scrutinized. First, it should be reiterated that Noriega had worked with the CIA since 1960, when, as a cadet at a Peruvian military academy, he had provided information on left-wing students to the U.S. Defense Intelligence Agency. For nearly three decades he regularly reported to the U.S. government and the CIA. He also became a key asset in the U.S. war against Nicaragua, allowing the contras to train on Coiba Island off Panama when direct U.S. military support to them was prohibited.[9]

Moreover, journalists have reported U.S. agency involvement with organized crime in drug trafficking since just after the Second World War.[10] Records of the 1986 executive sessions of the Iran-Contra hearings have shown that covert operations to fund the contras were intertwined with drug trafficking on a large scale.[11] As Senator John Kerry put it in one session of the hearings, "it is clear that there is a networking of drug trafficking through the contras. . . . [and] in the name of national security, we can produce specific law enforcement officials who will tell you that they have been called off drug trafficking investigations because the CIA is involved."[12] The U.S. government's failure to prosecute any of its agencies or agents involved in drug trafficking problematized the rationale of the invasion as law enforcement. In fact, the government sought to enforce, under the guise of its antidrug rhetoric, Panamanian compliance with U.S. regional policy in Central America.

American control of Panama had begun to unravel with the 1968 coup that brought Torrijos to power and ousted Arnulfo Arias Madrid, Endara's mentor and a member of the oligarchy. Arias had dominated Panamanian politics up to that time by merging nationalism with ethnic chauvinism and a form of socialism. Domestically, Torrijos's economic and land reforms dismantled the hegemony of the Panamanian white oligarchy. Indigenous, African, and mestizo Panamanians began to make substantial gains in education, health, housing, and employment. New hospitals, health centers, houses, schools, and universities were built. More doctors, nurses, and teachers were trained. In just under two decades, infant mortality declined from 40 percent to 19.4 percent, and life expectancy increased by more than nine years.[13] Indigenous communities were granted autonomy and protection for their traditional lands.[14]

Foreign policy under Torrijos was just as radical a break with the past. His policies of Panamanian sovereignty over the canal and military bases, and of regular contact and exchange of information with the Cuban government, directly threatened U.S. hegemony in Central America and contradicted U.S. regional policy. Increasing Panamanian nationalism and protest, including Torrijos's threat to blow up the canal locks if the United States did not comply, led to the signing of the Panama Canal Treaty in Washington, D.C., on September 7, 1977, by President Carter. Under this treaty, the canal and all military bases were to be transferred to Panama by the year 2000. Unsurprisingly, the treaty was extremely unpopular with U.S. conservatives.

What placed Torrijos and later Noriega on U.S. assassination lists was not the alleged criminality of their governments but their circumvention of U.S. policy in Panama and the region—a policy marked by anticommunism, racism, and intervention under the guise of a war on drugs. Omar Torrijos died in 1981 in a mysterious plane crash, which a former Panamanian army officer later attributed to the CIA. In addition, according to Amnesty International, in June 1987, Colonel Roberto Díaz Herrera, second in command of the Panamanian Defense Forces and a close relative of Torrijos, accused Noriega of electoral fraud, political murder, and plotting with the CIA to assassinate Torrijos. As in most political assassinations, such claims are rarely substantiated. What is easily discernible, however, is the fact that the reforms of the people's power movements, developed during the Torrijos regime, were blocked. Noriega eventually became the de facto head of state. With the untimely death of Torrijos and the change in the Panamanian government, the progressive reforms of the 1970s came to a halt. Despite the corruption of the Noriega government, however, a number of Torrijos's policies were allowed to continue. For example, benefits such as mandatory social security, vacation time, a bonus of one month's pay each year, insurance, and labor codes remain largely intact.

Race, Class, and Destabilization

The 1989 invasion was the culmination of the American economic war against Panama. The standard of living for the majority of Panamanians had already begun to drop from the mid-1980s onward as a result of the International Monetary Fund austerity programs implemented by President Nicolás Bartletta, who was elected in 1984. In an October 9, 1994, article that legitimized the invasion, the *New York Times* noted that more than 50 percent of Panamanians lived in poverty, with official unemployment at 14 percent.[15]

Government revenues before the invasion were down by 45 percent because of punitive U.S. policies toward Panama. For instance, the United States paid neither its assessments for using the canal—the treaty called for U.S. payments of $10 million each year for services—nor fees garnered by the canal. American businesses were prohibited from paying Panamanian taxes, and ships bearing the Panamanian flag were denied access to U.S. ports. From 1987, economic sanctions and the embargo caused great hardship. Malnutrition began to develop among children, particularly in the countryside where land-distribution programs were rendered ineffectual. Panamanian working-class people who had acquired land in the 1960s and 1970s lacked the resources to cultivate it. In the Canal Zone, Panamanians employed by the United States were more financially secure. Yet racial discrimination meant that most of these Panamanian workers held low-paying maintenance jobs.

The two years of sanctions from 1987 to 1989 led to a 25 percent drop in economic production and rising unemployment. In an interview in Panama City in November 1989 with representatives of the 60,000-member Federation of Workers of the Republic of Panama (an estimated 30 percent of unionized workers were in its ranks), members explained that unemployment increased from 10 percent to 11 percent in 1987 and 11 percent to 16 percent in 1988, and they projected it at 17.5 percent for 1989.[16] Poverty rose steeply: before 1987, 33 percent of the population lived below the poverty line; in 1988, 40.2 percent; 44 percent by 1989; and 50 percent in 1995. Increasingly, trade unionists also grappled with union busting. According to the federation, as the embargo took effect and unemployment grew, unions were weakened or destroyed. Collective bargaining was suspended, and campaigns were initiated against trade-union officials. Until the conflict with Noriega, the American Federation of Labor and Congress of Industrial Organizations (AFL-CIO) financially supported the federation's Institute of Free Labor Development. According to federation representatives, as the crisis developed the Panamanian union was told to protest in the streets against Noriega or lose its economic support from the AFL-CIO; union leaders refused and thus lost financial backing.

Rural workers fared no better than city workers. By 1989, production was down 50 percent as agricultural workers lacked farm machinery, fertilizers, and resources derived from petroleum, which Panama does not produce. As with Cuba, the U.S. embargo and economic sanctions prohibited the importation of fertilizers from the United States and Europe and the exportation of agricultural products like beef and sugar to the United States. Panamanian small-scale farmers faced increasing hardships with the embargo, as did rural indigenous communities. As Peter Herlihy explains, indigenous rights to autonomous land control and special government assistance, which had been granted under Torrijos, continued in varying degrees under the administrations of General Ruben Darío Paredes and Noriega. Political unrest and economic restraints in Panama since mid-1987 hindered government assistance to maintain rural Indian lands.[17] Before the U.S. embargo, indigenous workers moved to Panama City in search of jobs; in the aftermath of the war, urban indigenous populations are returning to their traditional land for economic self-sufficiency. Their economic autonomy is now threatened by militarists, real-estate developers, and government encroachment on their land.[18]

Women, National Crisis, and Nationalist Resistance

Whether in the urban or rural areas, the economic crisis was and continues to be borne most heavily by black women. Women workers in Panama, as in the United States, are primarily segregated in low-paying service-sector jobs as domestics, cleaners, store clerks, manual workers, and office workers. American sanctions aggravated the situations of thousands of female-headed households. Malnutrition and starvation have been steadily increasing among the Panamanian poor.

El Frente Unido de Mujeres contra la Agresión (FUMCA) was formed in July 1987 in response to the U.S. economic destabilization of Panama; in this sense it was a nationalist women's group challenging U.S. interventionist policies. The coalition was composed of twenty-two community-based women's organizations by 1989. At its March 8, 1989, national congress in Panama City on International Women's Day, three thousand women were addressed by Commander-in-Chief Noriega. Most FUMCA women were members of the Partido Revolucionario Democrático (PRD), known as the party of Torrijos and Noriega. The leadership of FUMCA has described the organization as the Frente Femenina of the PRD, at that time a party of the military, workers, feminists, students, and intellectuals. As the party of progressive and conservative nationalists with different economic and political agendas, it was held together by the external threat of U.S. intervention. According to FUMCA, women had the most to lose under a *yanqui* pact that militarized Panamanian resources and placed them under foreign management. The economic effects of the intervention were clear. For example, FUMCA reported the minimum wage at 75 cents per hour, with women earning an average of $250 a month (U.S. currency is the paper currency in Panama), with a maximum of $450. Milk cost 65 cents a carton, a loaf of bread, 45 cents. Because of the embargo and sanctions, construction virtually stopped. The resulting housing shortage meant rising rents, overcrowded housing, and increasing renter migration—all disruptions of family life.

Before the invasion, FUMCA had organized around Panamanian national defense and its effects on the political and economic rights of women. It had also attempted, without success, to establish contact with women in the opposition and the Canal Zone. Few reportedly answered the call, through FUMCA's national radio program, to form a women's front against foreign intervention. Race and class divisions, the privileges of Civilista women, as well as ideological differences in terms of the government all worked to mitigate coalitions among Panamanian women. The organization also opposed the hierarchy of the Catholic Church, which according to then treasurer Isabel de Del Resonio aligned itself with the oligarchy, urging women to demonstrate against Noriega's government by banging pots in the streets as middle-class women had in the CIA-sponsored overthrow of President Salvador Allende in Chile.[19] Prior to the invasion, FUMCA collected and delivered clothes, food, and medicine to poor women and offered classes for women in physical and psychological self-defense in case of a military attack.

By 1989, the U.S. military presence in Panama—some thirteen thousand troops were routinely stationed there—had also increased sexual exploitation of and violence against women. American troops provided the base for the prostitution industry in Panama. According to FUMCA, the racial and sexual violence against indigenous women by U.S. soldiers proved particularly severe. As Del Resonio explained to me in an interview, "gringos would rape and kill women, but the U.S. army would just ship them out rather than allow them to be tried in Panamanian courts."[20] For decades, although maintaining the right to jurisdiction and extradition over Panamanians, the United States never gave Panama jurisdiction over U.S. troops stationed in Panama. Some women nationalists wondered if the U.S. military never turned over any troops accused of raping or murdering Panamanian women, why Panamanian women should turn Noriega over to the United States.

Sexual violence by foreign troops was only one of the problems that Panamanian women—particularly poorer and darker-skinned women— had to confront. Among the other difficulties facing women, FUMCA identified the large percentage of female-headed households and adolescents without jobs; nourishment pensions (*las pensiones alimenticias*) as the only subsistence for large numbers of children; women's exploitation in the labor market; and the fact that the weight of the economic crisis was borne most heavily by women. In response, FUMCA made specific demands on the government including social security as a right; the abolition of work codes that undermined workers' rights and wages; the expansion and development of family laws with community input; publicly supported programs for children and pregnant women in poverty; full health rights; the adjustment to economic crises without cutting services to women workers; collective decision making between government agencies and community groups; and the increased role of women in government leadership.

The policy proposals of FUMCA were not well received by the America-installed Endara government. After the invasion, many FUMCA women were reportedly fired from their jobs and went underground or into detention camps, according to Esmeralda Brown, coordinator of the New York-based Women's Workshop in the Americas, a sister organization to FUMCA. Members of FUMCA had also begun to develop a forum on national and international policies, working with the German Democratic Republic-based Women's International Democratic Federation and the Cuban-based Frente Continental de Mujeres contra la Intervención formed in Cuba at the 1988 Encuentro. The regional and international perspective of FUMCA and its stance against U.S. intervention in Latin America set it at odds with the conservative Endara government.

U.S. Militarism in Central America

The United States routinely violated the Panama Canal Treaty in acts prohibited by international law and the U.S. constitution. The Torrijos-Carter Treaty banned the use of the U.S. military outside the protection of the canal. Yet in January 1985, 1986, and 1987, the U.S. military and the Panamanian Defense Forces engaged in joint military exercises unrelated to canal security in Panama.[21] From 1987 until the invasion, no U.S. military operation had been coordinated with the Joint Panamanian Commission, although the Torrijos-Carter Treaty called for such cooperation. Uncoordinated U.S. military flights and sea operations jeopardized commercial Panamanian flights and damaged the fishing industry. On land, U.S. soldiers freely harassed Panamanians with military maneuvers in neighborhoods and city districts; such operations often obstructed traffic for hours in commercial districts in downtown Panama City. Psychological warfare against the population and invasion-training exercises left an estimated twenty U.S. troops dead before the invasion on December 20, 1989. Troops died not in confrontations with Panamanians but in combat exercises or friendly fire. One FUMCA nationalist woman wryly commented in 1989 that U.S. troops "crash and explode, and no one is confronting them. Bombs explode on base. . . . They fought with a coconut tree, and it resulted in three deaths."[22]

Panama was strategically important for the U.S. war against Nicaragua (then under a Sandinista government); but under Noriega Panama became a member of the Contadora group, which sought a resolution to the contra war. In 1985, U.S. National Security adviser John Poindexter met with Noriega in an unsuccessful attempt to negotiate Panama's departure from the group. Poindexter requested (again unsuccessfully) the use of Panamanian Defense Forces for a southern front against Nicaragua. Vice President Bush also sought the reinstatement of Nicolás Bartletta (a personal friend and former student of Secretary of State George Shultz) as president of Panama. (Late in 1985 Noriega had helped to organize the dismissal of Bartletta, who was elected in 1984 amid accusations of electoral fraud by the Panamanian Defense Force.) The Panamanian government refused these and other requests as violations of Panamanian sovereignty.

Nonetheless, as the congressional hearings on the Iran-Contra affair in Autumn 1986 showed, "the U.S. Southern Command, located in the zone, played a major role in coordination, intelligence gathering, and delivery of supplies to the U.S.-funded counter-revolutionaries attempting to overthrow the Nicaraguan government."[23] El Salvador's war was a factor as well: air bases and listening posts in the zone, according to John Weeks and Andrew Zimbalist's analysis of the U.S. military role in Panama, were significant factors in the civil war in El Salvador. And in the November 1989 FMLN offensive against the Salvadoran government, hospitals administered by the U.S. military in Panama were used to service wounded Salvadoran soldiers.

Another objective of the invasion downplayed by most media reports was the removal of Noriega for economic profiteering, which supported nations that the United States opposed. Noriega not only dragged his feet in the contra war, but he also provided Panamanian free-trade zones in Colón for the duty-free shipment of goods for Cuba and Nicaragua, thereby circumventing the U.S. trade embargo. A March 26, 1987, letter from Assistant State Department Secretary J. E. Fox to Senator Jesse Helms illustrates how the Reagan administration viewed Noriega as countering U.S. interests:

The State Department shares your view that when the Carter-Torrijos treaties are being renegotiated, the prolongation of the U.S. military presence in the Panama Canal area till well after the year 2000 should be brought up for discussion. The continuing power of the Sandinistas in Nicaragua, the activities of the Salvadoran insurgents and the influence of communist Cuba in the region make it urgently necessary for the United States to strengthen its position in Central America. The continuing polarization of the political forces in Panama may lead to a crisis in the country which would pose a serious threat to stability in the region.[24]

The letter went on to call for steps "to bring about the resignation of General Noriega and to set up an interim government" that would safeguard "U.S. strategic interests." In the view of a fact-finding delegation, sponsored by the Black Veterans for Social Justice, that visited Panama in September 1989, the Bush agenda would finally turn out to be "a swap of the Canal for long-term, guaranteed U.S. bases in Panama," and the crisis would be escalated "until a Panamanian government renegotiates the Torrijos-Carter treaty, and the U.S. presence in Panama becomes permanent." (The usefulness of the bases after the invasion was demonstrated in the summer of 1994 when the United States "hosted" or, rather, detained Cuban refugees in Panamanian camps following a mass exodus from Cuba.[25])

Policy makers presented the U.S. military presence in Panama as crucial for influence in the region. Within one month of the passing of the Carter-Torrijos Treaty, presidential candidate Ronald Reagan, warning of the potential loss to U.S. security and financial interests, campaigned for the abrogation of the treaty. Under the provisions of the treaty, December 1989 proved a critical month in the progress toward Panamanian decolonization. Not coincidentally, it was the month in which the United States escalated the war. According to the treaty, as of December 31, 1989, the Panamanian government was to establish its own appointee as head of the Panama Canal Commission. The commission chair was then to implement plans for the December 31, 1999, transfer of the canal and all its property and assets (including military bases) to the Panamanian people; all U.S. bases are to cease operation in Panama by January 1, 2000. But on December 4, 1989, in clear violation of the treaty, President George Bush appointed his own nominee as head of the commission. One week later, the Panamanian National Assembly declared Panama in a state of war and named Noriega, commander in chief of the armed forces, as head of state. The U.S. State Department and major media routinely reported this as Panama's declaration of war against the United States.

Days prior to the invasion, media reported Secretary of Defense Dick Cheney's statement that a military wife had been threatened by the Panamanian Defense Forces, suggesting a provocation for military action. On December 16, 1989, a U.S. officer was killed in a confrontation with Panamanian Defense Forces. Four U.S. officers in civilian dress had entered a neighborhood that housed the Panamanian command, where on October 3 a coup attempt had been made. (Since that date, a U.S. curfew prohibited its soldiers from entering Panamanian territory without authorization from commanding officers.) The account of the shooting given in American sources stated initially that the officers were unarmed. But the Panamanian government maintained that they were armed and that the U.S. officers had opened fire first, shooting a woman, child, and elderly man. (The compound was located in a poor, black, and indigenous neighborhood.) Two days after this incident, on December 18, a U.S. soldier, who reportedly felt threatened, shot a Panamanian police officer who approached to question him in a laundromat. Two days later, the United States invaded.

The Invasion

On December 20, 1989, following a long history of U.S. intervention, came the last U.S. invasion of Panama. General Noriega was ousted and taken back to the United States to stand trial on drug charges, and opposition leader Endara was installed as president. The invasion of Panama was at that time the largest U.S. military operation since the Vietnam War, involving some twenty-six thousand troops with the largest parachute drop since the second World War. For weeks, the United States had been mobilizing troops at Fort Bragg in North Carolina. Congress, however, was informed of the attack only hours beforehand. In one sense, the invasion was a last resort, following the failure of U.S.-backed opposition parties— despite the millions of dollars invested in them—to challenge the Panamanian government seriously, and the failure of U.S.-backed coups (the most recent of which occurred on October 3).

But the invasion was not the bloodless walkover that the State Department portrayed it to be. Civilian neighborhoods were carpet-bombed. The Dignity Battalions, nationalist pro-government paramilitary squads developed by Noriega after the October 3 coup attempt, put up a strong resistance, despite being inadequately armed. While the State Department claimed some three weeks after the invasion that civilian casualties numbered just two hundred, the Spanish-language press both within and outside the United States, including the Inter Press Service and *Echo of Mexico*, cited more than two thousand civilian deaths and approximately seventy thousand military casualties. Initially, in New York only the Spanish Press (*El Diario*), the African-American Press (*Amsterdam News* and *City Sun*), and alternative media (WBAI-NY Public Radio) bothered to report Panamanian civilian casualties. New York City's *El Diario* carried photos and reportage of mass graves dug by the U.S. army to conceal the actual death count. The National Lawyers' Guild, returning from a fact-finding mission in Panama in early February 1990, and the Center for Constitutional Rights also reported the presence of mass graves.

On December 27, 1989, the *Wall Street Journal* ran a story describing how the possibility of a protracted guerrilla war—something that, according to press reports two days after the invasion, the Pentagon and Southern Command had feared—was dispelled by the surrender of key Panamanian forces on December 26. The *Journal* quoted U.S.-trained Major Ivan Gaytan, who surrendered a vital base: "I personally know the Americans quite well. They aren't going to put troops up against our guerrillas because they wouldn't put soldiers in another Vietnam. We feared they would simply bomb the hell out of our area."[26]

Media depictions of mostly adult male casualties obscured the realities of large numbers of children and women civilians injured or killed in the war. The bombing of Chorillos and other poor neighborhoods left nearly twenty thousand people homeless and food supplies scarce. American reports also obscured the fact that women were part of the national resistance, participating not only in the Dignity Battalions (as did some children) but in the military as well. The Base de Instrucción Femenina Rufina Alfaro, the women's military detachment, was named after Rufina Alfaro, the woman who made the first call in 1821 for Panamanian independence and sovereignty from Spain. Before the invasion, in the neighborhood where Rufina Alfaro is located, U.S. troops made several incursions in one week, pointing artillery at homes and flying low over houses in helicopters in predawn maneuvers. The women's military center was surrounded by a high fence, and across the street another fence was erected around an empty lot. On both fences and the front of the building were cloth banners in Spanish and English. Put there against harassing U.S. troops, one banner read Ay Que Miedo, Gringo, Ja Ja Ja (Oh What Fear, Gringo, Ha, Ha, Ha), another in English read, Don't Forget Vietnam.

The Panama invasion revealed a further adaptation of military technology to low-intensity conflicts against Third World countries. Although such conflicts usually involve proxy soldiers, contras, or mercenaries, in this case U.S. troops and the Pentagon were directly involved. Soon after the invasion *U.S. News and World Report* quoted General Edward Meyer, former army chief of staff: "This is the first time in the new post-cold-war world there has been an operation by any country where a mixture of conventional and unconventional forces was used in a measured way against the type of threat the U.S. will face in the future. The Panama operation outlined the rationale for the type of forces we will require."[27]

The type of forces required revealed an obsession with high-tech militarization: the Pentagon used eight $50-million F-117A Stealth fighters to drop two 2,000-lb. bombs on a communications site near Río Hato.[28] Initially, the Pentagon reported that the bombs were dropped in an open field causing no injuries; weeks later, new reports stated that the Stealth bombers had also hit communications centers in Panama City. To patrol the cities, the Seventh Light Infantry Division, trained in urban warfare, used night-vision equipment developed in the 1980s, allowing soldiers to see and shoot in the dark. Stun guns were also used. In the words of former chief of the Southern Command, General Frederick Woerner: "Low intensity conflict does not mean simplistic equipment. In Third World conflicts, the importance of sophistication increases, rather than decreases, since you're dependent on a more precise, not massive, application of force."[29]

After the invasion, Panama was policed by the Southern Command. During the postinvasion months, the U.S. government and major media reported that approximately 5,300 Panamanians were being detained for questioning in camps. Progressive activists cited higher figures. A January 19, 1990, *New York Times* article, "US Is Releasing Invasion Captives," failed to note that after releasing some Panamanians the United States rearrested or detained them.[30] Detainees were held without charge; more than a year after the invasion, the names of prisoners had not been released. Americas Watch, a human-rights organization, reported U.S. violations of Geneva Convention accords on the treatment of prisoners and the denial of basic rights of due process in preventive detention. Because the United States had never declared war on Panama, those incarcerated were not referred to as prisoners of war but as detainees. If someone's name appeared on a list (the United States had already developed a list of some six thousand government employees, civilians, educators, and nationalists who were prohibited entry into the United States), then he or she could have been picked up and detained without charge. The *Times* recounted the story of one Panamanian doctor who, after receiving a telephone call to go to the local police station for questioning, was arrested by U.S. troops upon his arrival and flown by army helicopter to the Empire Range detention camp.[31]

In 1990, the Center for Constitutional Rights filed the suit *Salas v. United States* on behalf of the families of 272 Panamanian civilians. In 1993, the Inter-American Commission of the Organization of American States agreed to hear the case on the basis of international-law violation and victim compensation. On the fifth anniversary of the U.S. invasion of Panama, the center issued a 1994 update reporting that *Salas v. United States* marks "the first time in history [that the United States] was formally obliged [to] respond to civilian allegations of human rights violations due to armed intervention in Latin America."[32] The suit was based on reports that two thousand civilians were killed, five thousand illegally incarcerated, eighteen thousand left homeless, and estimated billions of dollars in damages to personal and business properties stemming from the 1989 bombings and invasion. The center reported in 1994 that 80 percent of those affected in the invasion have not returned to work, and malnutrition and suicide have increased, with women and children the most adversely affected medically. Less critical assessments on the fifth anniversary of the invasion appeared in more influential media sources. For instance, the *New York Times*'s October 1994 article, "In Panama, a New Day Arouses Old Soldiers," reported that the two objectives for the invasion were to install a democratically elected government by deposing Noriega and to halt the flow of drugs into the United States via Panama.[33] Media reports not only shaped perceptions of the rationale for the invasion; they also influenced social perceptions of the legitimacy of state violence waged against Panama.

Valorizing State Violence in U.S. Media

American media coverage of the invasion signified overwhelming approval by both U.S. and Panamanian citizens. Bush's dramatic rise in the opinion polls was demonstrated on January 31, 1990, by ABC, which ran its stories on the invasion under the title "From a Wimp to a World-Class Leader." It is unclear who was interviewed by *New York Times,* CBS, or Gallop pollsters in the United States or Panama. Consider the Panamanian polling, for example: a poll taken in January 1990 by CBS News stated that 92 percent of Panamanians interviewed approved of the invasion. What many news sources failed to report was that the interviews were conducted in affluent (largely white) neighborhoods, probably the least hostile neighborhoods for U.S. news reporters in the wake of the bombing of poor (largely brown and black) neighborhoods.

One of the most frightening assumptions promoted in major media coverage was the right of the U.S. government to attempt to assassinate the leader of another country or region. Most of the major networks un-questioningly reiterated the idea that assassinations are legitimate government operations and that invasion is a valid way to implement them. Throughout the five hours of live coverage on December 20, ABC News anchorman Peter Jennings presented the position that the problem of Panama was not the invasion of a sovereign nation to eliminate its head of state and the bombing of a civilian population (the public seemed indifferent to this, given its passive reaction to Reagan's bombing of Libya), but that the "hunt for Noriega"—as Jennings described it—was not immediately successful.

Control over media coverage was strict. American journalists in the Pentagon pool—those flown into Panama by the Bush administration to cover the invasion—were restricted to U.S. military bases during the first hours of the invasion, thus ensuring that there would be no coverage of civilian casualties and bombings. Only the coverage of the bombing of Iraq several years later would exceed the restrictions.[34] No other U.S. press outside the Pentagon pool of journalists were allowed into Panama, and a Spanish photographer who sent photos of casualties to U.S. Spanish-language papers was killed by U.S. troops in cross fire outside a tourist hotel.

American media coverage of the invasion failed to question the U.S. assumption of international jurisdiction over drug-law enforcement as a pretext for violating its 1977 Panama Canal Treaty and Panamanian sovereignty. Nor was the use of Panama as a military base for U.S. intervention in Central America examined critically. Although there were critics of the invasion, as well as antiwar and anti-intervention demonstrations, the failure of mainstream institutions to raise concerns combined with the fervor of patriotic nationalism curtailed resistance to U.S. anti-Panamanian violence.

Part of the general acquiescence to state force stemmed from the media's projection of racial obsessions. Racism in reports of the invasion was constant. In *Newsweek*'s January 15, 1990, issue, Frederick Kempe described Noriega at the time of his surrender and arrest as "a whipped and beaten little man" and "a mere shadow of the machete-waving gringo-hating dictator."[35] The use of sexist imagery to support the invasion was also revealed in Bush's pronouncements that the United States invaded to save American lives and American womanhood; or, as Secretary of Defense Dick Cheney phrased it, the Panamanian Defense Forces (racialized brown) had sexually threatened a military wife (racialized white). In contrast, the United States has not invaded El Salvador or Guatemala or attacked the contras to safeguard American lives, although those governments and the contras have been responsible for the deaths of U.S. citizens, as well as sexual assaults on and the political torture of American women and religious and peace activists.

Perhaps no report reveals the convergence of classism, racism, and sexism that shaped the invasion and its representations better than Kempe's article. According to Kempe, "Noriega's continued survival blemished Bush's anti-drug efforts and underlined increased American impotence in the region" (20). Kempe describes Noriega as a "two-bit intelligence chief from a Banana and Banking Republic" (19). His depiction of Bush's December 1976 meeting with Noriega (when Bush was CIA director), subtitled "Bully vs. Brahmin," is revealing:

> The two intelligence chiefs contrasted in style and substance. Bush was lanky and refined, raised by a Brahmin New England family. He

towered over the five-foot five-inch Noriega. Noriega was mean-streets Mestizo, the bastard son of his father's domestic. Noriega offered his usual damp, limp handshake to Bush's firm grip. They were clearly uncomfortable with each other. (19)

Sensationalized as a safari hunt, with international law and state violence treated as no more than factors in a game between the romanticized hunter and the animalized hunted, the invasion of Panama and the devastating effects on its people, democratic law, and policies were trivialized.

Conclusion

State department and media information (or more accurately, disinformation) set the stage for and rationalized the invasion of Panama. Nationalism and racism provided the symbolism for violence in U.S. foreign policy. The invasion carried the markings of symbolic outrage at Noriega's criminality, state protective concern for U.S. personnel and families, and contempt for so-called banana republics. The confluence of such national sentiments allowed a military intervention to unfold with little significant domestic resistance. Like the threats of communism and terrorism, "narco-terrorism" provided the apologia for U.S. state violence. The public's voluntary ignorance of the canal treaty, drug trafficking, and the U.S. employment of Noriega allowed the circumvention of law, repressive and racist practices, and militarization.

As the Center for Constitutional Rights noted in its update on the fifth anniversary of the invasion, as usual, women and children bear much of the brunt of war.[36] Before the 1989 invasion, FUMCA's organizing pamphlet *Porque Las Mujeres Somos Parte de Esta Lucha* maintained that defending national sovereignty was part of women's political history in Panama—citing among other things Rufina Alfaro and women's leadership in the popular power movements in the 1960s and 1970s. The FUMCA pamphlet stressed that the conditions of women's lives demand activism: "Women, half of the population, realize that foreign aggression threatens the stability of their homes and their children's futures."[37] And at the November 1989 conference attended by U.S. educators and political and religious leaders, Panamanian women warned how deadly U.S. policy in Panama was and made this plea to U.S. women: "There are many U.S. women whose children are here and they do not know what they are doing or what the U.S. government is doing. . . . We're trying to bring about a rebirth of our culture . . . and they [the U.S. government] are thinking about killing our people."[38] During hunts and assassinations, invasions and bombings, protection is the justifying logic for U.S. violence directed at its external threats—in this case, nations and peoples who constituted the Other in the American mind. Violence, however, bleeds across borders. It migrates with mercurial fluidity with an unpredictability that cannot be easily contained once deployed: in May 1995 in the wake of various armed assaults on the presidential mansion and its guards by U.S. citizens attempting to exercise their right to assassination, the White House took the unprecedented action of permanently closing Pennsylvania Avenue to the public.

4 / The Color(s) of Eros:
Cuba as American Obsession

Eros, *n.* 1: *the ancient Greek god of carnal love.* 2: *physical love; sexual desire.*
3: *Psychoanal. a: the libido. b: instincts for self-preservation collectively*

Cuba, like Panama, has been the object of unwanted attention from U.S. interventionist policy makers. Unique to Cuba, however, is its historical role as an exotic locale for the U.S. imagination. Before 1959, as the site of American fantasy and fetish around a dark and sensuous culture, Cuba and its inhabitants were exploited and commodified in gambling, prostitution, and tourism, regulated by organized crime, that contributed to the gross national product. Today, films such as the *Mambo Kings* and *The Mask* encourage audiences to long for a nostalgic, romantic Cuba, where, as with the mythical, sexualized black, one finds and imbibes carnality and passion. In a sovereign state such as Cuba, the only remaining socialist state in the hemisphere, one also finds other forms of eros, including tenacious instincts for self-preservation. It is this form of libido that has so incensed some U.S. policymakers who encounter a political will that belies the image of the passionate, hedonistic Latin.

U.S. Destabilization . . . Cuban Resistance

"Ladies and gentlemen, there is an economic embargo against Cuba," warns the U.S. Department of Treasury announcement detailing travel restrictions for U.S. citizens and residents. Writer Gabriel García Márquez describes the blockade's initial effect on Cuban dependency:

> That night, the first of the blockade, there were in Cuba some 482,550 cars, 343,300 refrigerators, 549,700 radios, 303,500 TV sets, 352,900 electric irons, 288,400 fans, 41,800 washing machines, 3,510,000 wrist watches, 63 locomotives and 12 merchant ships. All these, except the watches which were Swiss, were made in the United States.[1]

Prohibiting all aid to and trade with Cuba, as well as tourism and business ventures, the United States pressures other governments and international institutions to deny credit to Cuba. American citizens engaged in research or academic exchanges are permitted to travel; with the latest travel restrictions imposed in 1994, however, educators and journalists must fulfill bureaucratic requirements (including the submission of curriculum vitae and research proposals). The blockade makes it difficult to receive phone calls from the United States, and mail from there is also unreliable. The obstruction of intellectual exchange restricts the speech of Cuban politicians, educators and intellectuals, and artists in the United States. Given the embargo and travel restrictions, the U.S. public relies on mainstream media for information and coverage. Often, these reports construct images of Cuba that are based on White House and State Department communiqués. Few mainstream media sources routinely depict the historical and contemporary U.S. destabilization of Cuba and its impact on social and governmental practices on the island.

Although the United States has established diplomatic and economic relations with former Soviet states, communist China, and communist Vietnam, Cuba is its last Cold War target for punitive economic policies. The thirty-three-year-old anti-Cuba trade embargo was intensified by a 1992 bill introduced by Robert Torricelli (Dem., N.J.) which prohibits foreign subsidiaries of U.S. corporations to engage in business transactions with Cuba. The blockade produces extensive food and medicine shortages; even Oxfam of America is considering providing assistance, as National Public Radio reported on May 23, 1995. Interracial Foundation for Community Organizing (IFCO)-Pastors for Peace and other religious and civic organizations have denounced the embargo as a form of economic warfare and, as intervention into the affairs of a sovereign nation, a violation of international law and U.S. treaties. According to an IFCO-Pastors for Peace newsletter, in the November 1993 UN condemnation of the embargo, which stemmed from a vote of 88 to 4, only Albania, Israel, and Paraguay—"none of them considered champions of human-rights,"—voted with the United States.[2]

Congressional members have joined activists in organizing to lift the embargo. Democratic House Representative Charles Rangel's Free Trade with Cuba Act (H.R. 2229) calls for lifting the embargo and has thirty-two cosponsors.[3] Pastors for Peace, the Venceremos Brigades, the Radical Philosophers Association, and the Cuba Information Project, among other groups, provide opportunities for North Americans to learn about the nation and, although this is becoming more difficult with increasing U.S. restrictions, to travel there to understand more about Cuban society and the impact of the embargo on Cuban lives.

Conservative projections of the United States as a legitimate intervener seeking to democratize Cuba problematize lifting the blockade, even though progressives, such as the groups cited above as well as media and corporate leaders, increasingly suggest that measure as the only rational policy. Activists have practiced civil disobedience by intentionally breaking the blockade. In 1992, Pastors for Peace transported medicine and supplies in a caravan from the northern United States to Mexico to be shipped to Cuba. Having detained the caravan at the Laredo border, federal agents, following a hunger strike by clergy and laity, finally allowed the caravan to travel into Mexico where its cargo was shipped on to Cuba.

In addition to the embargo and blockade, U.S. destabilization of Cuba has ranged from the State Department's 1960 harassment of the Cuban UN delegation to the 1963 failed military invasion at the Bay of Pigs, as well as alleged covert U.S. support for Omega 7, a terrorist organization of Cuban exiles, which in the 1970s was linked to assassination attempts directed at Fidel Castro and the downing of a Cuban airliner and the deaths of its passengers. The United States still illegally occupies Guantánamo Bay, and at its military base there military personnel detain Cuban boat people.

In June 1994, CUBA *Update* editor Sandra Levinson noted that the embargo and the United States' refusal to issue permanent visas to Cubans seeking to enter this country precipitate dangerous confrontations. For example, Levinson reports that "100 Cubans broke into the Belgian Embassy in Havana seeking asylum"; Cubans were injured or arrested when the military police attempted to stop the hijack of boats or planes; two leaders of a recently formed exile group, Commandos F-4, were arrested in Miami for attempting to purchase "a Stinger missile and other advanced weapons to launch an attack against Cuba."[4] Levinson maintains that normal diplomatic relations with Cuba would have prevented these occurrences. Normal diplomatic relations, however, have not existed for nearly a century.

In 1898, after a three-year war of independence, Cubans defeated Spanish colonizers, only to have their country immediately occupied by the United States, postponing a national liberation victory until 1959. For half a century, the U.S. occupation and "administration" of Cuba worked to convert the island into a plantation for U.S. sugar corporations and Havana into a Mafia-controlled tourist playground internationally renowned for its prostitution and gambling.

Before 1959, the Cuban majority, particularly dark-skinned Cubans and women, struggled for subsistence as impoverished illiterates. Most served foreign and local elites who prospered under the repressive, United States-backed Fulgencio Batista government. After the success of the second anticolonial struggle, the revolutionary government implemented comprehensive health care, free and universal education, social security, and free and subsidized housing. To address postrevolution expectations for better living standards, the Cuban government financed its redistribution of wealth by nationalizing the holdings and property of U.S. corporations and affluent Cubans who emigrated to the United States. Many local elites, white, and affluent Cubans fled the island for the United States during and after the revolution. Largely professional and middle-class, those who fled the revolution were criticized not only for their refusal to stay and build a more just society but also for darkening or "haitianizing" the island by leaving—the Cuban version of white flight, with Miami and New Jersey as U.S. suburban havens.

In the early years of the new society, Cuba sought political and economic ties with many nations, especially the United States. Fixated on its defeat by a national liberation struggle waged by (at that time) noncommunist rebels, the United States rejected Cuba's reconciliatory overtures and imposed the embargo and blockade. With the Cold War (and a neo-Monroe Doctrine-Manifest Destiny policy), the United States cut diplomatic and economic ties. The Soviet Union filled the void, becoming the newly independent nation's political and economic pillar. Cuba's pre-revolution economic dependency on the United States faded. Ninety miles from the Florida coast, the former site of U.S. militarism and tourism became, in U.S. parlance, a "Soviet satellite." Representations of Cuba as an appendage of Eastern European communism furthered the embargo and blockade; at times, ideological posturing led to near cataclysms, such as the Cuban missile crisis during the Kennedy administration. Since the fall of the Soviet constellation, U.S. state discourse has continued to represent Cuba as a communist satellite, although no configuration of communist states vying for its allegiance exists.

Before the Soviet demise, Cuba attained the highest standard of living in Latin America—in spite of the U.S. embargo. Supported by its trade with former socialist Eastern European countries, it escaped the devastating underdevelopment of Third World nations, which were penalized by the debt crisis and International Monetary Fund austerity measures. Unlike others in the region, Cubans enjoyed a high life-expectancy rate, 73.4 years, comparable to the U.S. average and exceeding the life expectancy of Native and African Americans in the United States. Cuba also developed one of the highest literacy rates in the Americas, 96 percent, with the ninth grade as the average educational attainment, surpassing the U.S. literacy rate.

Urban Cubans' expectations and desires around consumerism and materialism were rarely constrained by a notion of being a Third World country, much less a colony. Cuba's standing was that of a Second Worlder, able to best some First World nations, including the United States, by providing comprehensive social services for its population, and even defeating destabilization attempts from the most formidable First Worlder. In his 1994 keynote address to the sixth conference of North American and Cuban Philosophers and Social Scientists at the University of Havana, economist Alonso Casanova reported that in the 1980s, Cuba was the only Latin American country to increase its per-capita gross material product, by 33 percent; in 1983, with a strong economy, Cuba was 75th in the United Nations Human Index for quality of life in respect to education, health, culture, and social stability.[5] Cuba's workforce was considered to be one of the healthiest, most qualified and literate labor forces in Latin America and the Caribbean. That all changed in the late 1980s. Today, social services have collapsed, consumer desires can no longer be met, and discontent runs high.

According to Casanova, Cuba's economic structures "have not been good at producing wealth, but excellent in redistributing [it]." Central planning gave Cuba the most developed technological society in the Third World. Excellent highways and port facilities augment a textile industry capable of producing textiles for forty million people and a construction industry able to produce more than six million tons of oil per year. Trading four million tons of sugar for twelve million tons of refined oil annually, Cuba geared its economy for producing sugar for barter trade with Eastern European countries. The costs of producing oil and sugar were considered irrelevant because of this fixed-market or barter system between states. Productivity and quality were also not pressing concerns for the trading nations because of the guaranteed market, stated Casanova.

As the Soviet bloc disintegrated in the late 1980s, so did the Cuban economy. When the Soviet Union collapsed in the early 1990s, Cuba was catapulted into what it now calls its "special period," during which scarcity and hardship were intensified by the U.S. embargo and blockade. For Cuban writer Reynaldo González, however, the special period "was before the crisis and not now, when we [Cubans] have been returned without appeal to our condition as a Third World country."[6] In general, Cubans are adapting; for example, in medicine, more people are resorting to herbal and homeopathic alternative treatments such as acupuncture in place of anesthesia. Through the 1989 crash, Cuba lost 80 percent of its raw materials and 85 percent of its foreign trade—90 percent of which was in rum, tobacco, and sugar, and 10 percent in electronics, pharmaceuticals, and chemical products. Its decades of dependency on Eastern European technology left few spare parts or replacements for machinery: between 1991 and 1994, for instance, more than 50 percent of Cuban industrial facilities were closed. Unable to receive aid, Cuba's foreign debt principal, 7.5 billion, remains fixed as its interest increases from the International Monetary Fund and World Bank: the blockade makes converting the economy and technological and industrial equipment a tremendous feat without capital.

Post-1959 Cuba depended heavily on sugar cane as an economic mainstay; the first U.S. Venceremos Brigades of U.S. progressives supporting Cuban independence worked to harvest the sugar fields as a sign of political solidarity as well as economic support. Increasing trade with China (an estimated $420 million in 1994), exporting sugar for bicycles and technology, has mitigated the loss of the Eastern European market.[7] Cuba has also developed economic alternatives to sugar production. Its genetic engineering industry is considered to be one of its most economically successful ventures, although the dominant economic venture is tourism. Despite these endeavors, the needs of most Cuban citizens are not met.

For example, Cuba's universal ration book used to guarantee a certain amount of beans, rice, eggs, fish, meat, and household necessities for everyone, whether they could (or would) work;[8] with the current shortages and illegal marketeering, however, food supplies are now often depleted before the end of the month. Cuba's free health-care system is hampered by inadequate medicines and supplies. Cubans spend months without toothpaste and bathing soap. There is acute rationing of gasoline for cars and often twelve consecutive hours of blackouts; some neighborhoods go without electricity for days. Milk previously available to schoolchildren to the age of fourteen is now only available to those seven and younger, although it is still provided to adults over fifty-five years old. In the countryside people's access to gardens, oxen, and horse-drawn carts means fewer food and fuel shortages.

Survival with dignity is problematized by gender roles. As in the United States, women are the mainstay of the Cuban family. Overwhelmingly, women struggle with the effects of the special period on Cuban families. During times of scarcity and economic instability, the burdens of coping with inadequate supplies of food, domestic goods, and transportation, which largely fall on women who manage households and raise children, intensify. Fuel and food scarcities, water shortages and stoppages, and difficulty in finding children's shoes and clothing have made domestic life a nightmare for many women. Casas de las Mujeres y las Familias as women's centers have been formed to help city women meet to discuss and find solutions to their new domestic problems. Although Cuba has a law that makes it a social crime for men to not share in household duties and childrearing, it is difficult both to enforce it and to make men understand that they have to share in the reproduction of the family. As well, Cuban women note that local planning boards are still not responsive enough to community needs. Typically, the Cuban woman is also held responsible for the state's desire and need for her to be the resourceful and unwavering mother, wife, daughter, and comrade in times of economic crisis.

Today, the U.S. dollar reigns as hard currency in Cuba. In July 1993, the Cuban government decriminalized the possession of U.S. dollars in order to increase the flow of currency from Cubans in other countries, specifically the United States, to Cubans living on the island. That flow has been impeded by the restrictions on currency exchange and travel introduced by President Clinton following the mass immigration of Cubans to Florida in the summer of 1994. At a time when the United States is becoming more stringent about the flow of Cubans and currency, Cuba allows 100,000 Cuban exiles a year to return for family visits and has opened up restrictions on travel for Cuban citizens. At a June 1994 meeting with a small international delegation at Havana's Martin Luther King Jr. Center, National Assembly President Ricardo Alarcón—who holds a position equivalent to that of the U.S. Speaker of the House—explained that by restricting Cuban residents in America in sending financial aid to their families on the island, the U.S. government is infringing on their human rights.[9] American residents with family members in Mexico, Canada, Jamaica, and Israel, for instance, face no such restrictions.

Furthermore, the 1994 Clinton policy restricting Cubans who are traveling from the United States to the island to carrying out only $100 not surprisingly has resulted in money smuggling. Officially, the exchange rate is one dollar to a peso, but the underground market in 1994 trafficked 100 to 135 pesos for a dollar. University professors earn 600 pesos a month, while the approximately 300,000 workers in the sugar industry earn 150 pesos a month—less than $2 on Havana's underground market. Certain items in the new retail stores can only be purchased with dollars, legally sold in dollar stores and illegally sold in the underground market. In the past these were mostly luxury goods; now they include certain foods as well as soap and shampoo, which if cheaply purchased sells for $2 a bottle. In September 1993, Cuba legalized self-employment in approximately 140 occupations. Self-employed or independent workers—for instance, dollar-only taxi drivers or those whose private cars moonlight as gypsy cabs—constitute a relatively affluent sector of Cuban society. It is a sector in which largely unreported income goes untaxed. (The National Assembly passed an economic policy program that includes the creation of tax policy and incentives for savings.)

Rectification and Economic Chaos

Before Soviet reformers initiated perestroika and glasnost under the leadership of Mikhail Gorbachev, Cuban scholars maintain, there was the Cuban "rectification program." The third Congress of the Cuban Communist Party adopted the rectification program in 1986 in its own version of the opening process. Whereas the new Soviet openness and the Reagan-Gorbachev rapprochement received considerable play in the U.S. press, similar processes and restructuring in Cuba garnered little attention. In this rectification period, responding to economic and social crises, Cuban leaders began expanding their decision making and power base beyond the Communist Party and its traditionally light-skinned or white male leaders.

According to economist Casanova, the rectification program emerged from the government's recognition in the mid-1980s that the economy needed reform.[10] By opening up the decision-making process, rectification leaders acknowledged some of the liabilities of overly centralized, bureaucratic governments, which limit direct input from the community and nonparty members. The program dealt with not only the economic and political structures but also with the social inequalities based on gender and skin color that persisted in contemporary Cuba. In redressing such inequities, program officials expressed a commitment to increasing the numbers of women and black Cubans in leadership. Yet because salvaging the economy is a priority, providing equity for the most disenfranchised—blacks and women—is somewhat peripheral in rectification. The democratization of Cuban political and economic institutions does not in itself address the marginalization of women and blacks. The contemporary economic crisis has shifted the focus to economic survival, although social inequity determines who is most likely to survive at below-subsistence levels.

There are obviously problems and deficiencies in Cuban social and economic policies. Some U.S.-based intellectuals writing in popular media sources are able to describe the errors and limitations of the Cuban government while acknowledging its right to self- rather than U.S.-determination. For example, Isel Rivero y Méndez, a Cuban living in New York, recounts the unequal status of Cuban women and repressive treatment toward Cuban women dissidents while critiquing the macho politics of the United States and its embargo to impoverish Cuban people.[11] Since the Reagan administration initiated a campaign censuring Cuba for human-rights violations (while simultaneously dismissing UN human-rights covenants as applicable to the United States) against free speech and antigovernment dissidents, Cuba has been addressing criticisms of human-rights abuses such as those cited in Amnesty International's report on prison conditions.[12] In

1996, when the Cuban military shot down two Miami commuter planes distributing antigovernment leaflets, the deaths of the Cuban American pilots created a backlash that facilitated the passage of anti-Cuban legislation through Congress and Clinton's signing of the measure into law. As important as specific criticisms concerning the nation's practices are in respect to civil and human rights, generalized condemnations of Cuba for obstructing freedom of religion, democracy (construed as electoral politics based on a U.S. model), and the free markets obscure Cuba's broadened policies for religious practices, elections, and economic decentralization.

For example, in 1991 the fourth Congress of the Communist Party voted to open membership to Christians and non-Marxist-Leninists, disavowing its past discriminatory practices. In the early 1990s, Reverend Raul Suárez of Ebenezer Baptist Church in Havana became one of the first clergy elected to the National Assembly. According to the staff at the church's annex, Havana's Martin Luther King Jr. Center, the government increasingly seeks out religious leaders, Catholics, and Protestants as well as those in traditional African-based religions, Santería and Palo Monte, to be included in decision-making processes at local and national levels. Cuban scholars attribute the more public practices of religion in general and the growth in popular religiosity in Santería or Palo Monte to the assertion by the fourth Congress of the importance of understanding people's needs to practice their religions, which was debated in the 1993 Conference Commission on Gender, Race, and Class by social scientists.[13] Cuban Christianity often coexists in a syncretic form with the popular religiosity of African-based religions: for example, Havana's Ebenezer Baptist Church stands adjacent to the Martin Luther King Jr. Center, where traditional orisha dances and songs are performed by local youth maintaining their cultural and religious practices in Santería (Yoruba) and Palo Monte (Congo).

Changes in 1992 electoral laws revised the system in which members of municipal assemblies elected representatives to provincial assemblies, who in turn elected National Assembly deputies. In February 1993, Cubans held the first direct elections to the National Assembly since 1959. Of the new parliament elected in 1993, 83 percent are first-time delegates to the National Assembly, increasing the participation of youth, blacks, mestizos, and women, as well as deputies with international work experience.[14]

While it searches for foreign capital and investors, Cuba promotes decentralized local markets in a newly mixed economy struggling to survive. According to Alonso Casanova, 70 percent of Cuba's industries are inefficient partly because of past practices of withholding decision-making power from local managers.[15] Citing inadequacies as well as present resourcefulness, Casanova recounted how, after the confiscation of idle land held by American corporations in the 1960s, Cubans found that much of that same land, when controlled by the Cuban government, was still idle and poorly managed in the 1980s. The government began to redistribute tracts among local farming cooperatives; in September 1993, the government reorganized state farms, converting 75 percent of Cuba's agricultural land into smaller cooperatives called basic units of cooperative production.[16]

Nongovernmental organizations are decentralizing as well. The state-supported national women's organization, the Federación de las Mujeres Cubanas (FMC), envisioned its 1995 sixth Congress as an informal and democratic gathering with few paper presentations. Attempting to invigorate a national women's organization and distance past elitism, FMC delegates anticipated that the Congress would "give the floor to women, let them say what they want, when they want," according to FMC representative Elsa Agramonte.[17] She observes that in the special period it is difficult for women to discuss gender equality when they are trying to deal with shortages and survival. Because of the general struggle to meet daily needs, smaller gatherings such as Casas de las Mujeres or the Consejo Popular (Popular Council) have replaced the mass rallies of the 1970s and 1980s, according to Agramonte.

Exotic Cuba

Constructed as an erotic and exotic nation, Cuba with its cash crops has historically served European and American pleasures (or decadence). Before the 1959 revolution, Cuba signified unlimited and unpoliced consumption of rum (during prohibition), commercial sex, and gambling. For those inclined to more respectable or legal pleasures, it traded in the aboveground markets of sugar, tourism, and cigars. Afro-Cuban dance and music provided the exotic allure of cultural primitivism for consumers in both the underground and legal economies. To satisfy American and European desires for a dark exotica, Cuban markets expanded to include the bodies of women and children in prostitution. Today, tourism has created new cash crops: the island itself, the nativism of its culture, as well as the skills and performance of its people. Cuban's highly trained labor force has produced the most overqualified tourism personnel in the world: increasingly, professionals, particularly those proficient in English, leave their jobs as academics, lawyers, and concert musicians, for instance, to work as tour guides. In short, tourism is an appealing field as the only industry that guarantees access to foreigners—in other words, access to dollar carriers.

Tourism in Cuba is largely about marketing desires and selling "island eros" to nonislanders. Although not yet economically profitable, tourism is viewed as the key to Cuba's economic future. The industry generates thirty-four cents for each dollar spent; as Alonso Casanova put it, the Cuban government spends sixty-six cents to acquire thirty-four cents.[18] As an investment, it seems promising because of the fixed market; further, a barter system based on the relative stability of Cuba's position is the embodiment of the European and American imaginary of colored eros. Currently, the primary investors in Cuban tourism are from Western Europe. Cuban economic planners are involved in joint ventures in hotels and emerging private beaches at Varadero and other sites, with corporations in Canada, Spain, Germany, Italy, and Mexico. The historic symbol of Cuban independence, the hotel Havana Libre, was leased in the early 1990s to Spanish investors. With European and Canadian money come new sensibilities around labor and racial and sexual politics. Rumors circulating in Havana intimate that Cuba's joint-venture hotels, under new management and restructuring, discipline their workers, reassigning and terminating employees. Darker-skinned Cubans are reportedly moved from front desks to back kitchens—or even let go. On the consumer side of the market, African American tourists, male and female, are questioned when entering hotel lobbies as either potential pimps or prostitutes, whereas their white North American counterparts are not bothered by plainclothed security guards, doormen, or desk clerks. In the context of white desires and designs on dark Cuba, sexual objectification and exploitation reflect the stereotypes of antiblack racism.

Nowhere is this more apparent than in the sex trade. The sex industry is an integral part of North-South tourism; historically, the island has catered to the tastes of nonnatives. Before the 1959 revolution, there were 100,000 prostitutes in Cuba, an estimated 10 percent of the female workforce, according to the Federación de las Mujeres Cubanas.[19] Abolished in

Cuba, prostitution has visibly reappeared in the economy's dependency on tourism during the special period. According to Elsa Agramonte, the FMC focuses on education rather than criminalizing prostitutes and polarizing women, following the theory that "all of us need all of us" and that "the survival of the people at dignified levels of subsistence are important to us."[20]

In the emerging prostitution trade linked to tourism, European and Canadian tourists seem to prefer black teenaged girls, while Latin American tourists prefer white Cubans, as Osvaldo Cárdenas from El Centro para Estudios de los Estados Unidos observed in June 1993.[21] This claim is statistically indeterminate but consistent with the exoticized concept of the Other. Cubans and non-Cubans argue whether most *geneteras* or jockeys—the majority of whom are not engaged in prostitution—are dark-skinned or black. Black Cubans, such as Pedro Pérez Sarduy, coeditor of AFROCUBA, assert that disproportionately they are.[22] The association of blackness with criminality and prostitution reappears in socialist policing. The social belief that the majority of *geneteras* are dark-skinned Cubans fuels old racial prejudices of the black harlot or the counterrevolutionary, as white Cubana academics in discussions at the University of Havana in June 1993 described such girls and women. In the reverse, some dark-skinned Cubans prefer the company of whites. Cárdenas, who is the father of a dark-skinned teenaged girl, has noted that black Cuban girls are often in awe of European and American men.[23] They are dazzled not only by dollars but also by the existential wealth of men with white skin. For girls who model the antithesis of a European-defined beauty, attention from white men means that mere desire and the status of being desirable—sometimes augmented by a trinket or a meal—are ample payment for socializing and/or sex.

Prostitution is only the most visible form of sexual objectification of Cuban people and culture. Sexual objectification is also evident in media representations. For example, consider the *New York Times Magazine*'s 1993 travel article on "Sun and Sin in Cuba," which featured photographs of Copacabana dancers in plumage and nipple tassles, as well as a beach photo of a white European man, sitting in a chaise longue facing the camera, with his hand on the bare, G-stringed bottom of his black female companion, who lies face down in the adjoining lounge chair.[24] The fully clothed image of the alluring, feminized Cuban also appears in progressive publications such as CUBA *Update,* which in 1994 featured on its back cover a photo of three young, chic women strolling together as a mocha Cubana version of Charlie's Angels.[25] Not only the feminine is represented with seductive allure in U.S. culture. The eroticized masculine Cuban is also peddled in the United States, from the goofy, green, wannabe Latin lover played by Jim Carrey in *The Mask* to a women's magazine, in which editors warned their largely white, affluent female readers of the seductive powers of the Cuban head of state, an erotically demonized Fidel.

Among women, the representation of the eroticized revolutionary surfaces in the most unlikely of sites, for instance, a 1988 women's anti-intervention conference. In 1988, I joined two thousand women who traveled to Havana to participate in the Women's Encuentro organized by the FMC on North American intervention in Latin America and the Caribbean. The meeting drew indigenous, black, *campesina* (trade unionists), movement leaders, as well as white, affluent Latin American women. In the opening session, presided over by FMC head Vilma Espín, President Fidel Castro addressed the delegates, discussing the international debt crisis as well as toxic waste and garbage dumped by the United States on Third World sites. At a closing reception, he appeared with a retinue of mostly male cabinet members. Latinas and white Latinas from Argentina and Chile mobbed Castro, following him like raucous groupies as he attempted to greet each national delegation of women. Castro eventually retreated to a dignitaries' meeting room, and the women and their unruly behavior were locked out. There, he met with small delegations, including Native American women from the United States and women active in Latin American and Caribbean liberation movements. One FMC member bitterly remarked to a small group of U.S. delegates that the mobbing women would never have greeted another head of state, say the President of Argentina, with such disrespect. Yet her expression of disgust for the white Latinas who eroticized and racialized Castro was contradicted by the desire seen in the face of other Cuban women. For instance, earlier in the day nonelite, non-FMC women opened their houses for a tour of Cuban homes; one woman seemed mesmerized by a well-to-do Argentinian's waist-length blond hair and billowing, white, ankle-length summer dress, as she stepped across the doorway.

During a night of block parties, small delegations of women gathered in neighborhoods throughout Havana. There was a delegation from the

United States including mostly African American and Native American women, some of whom had been radical activists in the black liberation movement of the 1970s, and a few who, targeted for their work by the state, had been incarcerated as political prisoners. Early in the evening, we heard rumors that Castro would honor attendees with his presence. For progressive women who were often politically isolated—some had been detained in the United States or in more dangerous sites such as El Salvador or Guatemala—a visit from President Castro was considered an auspicious sign. To U.S. radical black and red women, it was not often that a head of state financed and attended a party in their honor. When Castro appeared, he made a short speech of greeting and soon departed after shaking hands with African and Native American women delegates.

As his entourage departed, the eyes of most African American women were not focused on Castro, as they might have been at the reception. Rather, they gazed at his male, military attendants. The men guarding Castro that night were black—ebony, dark-skinned Cubans. Their statuesque militarism, for some, upstaged Castro, particularly in their departure: they ran abreast and behind the sedan, entering it two by two, looking over their shoulders in an elegant run-dance. The image was shockingly different from that of secret-service agents in beige raincoats jogging alongside Reagan's or Bush's limousines in that era. It is possible that the women's desire was inspired by only romantic eros. It seemed to be something more. Echoing what their foremothers and fathers must have felt on seeing the colored battalion that guarded Abraham Lincoln or the first African American troops, nurses, and camp aides in the Civil War, these African American women were transfixed by the imago of black resistance. Rather than focused on heterosexual fetish, this eros seemed filtered through the colors of black liberation. Such eros allowed more than one woman radical to see herself in the departing soldier and to see in Castro and his entourage an embodiment of private and politicized desires for radical, antiracist resistance and national liberation.

Political Eros: Nationalism, Antiracism, and Anti-imperialism

Cuba has no system for classifying races. The island's inhabitants refer to themselves as Cuban rather than Afro-Cuban or Asian-Cuban. Yet there is recognition of and identification as white, mulatto, or black Cuban, with social realities that reflect the hierarchy of these racial relationships. The census classifies Cubans as white or black. In the 1980 Cuban census, for example, 70 percent of Cubans were identified as white and 30 percent as nonwhite, that is, mestizo or black, although it is likely the reverse. Only a minority of Cubans are of purely European descent. In the absence of classified races, skin color becomes the marker for racism. According to researchers Pablo Rodríguez, Paula Izquierdo, Ana J. García Lazara Carrazana, and Lourdes Serrano, there are more marriages between social economic classes than between racial groups.[26] They identify the latter groups as whites, mixtas (Indian and Spanish or African and Spanish), mulattoes, and blacks. In a debate during the 1993 Conference Commission on Gender, Race, and Class, this question was raised: "Qué es mixta en Cuba?" (What is mixed in Cuba?). Rodríguez and his colleagues answered: "A mystery." Some felt that it was more accurate to speak of skin color rather than of race, the aesthetics of beauty, and racism. But in a society where white parents have dark children and mulattas give birth to whites (as one woman gave the example of her dark-skinned husband and their lighter-skinned sons), the concept of race is much more fluid. Castro, for example, describes Cuba as an Afro-Cuban culture. Many Cubans, like their U.S. counterparts, assert that only the right wing or conservatives talk about race in biological terms, and yet many claim to have a dark-skinned *abuelita* (grandmother) in the kitchen or closet but fail to explain why she is cloistered there. In Cuba, nationality and ethnicity are not synonymous; even among Latin Americans, as among North Americans, ethnicity and skin color influence social and family life.

Darker-skinned, female, and poor Cubans benefited greatly from the economic and social policies adopted after the 1959 revolution; these same groups, however, are most adversely affected by the U.S. embargo and the economic crises of the special period. As in the United States, increasing economic hardships fuel racism, even in the absence of quantified races. Black Cubans observe that in a society where people are no longer fearful of a weakened government and Committees for the Defense of the Revolution, they more openly express antigovernment as well as racist sentiments censured by the state. (Overt expressions of racism in Cuba do not approximate the resurgent neo-Nazi and hate groups in former Eastern bloc states, which had outlawed racist and anti-Semitic speech and organizing.)

Occupying the poorest strata of society, with few family members in

North America and little access to dollars, black Cubans lack material supplies. In this way, dollars increase the racial stratification of Cuban society. Acknowledging that Cuba's need for hard currency brings new problems, National Assembly President Ricardo Alarcón has pointed out that his neighbor, who did not necessarily support the revolution and maintained friendly ties with Miami relatives, ate better and could provide for his family better than he, who had no conduit for American dollars.[27] Stratification is not restricted to race but is exacerbated by it. Still, black Cubans say that because they are the poorest sector are used to struggling and improvising, they complain the least. (In contrast, the urban, Cuban middle class, which is experiencing the greatest decline in material standards of living, are often more vocal in their complaints).

Despite its social problems and its own colonial hangover of antiblack prejudice, Cuba is noted for being one of the most racially progressive countries in the Americas. To antiracist U.S. citizens, Cuba represents a social and economic model that places human concerns before profit, supports decolonization struggles, and condemns racism. For instance, U.S. progressives Edwin and Jo Ann Hoffman note Cuba's significance to those struggling in a racially and economically stratified United States:

> The contrast between the profound levels of racism in our own country and the essential egalitarianism of Cuba cannot be dismissed. Cuba has nothing like the oppression of blacks living in our inner cities—the challenges of joblessness, homelessness, drug addiction and gang wars, violence and police brutality, high rates of morbidity and mortality, a failed school system.[28]

Cuba's commitments have included supporting exiled African Americans from the black liberation movement and Independentistas of the Puerto Rican liberation struggles of the 1960s and 1970s, such as Assata Shakur and other political prisoners. For many American progressives during that period, being in solidarity with Cuba was a commitment to racial equality and economic justice. Cuba's appeal, particularly to radicals, continued because it provided personnel and material resources in international struggles for socialist and antiracist states and movements.

Cuba's stature among anti-imperialists and radical antiracists is partly based on its foreign-policy commitments. During its period of economic prosperity and stability, Cuba spent considerable resources supporting decolonization and independence struggles in Latin America, the Caribbean, the Middle East, and southern Africa. The Nicaraguan Sandinistas, Salvadoran FMLN, the PLO, the ANC, and Namibia's SWAPO all benefited from Cuban educators, medical technicians, engineers, and other support. Such support did not greatly endear it to the United States, which subsidized the military in El Salvador, the contras in Nicaragua and southern Africa, the South African apartheid regime, and Israel's occupation of Palestine. Each of these racialized struggles was fought to some degree symbolically and literally against economic domination and racism.

The disapproval of Cuba's support of liberation movements even reverberated into U.S. mayoral politics. In 1990, Miami's mayor, Cuban-born Xavier Suárez, refused to meet with Nelson Mandela—touring the United States after twenty-seven years as a South African political prisoner—because of Mandela's meeting with Castro and Cuba's decades-long support of the ANC. That Suárez was the only U.S. mayor to snub Mandela may reflect not only his foreign-policy stance as a Cuban exile but also, as local activists contended, the racist politics of Cuban emigrés.

In contrast to the often tense relations between Miami's African-descended and (largely white) Cuban populations—relations exacerbated by antiblack police brutality and the Immigration and Naturalization Service's previous policy of welcoming Cuban immigrants as political refugees and dispatching Haitians as economic refugees—there have been decades of progressive alliances between African Americans and Cuban nationals. Although more brown and black Cubans live in Miami since the Mariel boatlift in the 1980s and the increasing exodus of darker-skinned Cubans, the city's Cuban population still manifests as and considers itself to be white, middle class, and conservative, particularly in respect to U.S. foreign policy toward Cuba. Lisa Brock notes the ties of black Americans to the island:

> Long before 1959 Cubans and African-Americans had forged working relationships: abolitionists jointly formed organizations, leftists and trade unionists exchanged strategies, and journalists, novelists and poets aroused mutual sensibilities. On a mass level, musicians and baseball players actually shared the same cultural venues, entertaining millions of regular Black folk in Cuba and in the United States. When the Cuban revolution culminated in 1959 most Blacks applauded its success.[29]

Since the 1959 revolution, according to Brock, the connections between African Americans and Cubans have been strained by the blockade, as well as racial polarization and antiblack racism among white Cuban exiles.

Particular historic events have emphasized the interrelations between revolutionary black nationalism in the United States and revolutionary Cuban nationalism, undergirding these ties and African American desires for an independent Cuba. A momentous episode, one promoting such coalitions, crystalized in 1960 with Castro's visit to Harlem and his meeting with Malcolm X. The September 24, 1960, meeting between the two leaders, documented in Rosemari Mealy's *Fidel and Malcolm X,* was a brief but important encounter that strengthened the bond between progressive African Americans and progressive Cubans.[30] This *encuentro* also became a symbol for resistance to imperialism and white supremacy. Ironically, the meeting occurred at the instigation of the U.S. State Department (much to its chagrin), which had pressured the Shelburne Hotel to cancel accommodations for the Cuban delegation, headed by Castro. Having just successfully waged a revolution for independence within the U.S. sphere of influence, the Cubans, who were scheduled to participate in international meetings at the United Nations, were harassed by the U.S. government during their stay. At the suggestion of Harlem activists, the disruption in accommodations was transformed into a cultural and political expression of solidarity and antiracism. When the Cuban delegation accepted the warm welcome of the Hotel Theresa's owner Love B. Woods and relocated to Harlem, ideological and political ties between progressive African Americans and Cuban revolutionaries were cultivated.

In *Fidel and Malcolm X,* recording both men's reflections on their meeting, Mealy quotes Malcolm X's observation that "the Theresa is now best known as the place where Fidel Castro went during his UN visit, and achieved a psychological coup over the U.S. State Department when it confined him to Manhattan never dreaming that he'd stay uptown in Harlem and make such an impression among the Negroes" (58). At a December 13, 1964, meeting where he discussed Che Guevara's aborted visit to Harlem (a visit canceled in response to antirevolutionary Cuban and U.S. Americans), Malcolm X repeated his assertions. With characteristic defiance, Malcolm X prefaced his reading of a note from Guevara (in which the Argentinian explained the reasons for his absence) by warning the gathering: "Don't let somebody else tell us who our enemies should be and who our friends should be" (quoted in Mealy, 59). Referring to Guevara, Malcolm X said, "I love a revolutionary. And one of the most revolutionary men in this country right now was going to come out here"(59). Advocating African American independence from the U.S. government's policy on Cuba, Malcolm X and his resistance to antiblack racism fused contemporary black radicalism and solidarity work with Cuba:

> You don't see any anti-Castro Cubans around here—we eat them up. Let them go and fight the Ku Klux Klan, or the White Citizens Council. Let them spend some of that energy getting their own house in order. Don't come up to Harlem and tell us who we should applaud for and shouldn't applaud for. Or there will be some ex-anti-Castro Cubans. (58–59)

Twenty-five years after the assassination of Malcolm X, at the May 1990 symposium "Malcolm X Speaks in the '90s," Castro reminisced about his meeting with the radical leader in Harlem:

> I always recall my meeting with Malcolm X at the Hotel Theresa, because he was the one who supported us and made it possible for us to stay there. We faced two alternatives. One was the United Nations gardens—when I mentioned this to the Secretary-General, he was horrified at the thought of a delegation in tents there. But when we received Malcolm X's offer—he had spoken with one of our comrades—I said, "That is the place, the Hotel Theresa." And there we went. So I have a personal recollection very much linked to him. (quoted in Mealy, 61)

Castro's reflections illustrate Cuba's attraction to progressive blacks and radicals, and how a small island nation came to symbolize resistance to a state constructed as an imperial behemoth. Obviously, to some degree the attraction also revolved around a black eros. Although sometimes romanticized, this eros is not necessarily a sexualized sensibility, for it is connected to Cuban culture's strong roots in political resistance as well as African music, dance, and religion. The Venceremos Brigades, historic African American Christian delegations, Pastors for Peace, study and exchange delegations on Afro-Cuban culture, women's and academic delegations—all have provided opportunities for (black) Americans to encounter Cuba. For nearly four decades, there has been an audience of progressives—and nonprogressives—attentive to the words of Cuban socialists, communists, and the Cuban head of state. For progressive African Americans and antiracists, this focus (and sometimes fascination) intensifies when Castro, departing from the position of most heads of state toward racially oppressed U.S. minorities, makes declarations of solidarity such as those expressed in his symposium speech:

> We have always been in solidarity with the struggle of Black people, of minorities, and of the poor in the United States. We have always been in solidarity with them, and they have been in solidarity with us.
>
> We must fight to defeat the campaigns, the schemes, and the lies, all that is aimed at separating us. I think that in these times we need that friendship more than ever, and we need your solidarity more than ever. And we fully appreciate it, because we understand that one has to be very courageous to [support] . . . Cuba in the United States. (quoted in Mealy, 59)

The bond between Cubans and black Americans no longer appears as close. The unraveling of this connection is a byproduct of black conservatism and the special period. Some Cubans have privately stated that in this era of economic crisis, they see African Americans as wielding little economic or political power in the United States and that powerful political allies and capital are what Cuba desperately needs at the moment. This perception of powerlessness on the part of poor and ethnically oppressed peoples (whose desires and agency are thought to be nullified by the state) is contested by more radical Cubans.

Conclusion

On November 18, 1994, National Assembly President Alarcón became the first Cuban official to speak at the National Press Club in Washington, D.C., since Castro's appearance in 1959. In the c-SPAN-televised address, Alarcón reiterated a long-standing statement by Cuban officialdom: as long as Cuba suffers the threat of foreign intervention, it will follow the assertion of its historic leader Carlos Manuel de Céspedes that a unified party is necessary for a sovereign and independent state. Reminding the audience and media viewers that the U.S. could not dictate Cuba's political, economic, and social affairs, Alarcón said that "Cuba is simply not a U.S. colony."[31]

American desires built around Cuba swing from reactionary and conservative designs of destabilization and neocolonial economic dependency to radical and liberal hopes for the sovereignty of a socialist state. The United States has spent tens of millions of dollars funding antisocialist Cuban organizations such as Radio Martí and several Miami-based organizations. It has also circumvented international law by implementing the embargo and punitive measures against other nations that trade with Cuba.

Despite U.S. investments against Cuban independence, it is still uncertain whether former Secretary of State Henry Kissinger's assertion about dominance—that power is the greatest aphrodisiac—is a formal reflection of U.S. state eros capable of crippling Cuba's sovereignty. What is clear, however, is that Cuba's efforts, aided by U.S. solidarity groups, to chart its own economic and social development continue among contemporary revolutionaries who, in some accordance with their head of state, assert national aspirations and international obligations. American desires for Cuba are framed by the words of Castro, quoted in *Fidel and Malcolm X:*

> Cuba has an important role to play, a very big responsibility, because there were people who thought that the revolution here would collapse just like socialism [in Europe]. . . . But of course, this country will resist. We are waging three great battles: the political battle . . . [for] the support of the people . . . the economic battle . . . and the battle for defense.
>
> We have to work in these three directions. But we are not doing this for ourselves. We are doing it for all the just causes of the world, at a time of skepticism. Optimism and the hope of the peoples will again be born, because the negative forces will not prevail. (59–61)

5 / Border-Crossing Alliances: Japanese and African American Women in the State's Household

We have to stem the tide of polarization; we must close the gaps, bring down the barriers, and make bridges instead of walls. —Yuri Kochiyama

Ms. magazine's 1993 profile of Yuri Kochiyama presents a model for inter-ethnic alliances and coalition building.[1] Having survived a U.S. internment camp during World War II, Kochiyama moved to Harlem in 1963 where she organized as a civil-rights activist. Kochiyama, who states that she was politicized by Malcolm X and other black radicals, engages in grassroots activism and coalition building in New York City, organizing within the Japanese American redress movement and amnesty campaigns for political prisoners. Her work builds bridges between some of the most polarized ethnic populations in the United States—African and Asian Americans.

Portrayed as deviant and model minorities, respectively, African and Asian Americans are the U.S. cultural caricatures of intellectual under- and overachievers. In a society that depicts the African as the embodiment of the worst traits of nonwhites and the Asian as the ideal nonwhite, the model minority par excellence is the Japanese American. Yet the title is deceptive. During the twentieth century, the U.S. government alternately incarcerated Japanese Americans in concentration camps and hailed them as white people. According to Carole Marks, Japanese American citizens were conferred the status of honorary white people during the gentlemen's agreement period between the two World Wars.[2] (Under apartheid, the South African government also granted this distinction to the Japanese.) As honorary whites, Japanese Americans were exempt from severe residential segregation and employment discrimination.

This mythology of the model minority at once dehumanizes those not part of this group and obscures struggles against poverty and cultural and language discrimination in nonmonolithically constructed Asian American communities. In a June 1990 *New York Times* letter, Ronald Takaki observes: "Most Asian-Americans know their 'success' is largely a myth. They also see how the celebration of Asian-Americans as a 'model minority' perpetuates their inequality and exacerbates relations between them and African-Americans."[3] Asking for whom Asians are to be models, Takaki notes that "such comparisons pit minorities against each other. . . . [while] the victims are blamed for their plight, rather than racism and an economy that has made many young African American workers superfluous" (21).

Nonwhites are differently valued yet share diverse standings as superfluous, marginal interlopers in a racialized society and culture. Jessica Hagedorn describes how American cinema stereotypes of Asian women are analogous to the American Africanisms critiqued by Toni Morrison:

> Asian women are the ultimate wet dream in most Hollywood movies. . . . we exist to provide sex, color, and texture in what is essentially a white man's world. [This] is akin to what Toni Morrison calls "the Africanist presence" in literature. She writes: "Just as entertainers, through or by association with blackface, could render permissible topics that otherwise would have been taboos, so American writers were able to employ an imagined Africanist persona to articulate and imaginatively act out the forbidden in American culture." The same analogy could be made for the often titillating presence of Asian women in movies made by white men.[4]

The Asianist presence, like the Africanist presence, sketches a civilized whiteness against the backdrop of the racially sexualized other.

Alliance building entails more than white and colored polarities. Anti-Asian sentiments in black communities focus on economic competition, which is often expressed in boycotts of Asian groceries and businesses in black neighborhoods as well as in general attitudes of ethnic chauvinism and xenophobia. Anti-African and black sentiments in Asian communities are less tied to economics than to the mythologized portrait of blacks as the embodiment of violent criminality, which in turn leads to sentiments of Asian racial superiority to blacks. African American perceptions of an antiblack racism among Asians fuels the divide between the two populations. For instance, black media sources for the last decade have reported on African American bashing in Japan where white supremacist depictions of African Americans have been adapted for the Japanese culture. The original Darkie toothpaste, now called Darlie, is marketed in Asia by Colgate-Palmolive with the caricature of a black minstrel figure. Other sources have exposed anti-African-American racism in Japanese business, for instance, in the tourist industry where a Japanese magazine reportedly issued a map of Harlem illustrated by a mammy figure. A February 1990 *Newsweek* issue published a survey of Japanese citizens in which 57 percent stated that too many racial and ethnic groups resided in the United States.[5]

Denigrating caste systems and the aversion to black physical characteristics are not uncommon in both African and Asian American communities, given that antipathy for blackness is held multiethnically. Conversely, shared political identity among people confronting racism encourages solidarity, coalition politics, and the formation of new languages of race in the resistance to subaltern states. For instance, *people of color, women of color* and *black*—denoting people stigmatized by white supremacy, the latter term was used by progressives in apartheid South Africa—are terms that exemplify these new antiracist racial groupings. Yet (re)naming one's individual self or group does not in itself address how national structures indoctrinate people into the race thinking and economic competition that are shaped by psychological insecurities and social ambitions. Solidarity is likely sustainable only where one confronts institutions that promote schisms between ethnic groups and where one can challenge the perception that the dominant state is both invulnerable and the only viable vehicle for safety and success.

Obviously, there are neither monolithic Asian and African American communities nor a monolithic class of women in general. Alongside color and caste divisions, class is also problematic in the forming of effective decolonizing alliances. Both the perceived and real economic and educational differences between the two groups complicate the union of progressive political groups. At times, Asian and African Americans may be able to unite along class and color lines in the United States. The same lines can allow them as colored elites to distance themselves from poor people and the political issues of those on the periphery of society. Given the international division of labor and classism, sharing the same skin tone or status as nonwhite does not necessarily align African and Asian Americans with exploited Third World peoples. Many struggle with and are shaped by the contradictions and ambiguities of a double consciousness and the multiple allegiances felt amid increasing class and color stratification among elite and neocolonized groups of people.

Despite the multiplicities of alliances, and the border crossings in different directions, one can explore—without romanticizing—the possibilities for strengthening political and interethnic coalitions in decolonization efforts. The romantic notion held in the 1930s and during World War II among African Americans that a victorious Japan, as a leader of the colored races, would liberate black Americans is argued half a century later by some African American academics who surmise that the postwar economic power of Japan signals the demise of white European supremacy.[6] What such arguments fail to consider, however, is that militarism, economic and racial hierarchies, sexism, and ethnic chauvinism are characteristics shared by both Japan and the United States. Irrespective of military and trade battles, the U.S. and Japanese governments have formed their own strategic alliances. One way to expand the connection between progressive Asian and African Americans is to examine these state alliances to see how such unions regulate women and other disenfranchised groups in each state's household.

State Alliances

American forces occupied Japan from 1945 to 1948, ousting right-wing militarists from the Japanese government, only to restore them in 1949 in the wake of China's communist revolution and the Soviet Union's acquisition of the atomic bomb. Like their Nazi counterparts, Unit 731 of the Japanese Imperial Army conducted biological warfare and, among other medical experiments, dissected Chinese prisoners of war, without using anesthetic. (An estimated twenty million Chinese died in the 1930s and 1940s from Japanese militarism and war atrocities.) Treating the Japanese much as it had Nazi scientists, the U.S. government covered up Japan's use of biological warfare in exchange for research gathered by Japanese scientists.[7] The United States freed accused war criminals like Nobusuke Kishi, who later became Japan's prime minister. Some rehabilitated politicians reputedly worked with organized crime groups or the yakuza. Yoshio Kodama, for example, was "a political fixer and later a major CIA contact in Japan who worked behind the scenes to finance the conservatives," according to a 1994 *New York Times* report.[8] Government documents, disclosed in the 1990s, revealed that in the 1950s and 1960s the United States channeled millions of dollars through the CIA to the Liberal Democratic Party to gather information, oppose communism in Asia, and undermine the Japanese left. Today, despite trade wars and escalating conflicts sparked by the 1995 $66 billion trade deficit with Japan, cooperation between the two states remains intact.

As economic and military powers, the United States and Japan have shaped sites of racial, sexual, and economic exploitation within their respective households and territorial spheres of influence through their domestic and foreign policies. Historically, each state has used mythologies of racial purity and superiority to rationalize foreign intervention. Both states have maintained domestic households—or internal colonies of ethnically, sexually, and economically oppressed peoples, largely sustained by women who labored in the family as well as formal and underground economies.

The similarities Japanese and African American women have, aside from not being white, most likely stem from the shared contradictions of living (for some in considerable comfort) in imperial states. Historically expansionist nations, the United States and Japan have two of the highest standards of living in the world. During the 1980s, U.S. life expectancy increased from 75.3 to 75.4 years for European Americans. Life expectancy is 78.3 and 73.1 years, respectively, for women and men in Japan. Japan's 120 million people have a similar birthrate (1.9 percent) to that of the United States (1.8 percent), and maternal mortality rates are low as well.

The living conditions of ethnic minorities in the United States and Japan are shaped by a color caste system. For some women and their families in Japan, the state, like its U.S. counterpart, differentiates services and equality. In Japan's internal colonies, for instance, minority women live unequal lives, much as American women of color. The Burakumin, Koreans,[9] Okinawans, Filipinas, and Ainu (the indigenous peoples of Japan), who collectively form a small percentage of the Japanese population, experience racism similar to that faced by African Americans: segregated and inferior housing; hiring discrimination and job segregation; disproportionately high unemployment and restriction from unions; poor health; poor performance on standardized educational testing (with a bias toward the dominant culture); and less access to university education. Underreporting in the government census minimizes state allocation of resources to marginalized ethnic groups.[10] According to a *New York Times* article, the Burakumin "were Japan's official outcasts for more than a century, given jobs that were considered unclean like butchering and leather work"; although this treatment officially ended in the nineteenth century, they remain the targets of discrimination and live isolated in close communities.[11] The lives of repressed ethnic minorities in Japan mirror those of their American counterparts who encounter discrimination, racial slurs, violence, and a general denial of the devastation wrought by racial and imperial policies. As in the United States, however, oppressed Japanese citizens organize against such racism. For example, Korean-born Japanese challenged laws that required them to register with the state as foreigners, to be fingerprinted, and to carry identification cards.

With the exception of the Konketsuji, the African Japanese community, most minorities could pass through assimilation; some, however, choose to organize for economic, cultural, and identity rights and have done so in coalition with people of African descent. There is an extensive history of African and Asian activism against some forms of racism and imperialism, for example, the Bandung Conference of African/Asian nations in Indonesia in April 1955 and other African-Asian solidarity conferences of nonaligned nations in Egypt, Ghana, Sri Lanka, Guinea, Algeria, and Cuba. More recently, in 1982 Burakumin Japanese and African Americans worked together at an international conference on combating racism in Japan, organized by educator-activists, the Kaiho Domei, and the Buraku Liberation League. Then and now, Burakumin and African Americans have shared strategies for fighting racism through curricular reform, nonracist and nonsexist schoolbooks, and the writing and publishing of history and stories about Burakumin culture and people. Today, Burakumin organizing continues through the International Movement against All Forms of Discrimination and Racism. Also, the Japan Pacific Resource Network (JPRN) works with African American and labor organizations such as the National Association for the Advancement of Colored People, the Hotel Employees and Restaurant Employees International Union, and the Japanese African American Association. The JPRN worked with the Coalition of Asian Women's Rights to produce "Migrant Women in Japan: Discrimination and the Struggle for Equal Rights," a Labor Video Project educational forum on the sexual and economic exploitation of Filipinas in Japan. These organizing and educational campaigns face states that increasingly form their own alliances of hegemony and domination.

Japanese and U.S. Polities: Managing Race in State Alliances

Protectionism and economic nationalism that view Third World imports and workers as competition are misguided because of the international nature of production and the global scale of multinationals.
— Annette Fuentes and Barbara Ehrenreich,
Women in the Global Factory

Combined, the United States and Japan form the world's largest economies, with one-third of the world's total gross national product. With Germany, they share the highest World Bank rankings. Along with Western Europe, North America and Japan, constituting 15 percent of the world's population, consume more than 70 percent of the world's resources, while controlling the world capitalist market.

Yet this is an uneasy partnership. According to an April 1990 report in the *New York Times,* in the 1980s as the world's largest debtor nation faced with declining exports, the United States had a purchasing power triple that of Japan; its gross national product was $5.2 billion to Japan's $1.9 billion. An average trade balance from 1981 to 1988 of –$97 billion for the United States to Japan's $52 billion, however, provoked incidents of Japan bashing. Economic nationalists decried Japanese penetration of U.S. markets and cited the U.S. trade deficit with Japan—$49 billion in 1989, half of America's $100 billion trade deficit. In contrast, Japan had a $400 billion trade surplus with the United States in the 1980s.

Japanese corporations have invested billions of dollars in the European Community, with Eastern European cities serving as the new *maquiladoras,* or low-wage industrial sectors in free-enterprise zones, for manufacturing and marketing cars and electronics to Western European cities. Japan bashing or anti-Japanese racism has become virulent in the United States and Europe. Seemingly, the rise of a dominant non-European economic power poses a threat to U.S. economic interests, although heavy German and Swedish investments in the United States have not led to any identifiable occurrences of German or Swede bashing. Fueled by economic interests, anti-Japanese nationalism has continued to spread throughout corporations, Congress, media, and marketing firms, and (kiddie) pop culture. Street violence informed by anti-Japanese sentiment has also risen.

In 1983 Vincent Chin, a Chinese American man mistaken for Japanese, was beaten to death with baseball bats by two unemployed white auto workers who blamed the car industry slump on the importation of Japanese cars. Although both men were convicted of murder, they received suspended sentences, with community work as part of their rehabilitation and parole. Sony Corporation chairman Akio Morita's *The Japan That Can Say "No": The New United States-Japan Relations Card* and Japanese statesman Shintaro Ishihara's *The Japan That Can Say "No": Why Japan Will Be First among Equals* countered anti-Japanese sentiment in the United States.[12] The latter book, which was reprinted in the *Congressional Record* argues that Japan has an obsequious relationship to the United States and that white European supremacy prevents America from accepting Japan as an equal partner in economic and political affairs.

While certain corporate and government sectors market racist nationalism as good business, others, particularly multinational corporations and banks, view anti-Japanese racism and Japan's anti-American response as potentially harmful to profits. Seeking to maintain their economic hegemony and to manage anti-Asian racism and xenophobia in the United States, corporate interests and policy analysts often try to prevent the potential disruption of capitalist economic growth with conflict mediation. Their proposals advocate healing the schism between the two dominant nations, with the reminder that this is, after all, a family fight. Conflict-mediation proposals by Japanese analysts also support the state alliance between Japan and the United States. Criticizing U.S. racism for contributing to the rise of American bashing in Japan, they argue for the creation of United States-Japan bilateral organizations, including an economic council and a trade court to depoliticize and depublicize trade disputes, and joint manufacturing facilities in the United States. Other policy experts have improved on the two-heads-are-better-than-one approach with a proposal of adding a third: the European Community headed by Western European elites. Such a triumvirate would then coordinate international economic policies concerning space exploration, sea mining, energy, refugees, drug trafficking, pollution and the global environment, and international human rights.[13]

Despite competitive economic wars, there are consistent calls for greater joint American-Japanese military operations in the Asia-Pacific region, where the United States and Japan control 70 percent of the economic activity.[14] Of America's estimated annual sales of more than $10 billion, Japan is a primary client, purchasing an estimated $570 million to $1 billion in weapons in the early 1990s. Although defeated in World War II, Japan had the world's fourth-largest military at the time of the disintegration of the Soviet Union. Historically, Japanese imperialism directed against Southeast Asian countries under the banner of Asia for the Asiatics coincided with the imperial wars of U.S. Manifest Destiny in the Americas. Currently, both states use military and police forces to control workers and destabilize self-determination activities. National economies and social orders are also integrated into the military as public monies are diverted from social programs to war efforts.[15] Japanese feminists argue in *Femintern: A Japanese Feminist Quarterly* that the Japanese economic miracle was "sparked by Japanese servicing of the U.S. military in the Korean War" and that Japanese investment and exploitation in Korea was facilitated by a U.S. military presence in both countries.[16] Simultaneously competitive and cooperative, U.S. and Japanese policies create colonial sites that profit from the degradation of women's labor, bodies, and families. Although popularly portrayed as antagonistic competitors, American and Japanese government and corporate leaders manage racist nationalism to control economic change and to retain a significant degree of power over resources and labor.

Working in the State's Household: Neocolonies in the Postcolonial World

Whereas the traditional forms of chattel slavery may have disappeared, the most widespread forms tend now to be debt bondage, exploitation of the prostitution of others . . . exploitation of child labour, and the sale and prostitution of chil-

dren. Other forms include the slavery-like exploitation of domestic help, forced labour and servile forms of marriage. Manifestations of apartheid and colonialism have also been classified as practices similar to slavery.
—Nina Lassen, "United Nations Efforts to
Eradicate Slavery and Slavery-Like Practices"

Nina Lassen's observations about contemporary labor exploitation are echoed by Mary I. Buckley's "Encounter with Asian Poverty and Women's Invisible Work," in which she argues that the work of masses of women "is all but invisible [which] . . . means that they are owned, possessed, appropriated like natural resources. . . . the bottom line for keeping them in submission is ultimately violence."[17]

In the late 1980s UNICEF reported that since the 1960s Third World countries have fallen deeper into debt and poverty.[18] International Monetary Fund and World Bank policies have maintained underdevelopment in Africa, Latin America, and the Caribbean, where individuals annually transfer more than $20 billion to North American and Western European banks—this outside investment in the face of increasing illiteracy, malnutrition, disease, and death in their own communities. As a region, Asia is exempt from increasing impoverishment, yet most Asian women and children workers do not share this exemption. Like other Third World women and youth, they labor at merely subsistence wages. In international production—more than a hundred free-trade or export-processing zones largely controlled by the United States, Japan, or the European Community—multinational corporations target women as docile workers for light-assembly work. Eighty to ninety percent of the workers in these zones are women, the majority of whom are sixteen to twenty-five years old. Citing the South Korean textile and Malaysian electronics markets as examples of industry developed with assistance from the U.S. Agency for International Development, Annette Fuentes and Barbara Ehrenreich maintain that the "most powerful promoter of exploitative conditions for Third World women workers is the U.S. government."[19]

In the international division of labor, most "black" women are segregated in low-paying, dangerous jobs. Here, the state oversees racial and sexual colonies that expropriate so-called women's work in biological reproduction and socialization; waged house, field, and factory labor; and the sex industries. Work is often synonymous with exploitation through inequitable wages, domestic or work abuse, physical danger in sweatshops, prison industries, and prostitution.

Reproductive labor and unpaid domestic work performed by women are mainstays of modern economic and political systems. As free labor, reproduction creates the family and workforce. Exploitation is the norm in household labor. Repressive, waged domestic work is disproportionately borne by women of color who are meagerly paid to reproduce and manage elite families and households. In 1980, for example, more African American women were employed as domestics than as professionals, according to Carole Marks.[20] The similarities in conditions of African American and Japanese American women workers are explored in Evelyn Nakano Glenn's work on Japanese American women domestics.[21] According to Glenn, despite significant differences in experiences in the United States, the similarities between the two groups are noteworthy: Japanese Americans have also faced institutional racism and segregation into low-paying domestic or agricultural jobs, even when they were college educated.

Glenn states that issei domestic workers, West Coast first-generation Japanese immigrant women, divided work into three categories: housework; unpaid work in a family farm or business; and paid work usually domestic in nature set by feudal relations. Even though subjugated by institutional racism, domestic work, and the strictures of issei family life, these women were not victims, according to Glenn: "The issei maximized autonomy in employment by choosing work situations in which employers were absent or inactive. . . . In the family, they went out to work secretly or withheld part of their wages as a means of gaining control over disposable income." Japanese and African American women struggle with the patriarchal restrictions of the state and family households, just as in Japan where Burakumin and Korean women are most often relegated to domestic work for employment.

Among African-descended legal workers in the United States, high infant and maternal mortality rates and falling life expectancy rates reflect the devastation of colonized life. The double shift—of unpaid domestic work and wage labor—has turned into a triple shift for a growing number of working-class women.[22] (With increased shifts come multiple exposures to overwork, ill health, and physical and psychological exhaustion.) The number of women holding two or more jobs quintupled from 1970 to 1990, from 636,000 to 3.1 million, while the number of men holding two or more jobs rose by merely 21 percent, from 3.4 million to 4.1 million. More and more women's earnings augment family incomes to stall the onset of impoverishment (or to enjoy a middle-class lifestyle). According to the Bureau of Labor Statistics, 1.5 million workers receive no more than the federal minimum wage, which was $3.80 per hour in 1990, less than California's minimum wage of $4.25 per hour. In the absence of meaningful assistance reform, women earning more than minimum wage are stripped of food stamps and medical care for children because of their higher income status. Given the racist wage differentials paid women and men of color, the earnings of women of color are essential to family survival, even in homes where men are working.

Employment segregation and differences in wage and education reflect the disparities in salaries. Among college graduates with one to five years of employment, black women earned $11.41 per hour and black men, $11.26 per hour; white women earned $11.38 per hour and white men, $12.85 per hour, according to an October 1994 *New York Times* report.[23] The same article concedes that wages for blacks with only a high-school education eroded during the 1980s. (According to Carole Marks, in 1990, 8.1 percent of employed African American women completed four years of college; 7.7 percent of African American men; 11 percent of European American women; and 22.1 percent of European American men.)[24] In 1987, although working more hours and more full-time jobs outside the home than European American women, African American women earned $1,664 less. Asian American women, in contrast, earned $1,000 more per year than European American women. Higher education levels and residency in high-paying states for Asian women (for example, in California rather than a southern state where wages are often depressed) contribute to these economic disparities. Women of color are rarely paid a wage comparable to that of a white European woman; nearly all women are denied equal pay with white European men.[25] And overwhelmingly, immigrant women of color are relegated to dangerous and unprotected types of work in the underground or illegal economy.

In the United States, labor conditions for African (Caribbean), Asian, and Latina illegal immigrant females mirror those in *maquiladoras* or fields in the Third World. In Florida, Haitian women, along with Haitian and Jamaican men, subsist in *bateys* (migrant farm camps) with conditions similar to those of slave-labor camps. The garment industry's sweatshops in Los

Angeles, New York, and Boston re-create the same severe economic exploitation and health hazards. Where 90 percent of sweatshop workers are immigrant women and children, subsistence wages in such workplaces in Los Angeles are reported to be as low as $50 for a sixty-hour week.[26] Without green cards, women who are threatened with deportation cannot obtain adequate medical services, legal representation, or state protection when they are denied or cheated on their wages, assaulted, or raped. These slavery-like conditions are exacerbated in U.S. prisons, where prison industries and workfare programs also represent an undocumented and unorganized labor force disproportionately made up of people of color: there, the state owns you. Convict labor, like the postbellum sharecropping that supplanted legal enslavement of Africans brought to America, places workers outside all law: even the United Nations does not recognize the right of incarcerated people to labor without exploitation, according to Nina Lassen.[27]

The most life-threatening work in the state's household is in the underground economy, namely, sexual work. The myth that men and women from nondominant ethnic groups are sexually deviant—rapists and whores, respectively—legitimizes sexual and racial violence. This myth also rationalizes the sexual exploitation of women and children in prostitution and other segments of the sex industry. Facing sexual imperialism that is reminiscent of slavery, African American women often find that their bodies are simultaneously reduced to units of labor and sexual commodities. The African American experience of dehumanized sexuality or sexual slavery as work is shared by Japanese Americans and Japanese minorities in Japan. After Japanese women achieved the vote in 1945, the women's movement there moved from advocating suffrage to campaigning to end prostitution and sex tourism. In Southeast Asia, the industry's sex tours service businessmen from Japan, the United States, and Western Europe. Thai, Filipina, and South Korean women and female and male children are sold, exported, and imported as commodities.

Femintern has reported that the sex industry and sexual slavery, as integral components of modern tourism, increased Japan's gross national product as well as benefited the country's military.[28] According to *Femintern*, prostitution serves as an income source for the Korean Central Intelligence Agency; in the 1970s two thousand Japanese men entered Korea daily, mainly for sex tours. When Koreans were forcibly transplanted to Japan as slave laborers during the war, Korean women were forced to service army men as prostitutes in camps. Half a century later, women still protest state imprisonment and sexual violence. In August 1994 women in South Korea threw eggs, chanted, and demonstrated in front of the Japanese Embassy in Seoul. Demanding direct compensation to Filipina, Chinese, and Korean survivors and their families, the women condemned the Japanese government's proposal to spend $1 billion over ten years to "finance cultural and student exchanges as atonement" for incarcerating 200,000 women to serve as prostitutes for Japanese soldiers during World War II.[29]

After its defeat, the government of Japan coerced geishas into serving as comfort girls to American occupation forces ("to protect the purity of 'respectable' Japanese women"), using its police officers to organize women as prostitutes.[30] Any geisha who attempted to run or hide was arrested and surrendered to U.S. troops. Asian feminists note:

> Both [Korean] kisaeng and the [Japanese] geishas have . . . been offered by their own governments as sacrificial lambs to men of invading foreign powers. . . . The outrages committed against kisaeng do not occur in a vacuum, they are profoundly related to the contempt shown by Japanese men for the women of their own country.[31]

Contempt is exacerbated when states portray women as "ethnic aliens" to increase the benefits of their exploitation. *Femintern* authors write that, whereas in the late 1960s South Korea sold young men as mercenary troops to the U.S. government for $1 billion to fight in Vietnam, now South Korea sells young women. In 1973, 700,000 tourists brought in $300,000,000: "With the profits reaped by paying minuscule wages to workers, foreign businessmen buy the bodies of South Korean women."

Twenty years later the industries of sexual exploitation thrive. Jacqui Hunt, president of the human-rights organization Equality Now, contends that the $1 billion offered by the Japanese government as compensation for the Asian women forced to work in brothels during World War II is more symbolic than real, given the trafficking and ongoing violence against women that continues in the Japanese sexual industry. Hunt recounts one recent atrocity:

> In April 1991, Maricris Sioson, a 22-year-old dancer from the Philippines, arrived in Japan to work at the Faces Club in Fukushima. Five months later she was admitted to a hospital, and on Sept. 14, 1991,

she died. Her Japanese death certificate listed hepatitis as the cause of death, but when Ms. Sioson's family opened her coffin back in the Philippines, they saw that she had been badly beaten and stabbed.[32]

A later autopsy by the Philippine National Bureau of Investigation indicated murder, yet Japanese police refused to release full medical and police records. Hearings in the Philippines determined that thirty-three Filipina entertainment workers, twelve under suspicious circumstances, died in 1991, according to Hunt; that year the Philippine Labor Ministry estimated that nearly eighty thousand Filipinas worked in Japan as "entertainers" unable to leave or move freely because of confiscated passports and salaries withheld until completion of their contracts. The yakuza, Japan's organized crime, is considered to be heavily involved in this labor trade.

Conclusion

The issues of sexual violence, forced and unpaid domesticity, reproductive rights, state discrimination, and social inequality are ties that bind all women together. When these ties are cut by racial and ethnic divisions, forming coalitions is problematic. Perhaps one of the more telling tests will be to see what partnerships African and Asian American women will form around U.S. foreign policy. The most critical connections will take place at home, however, given the resurgence of theories that purportedly explain the scientific basis of racial superiority.

Financed by the Pioneer Fund, which has historical and contemporary ties to neo-Nazism, the literature on race and intelligence by white male scholars, popularized in 1994 and 1995, constructs Asians and Ashkenazic Jews as intellectually (but not politically) superior to whites or Wasps. This postmodern Darwinian discourse on racial and economic supremacy posits a biological hierarchy that is supposedly revealed by genetics and intelligence quotas to reflect a political order, with blacks on the bottom and whites battling Asians for the top. In a society whose dominant racialized myths construct colored ethnic groups as inferior to white Europeans and European Americans (and hence, as a menace to society, civilization, and evolution), in its latest twist, this racist mythology offers seminal constructs that permit certain ethnic peoples to escape from a debased status. (Alleged Asian or Jewish superiority still is perceived as a threat to white civilization and white jobs.) Interestingly, the escape clause couples the racial mandate to rule with the sexual mandate to breed. The academic progeny of Thomas Malthus at City College, Harvard, University of California at Berkeley, Stanford, and other sites proclaims women as breeders, and thus strategic players in the race war. White males promoting these theories argue that because their more fertile inferiors are outbreeding them, white and Asian women (the intellectually superior females) must wake up to catch up. White men (mostly as conservative and rightist politicians) in turn contribute to responsible breeding by condemning abortion and reproductive rights while advocating sterilization or limited social benefits to nonwhite, immigrant, and poor women (especially those who have children while on public assistance).

Given this climate of organizing women for racially repressive mandates, coalitions, particularly among the marginalized, are essential for progressive movement. Despite compartmentalization, cultural ignorance, and interethnic conflict and violence, individuals do cross borders, thereby transgressing color and caste lines without reproducing abuse or oppression. Discomfort and friction are inevitable in such movement as activists and educators encounter and counter racial divisiveness. Urging coalitions to resist violence despite distrust among members means emphasizing commonalities and crossing borders into unfamiliar territories. In "Coalition Politics: Turning the Century," Bernice Johnson Reagon contends that coalitions are marked by low levels of comfort:

> Coalition work is not work done in your home. Coalition work has to be done in the streets. And it is some of the most dangerous work you can do. And you shouldn't look for comfort. Some people will come to a coalition and they rate the success of the coalition on whether or not they feel good when they get there. They're not looking for a coalition; they're looking for a home! They're looking for a bottle with some milk in it and a nipple, which does not happen in a coalition. You don't get a lot of food in a coalition. You don't get fed a lot in a coalition. In a coalition you have to give, and it is different from your home.[33]

Highlighting similarities in women's relationships to government policies and societies that are influenced by racial and sexual myths may not supply the warmth and familiarity that many desire. In a racially fragmented society, however, interethnic coalition building that includes African-Asian alliances could transform state households into spaces where more might feel at home.

III

Cultural Politics:
Black Women and Sexual Violence

6 / Anita Hill, Clarence Thomas, and Gender Abstractions

The spotlight on the 1991 Supreme Court confirmation hearings for Clarence Thomas and the gender consciousness raised in the media coverage have made Thomas's and Anita Hill's names symbols for reverence, respect, and ridicule in feminist and masculinist writings.[1] In the wake of his anti-civil-rights votes from the Court and his September 11, 1995, public claim that affirmative action is a Christian sin against whites, Thomas is more uniformly lampooned in the black press. Some of the reverence and ridicule surrounding both Thomas and Hill appears to be disconnected from reality and based more on gender abstractions—that is, on a notion of sexual politics conveniently and romantically severed from class and racial politics.

The respect given to Anita Hill, however, reflects the fact that she withstood the racist and sexist harassment of ultraconservative Senate Judiciary Committee members during the nationally televised hearings. Although their diatribes carried the virulent, authoritative contempt that only a fusion of racial, economic, and sexual elitism could manage to spew, Anita Hill maintained her personal dignity, which certainly deserves respect and praise. Still, both respect and praise in this case are weighed with irony: for Hill also worked to implement the policies of white privilege and patriarchy by eroding civil-rights programs redressing past and present discrimination. She harnessed her career to the ultraconservatism of the Reagan-Bush administration and its employee, her former employer, Clarence Thomas. To re-create Hill as a martyr heroine for mobilizing women and feminists is only possible if (a) one disconnects her from the singeing racial and class politics she embraced (and likely still embraces), and/or (b) one maintains that racism and classism are abstractions to—that is, irrelevant in—sexual politics. In other words, to make her a symbol or an icon, one must create a martyr heroine as a gender abstraction.

Throughout 1992, articles were written about Anita Hill as a feminist role model, a "race-traitor," and a "Republican traitor." These were part of the spillover of the hearings, as would be a number of books including two anthologies reflecting the debates on the hearings among African Americans—*Court of Appeal* and *Racing Gender and Engendering Justice*.[2] Allegations of sexual harassment by Hill, a woman from Thomas's caste, were able to delay the Supreme Court confirmation of Thomas when his own political record—antiblack, antifemale, antipoor and anti-working class, antiyouth, and antielderly—could not. The New York City-based Center for Constitutional Rights released a statement that Clarence Thomas was unsuitable for the U.S. Supreme Court because of his lack of experience (an unqualified candidate was being promoted by anti-affirmative-action politicians) as well as his antidemocratic bias. The center reported that under Thomas's directorship as chair of the Equal Employment Opportunity Commission (EEOC) class-action suits declined dramatically compared to individual cases; in 1988, 40 to 87 percent of cases were closed because they were improperly investigated by field offices and state fair-employment-practices agencies; case backlogs rose from 31,500 in 1983 to 46,000 in 1989; processing time increased from four to seven months in 1983 to nearly ten months in 1989; equal-pay cases declined from thirty-five in 1982 to seven in 1989. Concerning affirmative action, the center noted that Thomas changed the EEOC policy of establishing goals and timetables for businesses to open jobs to white women and women and men of color, re-instating the policy only after the Supreme Court's 1986 decision to uphold these guidelines. At the same time, the Court upheld affirmative action, which ironically enabled Thomas to further his own educational and legal career.

As Reagan's EEOC appointee and Bush's nominee to replace pioneer civil-rights litigator Thurgood Marshall, Clarence Thomas sparred his way through the hearings amid allegations of sexual harassment by portraying himself as a victim of "high-tech lynching." Historically, postbellum lynching victims were blacks (and whites) who resisted rather than collaborated with racist practices. Thomas's black-victim performance opportunistically appropriated lynching as a defensive strategy and metaphor and as such was ideologically compatible with the anti-civil-rights backlash of the recent Republican presidencies. Claims of innocence can be based either on symbolism or specificity. For Clarence Thomas, a man who faithfully executed the policy wishes of his conservative white employers, to assert during the hearings that he "wasn't harmed by the Klan [or] the Aryan Nation but by this process"—the high-tech lynching of an uppity black man—distorted the historical significance of racist killings as punishment for noncompliance with conservative, reactionary whites. Whatever one assumes about the charges, Thomas was able to co-opt antiracist and antilynching discourses because public critiques of racialized sexualities and fears are widely discouraged. Because Hill did not address the issues of race or how her sexuality had been racialized, this performance of a black male as racially sexualized captured center stage.

Surviving and refusing to be silent about sexual victimization are courageous acts. Yet survival or speaking out does not make one a public heroine; public responsibilities and commitments must be taken into account. In the making of heroines in gender politics, feminist or counterfeminist, race and class ideologies still count. For example, if a female staffer in David Duke's Louisiana gubernatorial campaign had courageously come forward with accounts of sexual harassment by Duke (who incidentally backed Clarence Thomas), although I would have supported her right to confront her abuser, I would not have named David Duke the only villain, given that they both share reactionary ideologies. Obviously the abuse of right-wing women building careers under the tutelage of right-wing men (who may implement racist, classist, sexist, and heterosexist policies) needs to stop. Eulogizing such women is extremely problematic, given their antidemocratic and retrogressive racial politics. Supporting Hill's right to a fair hearing on sexual harassment requires compassion and outrage over sexual abuse. But placing her on a pedestal reveals how inane analyses of sexual and racial abuse and democratic politics had become.

At that time, Anita Hill had implemented Reaganite anti-civil-rights policies, taught at Oral Roberts University Law School, and maintained that Robert Bork was unjustly denied a seat on the Supreme Court. To idolize Hill, therefore, one had to imitate Clarence Thomas, Orrin Hatch, John Danforth, Arlen Specter, Strom Thurmond, George Bush, and company in their wolfish cries of "lynching!"—this time with the added cry of "Harassment!" Following the opportunistic moves on political language, history, and reality throughout the hearings, one could first make trivial and then manipulate the lengthy red record of racial and sexual violence and imagery that African Americans struggle to survive. (Or one could have chosen to mimic contortionists' claims, in an episode of *Tony Brown's Journal* with Thomas supporters Phyllis Berry Myers and John Doggett, that Thomas was lynched while Anita Hill was raped—claims that thereby attain some false enclosure of unifying blackness.) Rape and lynching are tied together in the history of African American women who were tortured and raped prior to and during lynchings; black women were also lynched, along with African American men who assisted them, for resisting or avenging rape by white men. Because manipulating history is a useful tool for denying reality, it is unsurprising that the political history and reality of African American men's sexual abuse of African American women is equally manipulated and denied.

The Hill-Thomas hearings provided equal opportunity to create pedestals laden with right-wing role models—black and white, male and female. Anita Hill, who had overcome her personal victimization with dignity and restraint painfully lacking in Thomas and most of his multiracial, female, and male cheerleaders, was the most appealing. Consequently, in the November 12, 1991, issue of the New York-based weekly the *Village Voice,* African American columnist Lisa Jones, after describing the "Bush/ Thomas lynch strategy" and the racist and sexist vilification of African American women, wrote that "Anita Hill—shunning victimhood—is a role model."[3] And yet Hill—shunning or embracing victimhood—could not possibly be a role model if being one means having a responsible relationship to African American communities and progressive democratic politics. For Jones, the class and racial politics of Hill are as irrelevant as Thomas's sexual politics are for the editors of the African American, Brooklyn-based weekly *City Sun,* who superficially treated the charges of sexual harassment while focusing on the detrimental political relationship of both Thomas and Hill to African American communities: "The truth is that Clarence Thomas and Anita Hill are cut from the same cloth. . . . Black people's interests were not the motivating factor for either Thomas' or Hill's career move."[4] Such articles, based on gender abstractions, fail to present a discussion of sexual politics connected to racial and class politics or the ways in which black identification shaped responses to sexual abuse.

In the aftermath of the hearings, a televised spectacle that became popular entertainment much as the O. J. Simpson trial would in 1995, the veracity of Hill's courageous testimony has been disparaged by some and substantiated by others.[5] That neither Hill nor Thomas worked for the benefit of African Americans probably led to the more jocular attitude among a number of black male intellectuals in their commentary on the hearings. More somber attitudes among black male intellectuals were later expressed over controversies involving Benjamin Chavis, C. Eric Lincoln, and Mike Tyson. Chavis, the former head of the NAACP, was accused of sexual harassment. Lincoln was convicted on charges of physical assault of a black female Harvard divinity graduate student. Mike Tyson was found guilty of raping a black beauty-pageant contestant. Prominent civil-rights leaders, black scholars, and sports heroes clearly invite different forms of consideration.

Reductionism is endemic to discussions in which the politics of sexual harassment are isolated from racial and class politics. When the African American experience was reduced to the African American male experience opportunistically performed by Thomas (he also represented the transracial male because his accuser was black, not white), the woman's experience became reduced to the "whitened," middle-class female experience uncritically worn by Hill. The irrational and illogical commentary on the hearings underscored how prevalent reductionism is: white women commentators on National Public Radio stated that Clarence Thomas needed a black on the Senate Judiciary Committee, whereas Anita Hill needed a woman. Neither the fact that Hill is both black and female nor the fact that there is no monolithic black or women's voice or vote spared listeners the inanity of coverage lost in gender abstractions.[6] Much of the analysis obscured the political ties of gender to race and class and veiled the racial and class politics of women and men mobilizing under the banner of sexual politics.

The issue of class mystification routinely appeared in writings about this case. An October 1991 *Boston Globe* article argued that in confirming Thomas in the face of Hill's odious, highly detailed and credible story, the Senate's clear message will be that women who complain of sexual harassment are not to be believed. . . . if an upstanding, articulate law teacher who knows the rules cannot get a group of men to hear her, can a secretary have much hope?[7]

This passage suggests that Hill had no race (although credibility is tied to race) and refers to class in an incomplete way: the secretary is likely to be believed if she is white and accuses the black janitor. Women harassed by men of their race and class have little credibility before the law; women with race and class privilege are more credible than the accused if he is someone with a lower status in the social hierarchy—which is a significant part of the history of lynching. Referring to Hill as if she had no race or class interests gives her the guise of respectability, which in this society takes the form of middle-class, white, and heterosexual womanhood. Isolating sexual harassment from a race and class analysis thus reduces discussions of such harassment to abstractions.

The lack of a class and ideological analysis among some organizers and commentators in the Hill-Thomas hearings was critiqued by bell hooks's "Must We Call All Women 'Sister?'," an essay criticized by some feminists because of its rejection of a generalizing gender solidarity irrespective of politics.[8] In "The Invisible Ones: The Emma Mae Martin Story, the One Thomas Didn't Tell," Lisa Jones also offers a critique of class politics in the choice of Hill as a symbol of feminism and women's victimization.[9] According to Jones, that sexual harassment was a more appealing middle-class women's issue than welfare rights is the reason why fewer women rallied around Thomas's sister Emma Mae Martin. Thomas, in Lee Atwater fashion, publicly chastised her for welfare dependency: "She gets mad when the mailman is late with her welfare check." Noting how economics and class shaped women's mobilization in resisting sexual violence and harassment, Jones observes:

> Thomas's distortion of his sister's life says a lot about him, but it says even more about America. No child-care or health-care system, dead-end jobs, dysfunctional schools, yes. But what of the political/media value put on the lives of women like Martin? Especially black women like Martin. The Martins of this country are pigeonholed as sub-American, subfemale . . . subhuman. (27)

An ad hoc group organized by African American academic activists Barbara Ransby, Elsa Barkley Brown, and Deborah King pitched an educational and fund-raising campaign with a large ad in the November 17th, 1991, Sunday *New York Times.* Under the title "African American Women in Defense of Ourselves," their analysis demystified abstractions by speaking out against the partnership between destructive U.S. policies and the cynical posturings of Bush, Hatch, Specter, Danforth, and their employees. Excerpted below and signed by more than 1,600 women of African descent, it broke the routine rally around media heroes and heroines and the diversion of gender abstractions:

> As women of African descent, we are deeply troubled by the recent nomination, confirmation, and seating of Clarence Thomas as an Associate Justice of the U.S. Supreme Court. We know that the presence of Clarence Thomas on the Court will be continually used to divert attention away from historic struggles for social justice through suggestions that the presence of a Black man on the Supreme Court constitutes an assurance that the rights of African Americans will be protected. Clarence Thomas' public record is ample evidence that this will not be true. Further, the consolidation of a conservative majority on the Supreme Court seriously endangers the rights of all women, poor and working class people, and the elderly. The seating of Clarence Thomas is an affront not only to African American women and men, but to all people concerned with social justice.
>
> We are particularly outraged by the racist and sexist treatment of Professor Anita Hill, an African American woman who was maligned and castigated for daring to speak publicly of her experience of sexual abuse. The malicious defamation of Professor Hill insulted all women of African descent and sent a dangerous message to any woman who might contemplate a sexual-harassment complaint. . . .
>
> As women of African descent, we express our vehement opposition to the policies represented by the placement of Clarence Thomas on the Supreme Court. The Bush administration, having obstructed the passage of civil rights legislation, impeded the extension of unemployment compensation, cut student aid and dismantled social welfare programs, has continually demonstrated that it is not operating in our best interests. Nor is this appointee. We pledge ourselves to continue to speak out in defense of one another, in defense of the African American community and against those who are

hostile to social justice no matter what color they are. No one will speak for us but ourselves.[10]

This text is unique in that it addressed structural politics and racism as well as sexual abuse with some form of integrated analysis that was missing from camps that polarized both issues or from groups that treated the accusations and hearings as pure spectacle.

Conclusion

The selective use of black women as feminist icons reflects their abstract roles in American culture and the ways in which political ideology influences iconography. The extensive and multiracial rally around Anita Hill was not repeated in 1993 when President Clinton withdrew his support for Lani Guinier, his nominee for the Justice Department's civil-rights division, in the wake of a conservative backlash against her strong stance on voting rights for minorities. Nor did massive protests like those surrounding Hill appear in 1995 when Clinton fired Surgeon General Joycelyn Elders for her candid stance on the need for sex education in American schools.

Gender abstractions that reconstructed Hill and Thomas as icons veiled the antidemocratic politics upheld by both black Republicans. The construction of Thomas as a racial icon, simultaneously representing black victimization and resistance, mirrored the construction of Hill as a gender icon, representing female victimization and resistance. The disingenuousness of antiblack and anti-civil-rights politics among African Americans was highlighted in President Bush's selection of Thomas as the successor to a civil-rights leader who successfully argued *Brown v. the Board of Education* in desegregating American schools. Thomas's retrograde gender politics were inconsequential to his selection by a pro-choice president; his reactionary sexual politics could hinder, but not obstruct, a confirmation fueled by racial politics that were palatable to the far right who supported him. If allegations of sexual violence could have derailed such strong political commitments to reactionary racial politics, they would not have been accusations made by a black woman, who in the American mind embodies the racial-sexual Other.

7 / Symbolic Rage: Prosecutorial Performances and Racialized Representations of Sexual Violence

Symbolic Rage

Postbellum lynching—in which the general rationale for mob and state terrorism was that it countered black male sexual violence against white females—exemplified the symbolic rage and prosecutorial performances of the state. Symbolic rage is connected to such performance in that the symbols associated with one's fury supersede and determine responses to specific abuses that have allegedly sparked that fury. Violent anger is supposedly inspired by the myths and symbols that precede and take precedence over any specific criminal act.

Antilynching campaigns, led in part by Ida B. Wells, demystified symbolic rage—the white "civilized" fury against black "savagery." Noting that the charge of rape was used as the general apologia for mob violence and state complicity in or indifference to it, Wells proved that many of these accusations tended to be false and that the charge of sexual violence was only leveled in a fraction of lynching cases. Of white men, who as a caste were the prosecutors and executioners of sexual violence (as well as the perpetrators), Wells wrote in 1895 that to "justify their own barbarism they assume a chivalry which they do not possess."[1]

Designating interracial sex—specifically that between black men and white women—as the most heinous form of criminality, moral and social leaders based the legality of lynching on racial and sexual myths and on a white code of chivalry that featured a macabre duet played out in bipolar stereotypes of white knights and ladies pitted against the threat of black sexual brutes and savages. In Wells's era, European American women, particularly those from the propertied classes, were perceived as inherently virtuous, and thus absolved of any charges of sexual promiscuity or miscegenation; European American men, again particularly of the upper classes, were considered inherently chivalrous and thus absolved of charges of sexual violence or miscegenation. African American men, on the other hand, were identified as rapists; defined as inherently promiscuous, African American women could not be violated because they were said to be without virtue. A white man would not rape a lady (a white woman) and could not rape an object (a black woman). (Intraclass rape of white women, including incest, was usually represented as the seduction of the white adult male.) A white woman could not desire a brute or likely join in coalition with someone considered to be a sexual object. During the era of lynching, voluntary sexual associations between black males and white females were constructed as rape, and were punishable by death (of the African American involved). Wells and others argued that the mythology of black sexual pathology that motivated lynching functioned as the apologia for rape in a society where actual and alleged assaults against whites were prosecuted while convictions in cases of sexual violence against black women were rare.

Female African American antilynching activists confronted the convergence of racist and sexual violence, urging white women to respond to the political use of the rape charge in lynching cases. These activists argued that the prosecution of actual sexual violence for either white or black women was not the objective of the lynch law. The majority of sexual assaults were in fact intraracial. Although national crime statistics for sexual violence were not recorded in the nineteenth century, today's statistics are illuminating. Currently, the FBI reports that more than 90 percent of rapes are intraracial; in interracial rape cases, the percentage of white male assaults on black women exceeds that of black male assaults on white women. One hundred years ago, the percentage of black male assaults on white women was even lower, given racial segregation and the social restrictions on white women. While the percentage of white male assaults on black women was higher (as black women worked as domestic servants in white homes), white males had virtual immunity—as the caste that adjudicated, legislated, and enforced the laws—from prosecution for sexual violence against black women and near immunity from attacks on their female family members or on white women of the lower classes. In fact, the majority of sexual violence in Wells's era was committed by white men who were (and remain) the most likely assailants of white women and who were also responsible for a considerable amount of violence in the lives of black women.

A true correlation between the occurrence of lynching and the prosecution of sexual violence should have meant that the majority of those lynched in the postbellum era were white men. Yet the victims were largely African American. That collective punishment was inflicted on black communities (where property was stolen or destroyed by lynch parties); that the specificity of the crimes and their punishment was treated as inconsequential by mob and state prosecutors; that nonexistent crimes were alleged; and, finally, that the rare phenomenon of black male sexual assault on white females became the national marker for sexual violence—all these facts reveal how the state and society's outrage over sexual violence was based on symbols and mythology that justified the use of ritualized racial violence.

If perpetrators of state violence require demonization to justify their symbolic rages, then entertainment is indispensable to their prosecutorial performances. As spectacles, lynching and later legal executions racialized and politicized sexual violence. Sexual violence that violated classist and racist hierarchies was constructed as the most heinous form of abuse and so was given the most heinous form of punishment. Demonization of racialized sexuality as criminal promoted mass participation in lynchings and furthered indifference to intraracial sexual violence that did not reflect the racial mythology. Symbolic rage validated mob vigilantism, state malfeasance, and police violence in the name of "protecting" women. Prosecutorial performances rarely emphasized the specifics of the crime, the importance of just laws, or the rights of the accused or the survivors; instead, such exhibitions engendered a fixation on generic types of sexual beasts, heroes, and heroines.

Institutionalized, legitimized, and paternal, symbolic rage and state violence needed no specificity of crime because prosecution was directed by mythology. (Subaltern rage also entails demonizing but it is often grounded in the material conditions of oppression.) "Ordinary" sexual violence—that is, intraracial instances—became overshadowed by "extraordinary" racial violence—or interracial occurrences. Until sexual violence crossed caste borders, violating race and class hierarchies, it was considered private and commonplace; in its transgression of such borders, it became public and doubly offensive to state sensibilities. In general, the prosecution of private violence (when it occurs) is routine; the prosecution of public violence, in contrast, is highly ritualized in keeping with the symbolism. Lending itself to apathy and social denial of the prevalence of racial and sexual violence, symbolic rage in prosecutorial performance demands an audience. As I argued earlier in reference to Foucault's *Discipline and Punish*, public prosecutions and executions are essential to spectacles. In its larger-than-life punishment and ritualized pageantry, state violence provided the imagery, parameters, and meanings of prosecution and justice in lynching cases.

Prosecutorial Performances

I first began reflecting on symbolic rage in state prosecution when reading Ida B. Wells's political memoir, *Crusade for Justice: The Autobiography of Ida B. Wells*.[2] Yet it was my mother's unfinished autobiography, which described how a family tragedy of domestic and sexual violence transmuted into racialized spectacle and sport, that led me to reconsider the impact that race, rage, and the law have on our lives. Typically, my family never speaks of the incident; understandably, family elders do not keep alive a story that permits neither pride nor comfort in the telling. Although the persistence of the story counts for something, it reveals no resolve as in the stories of rage and resistance offered in Maya Angelou's autobiographical account of male relatives who buried her pedophilic rapist in a cornfield, or Wells's descriptions of black families who avenged white violence.[3] (The only story of outrage I recall from my mother described the night she spent roaming with her five-year-old twin sister and older siblings to decapitate black jockeys gracing the lawns of white homes.) Retelling parts of familial stories, freeing them to function with the best or worst of intentions, I reveal my own discontent, which is three generations removed from black Mississippi fear and white prosecutorial performances:

In the 1920s and 1930s, my mother's black-red mother, Mamie, raised her five children in rural Mississippi. Most of the time they lived in Holly Bluffs, sometimes on, sometimes near a plantation farm owned by her Choctaw mother, Virginia Elam, and her African American stepfather. (Not blood kin, and reportedly my grandmother's abuser, he remains nameless in my mother's book.) On that farm lived the children from great-grandmother's previous marriages and her current and last one. P was considered the favorite of my great-grandmother Virginia's sixteen children and was, writes my mother, a very beautiful, dark-skinned black woman.

My great-aunt was a favorite among not only black but also white people in Holly Bluffs. This was in small part due to her looks and in great part due to her character; generosity was one of her most striking features. Aunt P *never* (my mother's emphasis) had a relationship with a white man; her popularity with whites came from her culinary talents, charm, and strategic acumen: she baked well and often brought cakes to the local white sheriff's office. Aunt P was also given presents. Black men courted her with gifts. At nineteen, after receiving the gift of an automobile from one man, Albert, she kept seeing other Negro men. Having warned her of his jealousy, one day he took her life: with a shotgun, stepping from behind the bushes near my great-grandma's doorstep, he shot P as she strolled near home. Many in our family and its community who loved my great-aunt—including the other men she knew—were outraged at her death. None of these, however, sought the prosecution of her killer. Whites did. Within days, a posse, which likely included the sheriff, found where Albert was hiding, dragged him out, and lynched him.[4]

The lynchers marbleized murder into sport and spectacle. Leaving little space for mourning, they created—after the mess Albert left for my great-grandmother in her yard—another mess to clean up, another atrocity to contain. What was to be cleared and framed would shape the ground on which local Negroes stood in relationship to pain and punishment as state performance and white ritual. How to find and move to other sites without losing their footing must have bewildered black Mississipians standing so far from justice.

Sorting out the posse's public rage and my family's pain from my great-grandmother's private grief and anger is difficult. I imagine that rage without grief is a flight from pain; that symbolic rage is the antithesis of grief; that it preempts mourning and suggests that there is nothing to fear if demons are punished. Rage at the state seems to be deflected, its splinters strike subjects and objects at varying distances, reflecting how little trust there is in state protection. Rage at Albert fluctuates between rightly blaming him for my great-aunt's murder and wrongly blaming him for his own lynching (with the reasoning that any pre-World War II Negro stupid enough to murder a pretty, young Negress who baked for the local white sheriff courted death). The state proved that it did not need to bring Albert before family or community for sentencing, for grief, or for healing and thus excluded them from determining restitution. The state, embodied in the lynching mob and the court, owned Albert and could dispense with him—and justice—as it saw fit. Private rage and grief would be respectful to the memories of P and Albert; yet the numbing familiarity of symbolic rage is immediately forthcoming. I can use it myself: it is emotionally (although not always professionally) safer to rage at white and male abstractions. Neither attentiveness to details nor counterstrategies are required; while specificity does not anesthetize, abstract generalities bring relief from deep feelings, clarity, and responsible action. Understandably, one would be reluctant to feel an anger that could slide into fear, pain, and later, perhaps, resistance.

My great-grandmother and her family felt grief and a private rage that had no symbols for public expression in a white world. It was permissible for blacks to rage at Albert but not at his killers. Mississippi blacks could have vicariously participated in his pursuit and death or, like the black minister in Walter Van Tilburg Clark's *The Ox-bow Incident,* go along to pray for the departed and the living.[5] Either of those roles, expressing their rage or sorrow, would have been somewhat risky given the unpredictability of lynching mobs. This was true before the Civil War for whites, the majority of lynching victims then, and for postbellum blacks, the majority of victims after the war. In lynchings, there were no promises of safe return, especially for those whose status was more like the hounds than the hunters; black Mississippians, in fact, were given fewer guarantees of survival than the hunters' dogs. More than one black in Holly Bluffs may have cheered the posse. On the other hand, more than one might have quietly wished for Albert's escape, which could indicate either misogyny and indifference to sexual violence or a privileging of racist violence as more heinous than intraracial sexual violence. Hoping for his escape might also merely show that some blacks possessed a sense of justice not tied to a lynching rope; others may have dismissed the possibility of justice in that state where white vigilantes had immunity from prosecution, for black kin were at their mercy. Still others may have felt or feigned indifference to both victims and the mob; choosing to let go of the dead and those who might as well be gone, they offered no prayer of protection and buried the dead in silence. Disturbed by the executions, anyone praying for, cursing, or trying to ignore Albert's attempts to stay alive likely damned the authoritarian killers, whose rage was unlike justice and, by its excess, as identifiable as a lover's jealous brutality. Because killing Albert did not bring his victim back to life, the point of his death remains debatable: was the execution restitution or revenge? And yet, do not restitution and revenge belong by right to the sufferer or her/his family? Social punishment and execution, like self-punishment and suicide, seem to be both restitution and revenge. The posse's vengeance may have been an expression of its members' pain mingled with anger. Stories about Mississippi crackers suggest that the lynching party's emotions likely stemmed in part from indignation that any black man would dare take (away) a woman—even a black one—who belonged to them. Psychologizing a lynching party, however, does not obscure its omnipotent racial power vested by state authority.

Justice, of course, was the prickly issue. The posse killed as part of a law-and-order campaign. Yet the prosecutorial performance that led to the execution of a murderer did not inspire a great sense of safety among African Americans. Racial violence as public violation felt by a community (historically, lynchings included collective punishment) would eclipse sexual violence as personal violation felt by an individual. So what was initially my great-aunt's story becomes Albert's story; mourning P was supplanted by concerns over Albert's prosecution and punishment.

Not being white, Albert would have no trial date for legal prosecution, a custom recognized but not sanctioned by both whites and blacks. The law was white and so the punishment, although deadly and irrevocable, seemed whimsical, or unpredictable. Prosecution generally tends toward whimsy in respect to black life. Whimsy would have stood in his favor, although if Albert had been a "special" Negro, if he had had the good fortune to be popular among white men or to "belong" to some prominent white man in his hometown, men of influence would have argued for leniency. For instance, white folklorist Alan Lomax was successful in his pleas to the Texas governor for the pardon of blues singer Leadbelly (Huddie Ledbetter), who was incarcerated for murdering a black woman. Other white patrons have had less good fortune. After calling for the execution of black and Latino youths accused of brutally raping a white woman in Central Park, in an advertisement in the *New York Times,* Donald Trump unsuccessfully pled for boxer Mike Tyson before his conviction for raping a black woman, Desiree Washington. If Albert had been a popular entertainer of whites—for example, a military hero like Othello or a sports hero like O. J.—it is unlikely that he would have been lynched for killing a black woman, although he most certainly would have died horribly for killing a white one. But as an "ordinary nigger," Albert was also by definition unlucky: as entertainment rather than entertainer, he could not survive sport, which overtook tragedy.

Albert was transformed by spectacle and prosecutorial performance. Until the lynching party arrived, there was probably nothing particularly unique about this man. His newly gained prominence only highlighted his insignificance: Albert became special the day that whites decided to lynch him—not the day he killed my great-aunt. There was certainly nothing unusual about his crime. Because someone's woman kin is murdered daily by a male friend—every day four women die at the hands of their male partners—sexual violence seems a commonplace epidemic. Given the prevalence of domestic violence as a form of sexual violence, only the lynching seems extraordinary, uncommon. Today, Albert would not have been lynched or legally executed for killing a black woman, given the racial disparity in death sentencing. (If his victim had been white, sensationalism would have memorialized the spectacle so that future generations could use it to illustrate either black sexual or white racial savagery, depending on what point the writer wanted to make.)

The lynching moves to monopolize my attention, quickly dominating everything—except my great-grandmother's grief. Because of the lynchers, this man, not even a blood relation, upstages our family tragedy as both victimizer and victim. His image, as insecure parasite, feeds on that of my great-aunt. To jettison Albert, to throw him out like debris—or at least relegate him to a footnote in this story—however, would be in bad faith. On some level, we seem to occupy the same skin, uncut by gender and blood. Hortense Spillers writes that an enslaved African American female "shares the conditions of all captive flesh," as the "entire captive community becomes a living laboratory"; for such women the theft and mutilation of the body create a special condition in which "we lose at least gender difference in the outcome, and the female body and the male body become a territory of cultural and political maneuver, not at all gender-related or gender-specific."[6] In contrast, Zillah Eisenstein points out that these shared conditions erase neither the female body as a site for sexual violence nor gender specificity in violence;[7] the batterer, the rapist, the irate husband/lover/father/brother knows no ungendered female body. Still, to return to Spillers, the meanings of sexual abuse are shaped by the status of the "captive community's" members and the state's "laboratories" or theaters for punishment and discipline. Those who are doubly bound by racial and sexual violence seem timelessly stitched together. Yet ties to violent males and state executioners need not become entanglements that hide the commonalities between captive or captor communities, which can lead to organizing sites for safety and mourning and to confronting the specificity of crime without racialized mythologies and prosecutions.

Social Texts: Black Women and Sexual Violence

The common ties among women confronting sexual violence are evident. Several years ago, my godsister S. told me that when Tikki, a fourteen-year-old African American, immediately reported that she had been raped by a white transit policeman, her story was generally received as unreliable, even by her mother.[8] So Tikki went to a girlfriend's house and called the ambulance that took her alone to St. Luke's emergency room. Once there, she persisted until hospital staff eventually listened to and treated her, despite a white male intern's initial combative insistence that she had not been raped. As an upper-class white woman, S. brought a legitimacy to Tikki's story in retelling it to me and others. Affluent but female, S. could not translate her class status into enough clout to report a white, working-class male cop's crime against a black, poor girl to the New York Police Department. Unable to have the officer sanctioned, Tikki now finds an alternative route to and from school, selecting other subway stops to avoid the police officer assigned to her home station. S.'s intercessions for Norma, a fifteen-year-old Latina who was periodically beaten in the streets by her ex-boyfriend, were more fruitful; both were able to report the assaults to city agencies. But at the bureau desk that determines who qualifies for a hearing to obtain a restraining order, the woman behind the desk denied Norma a court date. Both S. and Norma were unable to sway juvenile authorities; along with some of Norma's girlfriends, these state employees insisted that Norma had walked not only in her ex's neighborhood but on his street at the time of the attacks, and so she courted her own abuse. Like Tikki, Norma also now finds other routes to travel.

Unsurprisingly, sexual violence is generally underreported. Survivors are more likely to tell their stories when they feel they will be believed and treated compassionately. Such treatment is somewhat difficult to find in a culture that desensitizes spectators to violence and markets violence as a commodity, particularly when sexual violence occurs in the lives of non-whites. Given the stereotypical projection of licentious, unnatural, and violent sex onto darker-skinned peoples as sexual reprobates, this deviancy is triply complicated by sexism, classism, and heterosexism. Black women's experiences of violence are shared with all women but magnified by racism and classism, given the stigma of an Africanist sexuality.

Subaltern or captive communities have little credibility, even among themselves. Generally, sexual violence is most believable if the survivor has privilege over the accused: those who are adult male, light-skinned, affluent, or heterosexual are considered more credible and authoritative than those who are young, female, dark-skinned, poor, gay, lesbian, or bisexual.

In his documentary *Ethnic Notions*, Marlon Riggs illustrates how cultural representations of racial and sexual others have rationalized atrocities against African Americans. Objectified as either hypersexual whore or asexual mammy (both eager to serve white males), the black female has been entwined in caricature with bipolar stereotypes of African American men as either aggressively oversexed (the black rapist) or neutered as the family retainer (Uncle Tom). The image of black women as promiscuous, which was manufactured by white males, deflected attention from racialized sexual violence inflicted by white men. Historically, the rape of enslaved African women was common. Not until the twentieth century did courts in general begin to recognize that black women could file charges against their assailants.

The construction of blacks as animals rather than humans shaped representations of sexuality, defining black female sexuality as a site of bestiality and illicitness. Black feminist writers have explored the devolving status of African women under enslavement as well as African American women's resistance to this oppression. Paula Giddings notes that changes in Virginia laws concerning indentured servants culminated in 1661, when Virginia officially recognized slavery.[9] African American women were subsequently referred to in law as "nasty and beastly." This new entity could now be impregnated to create a new "crop" of enslaved people because under the new legal statutes, children would assume their mothers' status. In 1691, law prohibited whites from marrying indigenous or African people.[10] In addition, "property" (slave, prostitute, wife, child, prison inmate) was said to have no legal rights; similarily, subhuman females had no virtue. The alleged absence of (sexual) virtue affected, and still affects, the legal standing of African American women. Europeans and European Americans cannot present the image of the black without the fantasy of black sexuality that is both titillating and terrifying for those who indulge in it. In popular mythology, African Americans were considered only capable of lust, whereas whites could love; still, sleeping with black females was seen as a rite of passage for white manhood.

Social respectability is premised on "proper" sexuality. White women commit racial and social suicide when they align themselves with black, brown, yellow, or red women against white men accused of sexual attacks. In other words, maintaining their personal integrity and morality is rewarded with a loss in conventional respectability. Not only are such women called race traitors, but by defending a historically virtueless victim, they also transgress white standards of sexual decency. For instance, Suzanne Ross, a white woman advocating fair proceedings for black and Latino youths accused of rape and battering, recounts how white women hissed "Race traitor!" at her as she took her seat on stage during a talk show about the Central Park rape case.[11] Conversely, women of color who join white women in confronting men of color accused of sexual violence are also labeled race traitors; the dominant society, however, grants these women the social respectability of sexual morality that it typically denies white women who support black or brown defendants.

Individuals without social, political, or economic equality have little legal equality; this is true not merely for defendants but for victims and survivors, too. Women without racial equality are not sexually equal to men or women of the dominant race; they subsequently have no equal legal protection in cases of sexual violence because prosecution is administered by the racialized state. The state's enforcement of their rights, therefore, is seen as whimsical. (Sexual equality between respectable and un-respectable women would, in the absence of gender equality with men, merely provide greater recognition of "other" women as spectacles in violence.)

Sexual reprobates have difficulty in proving themselves as victims. By definition, sexual deviants transgress social norms; thus violating such an aberrant person is seen as an oxymoron. This problematicized status, which places women outside the protection of legal and social concern, led to antilynching campaigns and African American women's historical critique of the sexual politics involved in racial violence and lynching. Although some veneer of sexual innocence can be maintained—the prostitute with a heart of gold, the loyal Pocahontas or Malinche—the public is not socialized to view black females sympathetically in rape cases, given their historical construction as whores. Maternity also works against black women, who are represented as a source of social decay; rather than mother, they are alleged to reproduce or breed criminals and deviants. Characterized as the quintessential bad or destructive mother, the black woman categorically lacks credibility as a victim of social violence. (The destructive mother image tends to be appended to women who advocate the right to choose to regulate childbearing: they are portrayed as the enemy of the child or fetus.)

Social bias is evident given how violence is considered newsworthy and then rendered sensationalist. Few of the sexual-violence cases reported in the *New York Times* in the late 1980s and early 1990s involved white males accused of assaulting black females. (The equal expression of national outrage for highly publicized trials of white men accused of sexually assaulting women of color is an anomaly.) Of those cases that did, the most notable were the Tawana Brawley investigation and the St. John's rape trial. In each situation, the black girl or woman involved had no credibility. Brawley's case, directed in the media by Alton Maddox, Vernon Mason, and Al Sharpton, was considered a hoax. (The television show *Law and Order* ran an episode on May 17, 1995, fictionalizing the Brawley case, with the message that even though the legal system is racially unjust, it is the best we have.) In the other case, white athletes from St. John's University were acquitted of charges of gang rape and sodomy of a black female student.

In both fictional and news accounts, some of the most sensational representations of sexual violence have depended on black characters and caricatures. White American pop-culture classics such as D. W. Griffith's *Birth of a Nation,* Margaret Mitchell's *Gone with the Wind,* and *King Kong* recycle images of white heroes foiling and avenging black demons who threaten or sexually assault infantilized white women. White male chivalrous knights, white female virtuous ladies, black male sexual brutes, and black female sexual objects all perform for a national cultural mythology that is the backdrop for social and symbolic rage against sexual violence.

Although the majority of sexual assaults are intraracial not interracial, the media reserves its most sensationalist accounts for those cases in which the accused or convicted is black. News sources often privilege accounts in which black assailants violate racial and class hierarchies. When the victim or survivor is from a privileged caste and the accused is from a marginalized class, the assault becomes one against caste and is prosecuted as such by the state. If the victims are socially subordinate to the assailants, the violence becomes a literal and figurative index of subaltern oppression by dominant groups.

Most of the infamous cases reported in the *New York Times* in the 1980s and 1990s centered on African American males who assaulted black or white females. (Where Asian, Latina, and Native American women appear in relationship to black males is obscured.) Blacks in sexual-assault cases serve as a catalyst for social reflection on and rage at sexual violence. Surreptitiously, they also serve as entertainment. Toni Morrison notes that "Africanism has become . . . a way of talking about and a way of policing matters of class, sexual license, and repression, formations and exercises of power, and meditations on ethics and accountability."[12] Africanisms provide the setting for racialized treatments of sexual violence and selective condemnation of it.

State Scripts: Crime, Punishment, and Performance

Between 1930 and 1964, ninety percent of the men executed in the United States for rape were black. One study of sentencing found that black men convicted of raping white women received prison terms three to five times longer than those handed down in any other rape cases. Yet, at the same time that black-on-white

rape evoked the most horror and outrage, it was by far the least common form
of violent sexual assault. An investigation of rape cases in Philadelphia in the
late 1950s found that only three percent of them involved attacks on white
women by black men.
            —John D'Emilio and Estelle B. Freedman, *Intimate Matters*

John D'Emilio and Estelle Freedman write that despite the infrequency of black attacks on white women, the image of the black rapist has been used to control black men and "instill fear into white women who moved too freely in the public world."[13] Interracial sexual violence is involved in less than 10 percent of reported rapes, according to the film *Rape Culture,* which states that white males sexually assault black females at twice the rate that black males assault white females: 8 percent and 4 percent, respectively. Interracial rape is the cultural marker of the horror of sexual violence. Representations of such violence as heinous rather than infrequent (less than one in six rapes are reported), makes it "extraordinary" and sets the stage for sensationalist prosecution. Freedman and D'Emilio write: "The fears and outrage that the rape charge elicited among whites was such that, initially, few responded to the moral challenge that lynching posed. Instead the accusation of rape encouraged the demise of white support for racial equality. At best, white leaders shifted the onus onto blacks and urged them to stem the tide of sexual assaults. But, more often, commentators accepted the truth of the charge and sought an explanation for the propensity of black men to commit sexual offenses" (217).

Increasingly, sexual pathology is understood to include all types of assailants; physical appearance, however, continues to demarcate savage or civilized sexuality, thereby implicating or absolving defendants in crime. According to Sander Gilman, "the Other's physical features, from skin color to sexual structures such as the shape of the genitalia, are always the antitheses of the idealized self's. . . . sexual anatomy is so important a part of self-image that 'sexually different' is tantamount to 'pathological.'"[14] Frantz Fanon's dramatic assertion—"Whoever says *rape* says *Negro*"— refers to the imago, in the white mind, of a black male with a white female.[15] Mythologized whiteness is a form of absolution in most state representations of sexual violence. Some subaltern communities reverse this process: whiteness becomes a marker of guilt, signifying the abuses of racial supremacy, whereas blackness represents resistance and exists as a marker of virtue. The black-power movement often cited misogynist passages of black men posing and posturing with Fanon's imago as weapon and security blanket. In the cultural imaginings of the white mainstream blacks symbolize sexual criminality. In this way, Fanon's generalization seems accurate, particularly if one restates it: "Whoever says *Negro* says *rape.*" That is, rather than reduce sexual violence to a type of being, one reduces the being to a type of violent act. For Fanon, whites in general are "convinced that the Negro is a [sexual] beast"; describing Martinican attitudes toward the Senegalese, Fanon also suggests that Negroes are similarly convinced (165). These images are replayed as a cultural constant both in fictive and factual accounts of reality: "European culture has an *imago* of the Negro. . . . on the screen the Negro faithfully reproduces that *imago*" (169). Fanon's reference to the movie screen can be extended to television and local and national crime news, in which the criminal incidents chosen for illustration seemingly prove the stereotype. Today, more than a few blacks and nonblacks suffer from a phobia of male blacks.

Ordinary violence is black on black, white on black, or white on white; extraordinary violence is black on white in mainstream representations or white on black in subaltern representations. Within these constructions, the rare is the most reprehensible, the symbol is the norm, and all are invited to express rage and fear as responsible acts. Even though state protection, if and when it comes, is desperately welcomed, it is not necessarily a manifestation of the state's interest in people's safety. Protection appears and disappears with the whims and interests of the state, as it regulates or deregulates violence, funds or defunds violence and antiviolence programs. Many seem to have given up on any hope of adequate state protection from and prevention of violence, particularly those who live in communities represented as either violent or deviant. The safety of captive communities rarely seems to coincide with state concerns. Safety becomes, like protection, a commodity that is sold to those who can afford to purchase it (or a possibility for those who demand it).

Conclusion

Today, women and people of color are invited to participate in determining legal action within the context outlined by the state. Feminist and antiracist perspectives on violence have influenced the media and laws on prosecution. The days of whites-only and men-only juries are past. Increasingly, women and subaltern ethnic peoples take part in trials as judges, district attorneys, and prosecutors. Wielding the state's police and prosecutorial powers, they assume and project the impartial objectivity of institutionally authorized voices. Where legitimacy relies on conservative ideology, however, the mainstream acceptance of feminists and blacks depends on their mirroring and masking of dominant biases. Speaking authoritatively may require asserting state fictions as fact. The appropriation of black and/or women's voices and bodies allows state prosecution to be colorized and feminized. When the state is feminized or racialized as victim, it garners a sympathy that deflects from its misrepresentations of sexual violence and its own implementation of violence. More often than not it is safer and more socially acceptable to participate in rather than oppose state prosecutorial whimsy concerning sexual and racial violence.

Sometimes indictments are just; other times they evoke morality plays in which symbolic rage incites and executes its own violence, rationalizing punishment as a form of protection. Supplanting the original violent act, prosecution carried out by a mob, the police, or the court may create new forms of violence. This kind of abuse differs from social violence in its hegemonic moralism and uncontested legitimacy. The historic, symbolic prosecution of sexual violence used as a weapon of terror against blacks has left a peculiar legacy for contemporary society in which the black remains linked to the image of concupiscence and violence. The fact that blacks are accused of being sexually violent and promiscuous has suggested that they have a greater "invulnerability" to injury that in turn has rationalized antiblack violence. Portrayed as naturalized by violence and impervious to pain, blacks allegedly invite abuse.

Valorizing the state as the natural prosecutor of and protector from violence requires ignoring its instrumental role in fomenting racial and sexual violence. Like the family, the state "protects" itself from exposure and confrontation by discrediting or muting stories (and erasing them in historical texts and news sources) that denounce the caprice in punishing sexual violence as spectacle. Stories that condemn sexual and racial violence are probably perceived as most disturbing, for they contest claims to moral legitimacy by the state. The possibility of criticizing prosecutorial performance that is shaped by racism and sexism while at the same time supporting survivors is an anomaly in the sporting arena of the court room. There, polarizing school-yard challenges mandate the choosing of sides: either one is pro-prosecution (pro-survivor and hard on crime) or pro-defense (anti-survivor and soft on crime). To question the function of punishment, rage, and symbolism as prerequisites for justice is cast as morally dubious.

The state defines the terms for the prevention and prosecution of and the protection from sexual violence. Its prosecutorial performances deflect social concern from the overwhelming majority of sexual-violence cases: most sexual assaults go unreported; only a fraction of reported cases go to trial; of those litigated, few end in convictions. Most often, the assailants are known by the victims/survivors and share their ethnicity, economic status, classroom, neighborhood, or even home. As a masking technique for states that refuse to grapple with the specificity of sexual violence, sensationalized show trials shield the state from critiques of racism, sexism, heterosexism, and classism in court. The mythologies unchallenged during such trials obscure racial and sexual violence.

Rather than advocate vigilante or privatized police forces (as diverse as white gangs or the Nation of Islam's patrols of urban neighborhoods), one could explore other forms of civic response to social and criminal violence—for instance, those guided by human-rights covenants. Many, particularly disenfranchised peoples, stand on shifting ground in relationship to state prosecutorial powers. Sometimes, police brutality and court malfeasance would seem to caution against coperforming in spectacles of rage; yet media demonization and social hysteria around crime support acquiescence to state violence as protection and prosecution. Fearing vulnerability to violence, some may yield to myth and moralizing in a state (which is unwilling to fund prevention, treatment, and support services adequately) in order to gain promises of safety and performances of selective, ritualized punishment. Front-row seats or stage roles in televised punishments offer the spectacle of show trials, which we may watch with the conviction that we are closer to the hunters than the hunted.

Sidebar: Private Traumas and Public Spectacles

Late for a women's soccer meeting in Manhattan, I accepted a ride after a night class with a fellow graduate student who assured me that he was heading my way. He was African, unlike the nameless white man who stopped at the San Antonio bus stop to offer me, a seventeen-year-old late for work at the mess hall, a lift. When I said to both that I would take public transportation, both insisted there was no inconvenience—each was going in my direction. Like the white good old boy, the black grad student drove several miles before hooking his arm around my neck to choke me. (More literate than the Texan, who only used physical force, my classmate attacked my resistance with psychoanalysis: "You probably prefer white men"; "You are incestuously enamored of your father." Unlike the "cracker" who pulled the car off the highway into a wooded area, the "brother" parked along north Central Park to rape me. While I was struggling with him, a patrol car pulled up alongside the car. Two white cops eyed us from behind their rolled-up window. Startled, we stopped fighting long enough to stare back. In those few seconds, I never thought to ask the police for help; they never offered protection. As they pulled away, I opened the door and began running, at 10 P.M., alongside the park toward the subway. Unlike my escape out of the woods onto the Texas highway, no black woman with two children in her car insisted on helping me as my assailant cruised beside me, apologetically assuring me that now he would drive me to work. (I missed work that day at the air-force base just as I later missed my meeting that night.) When I tried to report a white stranger's attempted rape, the police who came to the house reasoned that because it would be his word against mine, it was not worth filling out an incident report. Seven years later, I never bothered to report a black colleague's attempted rape. Instead, I just reminded myself to find other ways to travel.

Like Tikki and Norma, many might locate alternate routes, finding and believing themselves to be beyond state protection. Self-reliance, strained through fear and isolation, merely feeds rage and despair. Organizing a different route for travel also involves community. Building community resistance to violence is a way to move away from the symbolic rage of state prosecutorial performance, the titillation of racial and sexual spectacles, the criminalization and social neglect of racialized groups. In family tales and state spectacles alike, private and public violence intersect. Studying family stories and social analyses, one might construct narratives of racial and sexual violence that map roads other than those demarcated by the state. In fact, one could conceivably sketch the context for personal and political relationships to community and state that forgoes indifference to pain, grief, and justice.

Rarely told, frequently exploited, and rejected, stories about racial and sexual abuse are often unable to achieve even the best of intentions. Left dangling, narratives about personal violence fade as grief and anger recede to half-memories. Typically, many label their nonfictive stories as painful and embarrassing: rape, incest, domestic abuse. For poor and/or black families, the stories depict victimization by police, courts, and the occasional lynching mob. Unless implicated in the story, outsiders, spectators, and foreigners prove more attentive and sympathetic listeners; and yet, having little invested in the telling, many feel no obligation to respond beyond listening. Families and states often discourage storytelling that reveals their vulnerable proximity to, as well as culpability in, violence. For example, speaking out about incest or sexual abuse threatens to expose the less-than-ideal family or state; ironically, telling the truth about family violence is viewed as destabilizing the family just as vocalizing state violence and human-rights abuses is portrayed as destabilizing the state. Family and state may shield themselves from confrontation by curtailing the voices of protesters who seek an end to abuse. Victims and survivors are encouraged to protect others with their silences. Although this leaves them vulnerable to old abuse and denies them their own right to rage, it likely guards them from newer abuses such as social condemnation, isolation, and punishment for exposés in the classroom, courtroom, church/mosque/temple/synagogue, at the dinner table, as well as in the media, military, or government. Sometimes, a family or state deflects attention from its flaws by projecting a victim as its nemesis; then punishment becomes performance, electrified by symbols that promote the continuity of the romanticized entity. Such punishment, like the silencing of private stories of abuse, distances the victim from vulnerability and grief. The "some things better left unsaid" are generally those that cannot be glorified or celebrated by the idealized self, family, race, or nation. Likewise, the most marketed or exploited stories of violence are those that do not threaten fragile idealized identities.

At the intersections of racial and sexual violence, recounted in family tales, social texts, and state scripts, tragedies are dragged across borders, crossing over into silent denials or public spectacles. Whether abuse is silenced or sensationalized, each response erases grief and denies protection.

Building sites for mourning and safety, one may resist the muting and marketing of pain. To demystify racial and sexual mythologies as well as social contempt for and indifference to the violence in black and female lives, one must analyze state scripts in which symbolic rage masks stereotypes and contempt while suggesting that punishment serves as protection.

Personal tales and public texts interweave family stories and social spectacles. These narratives clear a space for reflecting on the ways in which private tragedy inspires and mirrors public horror. In their clearings they may create a moral for audiences, generating some compassionate thought or action: compassion brings the possibility of identification, and with it struggle, with the subject suffering—a connection that suggests more permanent ties than pity where one might feel superior to and so alienated from the sufferer. These tales are told in call-and-response fashion, with expectations, even demands, for action. Often these expectations are frustrated. Even for those who escape apathy, agency is problematic. Some survivors, particularly survivors of institutional violence, doubt their own strength and collective power; consequently, exhortations that they assume more responsibility in a world that is irresponsible enough to abuse them seem burdensome and accusatory. Nevertheless, many survivors speak about and organize to counter violence. Occasionally, their stories about sexual and racial abuse are received as instructive. On other occasions, these narratives are used to depressurize and legitimize everyday rage against violence and any group associated with inflicting it.

Sometimes those who reveal their stories see them turned into spectacles. The price for acceptance of the story, no longer rejected, is the marketplace. Functioning with the worst of intentions, commodified tales entertain and, in their performance, encourage detachment and passivity, the unengaged as amorally amused or morally bemused spectator. As discourse in community gatherings, news commentary, or surrogate event, the spectacle replaces political actor with social spectator. Those raised to "never put their business in the streets" avoid becoming spectacles and flee associative contamination from the indiscreet or unlucky. If ever implicated in the tale or confronted by an urgent request for assistance, thus cornered and unable to assume the role of detached viewer, one can suppress the story, deny its validity, and erase its danger. Seeking a safe haven as audience, shielded as an anonymous spectator, one can wield an illusory control over the tragedy-as-spectacle, turning pain into performance. This search for anonymity as a measure of safety in turn patterns our speech and acts. Many, even survivors, rarely discuss as engagés the events that highlight their vulnerability to violence. Those who do might find that sharing stories provides an essential narrative, an ethical text that deprivatizes pain to border-cross into public activism.

8 / Coalition Cross Fire: Antiviolence Organizing and Interracial Rape

Women's efforts to end violence often come out of coalitions.[1] In turn-of-the-century antilynching campaigns, Ida B. Wells enlisted the assistance of English women and men. Later, white feminists such as Texan Jesse Ames Daniels publicly opposed racist violence that was justified as the protection of white women from black men. In coalitions Wells, Florida Riffen Ridley, and Mary Church Terrell noted that the prosecution of rape was determined by the social status of the woman assaulted as well as that of the accused. Contemporary antiracist feminisms are rooted in and build on historical coalitions and analyses of lynching and rape. These antiracist campaigns were also waged against sexual violence, as women activists reasoned that an end to lynchings, as well as false and illegal prosecutions, would increase the likelihood of legitimate and legal indictments in rape cases.

In 1904, responding to an editorial vilifying African Americans, Mary Church Terrell of the National Association of Colored Women wrote: "[An] error on the subject of lynching consists of the widely circulated statement that the moral sensibilities of the best negroes in the United States are so stunted and dull, and the standard of morality among even the leaders of the race is so low, that they do not appreciate the enormity and heinousness of rape."[2] Four generations later, we appear to be still haunted by that error and the notion that most women of color protect men of color who rape.

Multiracial alliances in the United States are fairly difficult to sustain; racial antagonisms and distrust fray, if not splinter, coalition politics. When activists try to work together in polarized interracial rape cases in which the assault is marked by a ferocity of violence, the alliance can often resemble a battlefield. Amid these highly controversial cases, the work of women denouncing both sexual violence and racism in the legal system tends to become a casualty in the cross fire between divided camps of anti-racists and feminists.

In New York City in the late 1980s, diverse and multiracial groups of women formed around the 1987 Tawana Brawley case and the 1989 Central Park case. In the Brawley case, women agreed to stage a rally and march through the red-light district in Times Square with placards that read "Stop violence against women" and "Tawana is our sister/daughter"; yet no consensus could be reached to have a women's delegation meet with Alton Maddox, Vernon Mason, and Al Sharpton or even to support anti-hate-crime legislation (sponsored by David Patterson) then pending in the New York State Assembly. This so-called victimless crime against a black teen (Brawley accused several white policemen of sexual molestation and rape) was widely dismissed as a hoax; indeed, no evidence was offered by Brawley or her attorneys. Nevertheless, because those accused of the assault represented the bastion of white-male privilege to exercise violence with impunity and because the alleged victim represented those most vulnerable to sexual violence, progressive women sympathized and quickly mobilized around the case.

The Central Park jogger case proved to be much more explosive. Difficulties in organizing stemmed from the brutality of the assault. Unlike the Brawley case, this was no fabricated crime. The survivor was viciously attacked and left for dead. In addition, women activists had to contend with historical mythologies concerning racialized sexual violence that dominated this case: African American and Latino teenagers were arrested and convicted for the violent rape of the white woman survivor.

During the first collective trial, a local televison station aired a clip of a Latina spokeswoman for a gathering of black and Latina women demonstrating for the conviction of the defendants; in the clip she referred to Tawana Brawley and Al Sharpton as "circus animals." Earlier, Brawley and

Sharpton had visited the trial in support of the defendants, and in an interview with reporters, Sharpton maintained that the youths were being denied due process. Whether the Latina's statement reflected her personal sentiments of antiblack racism or her frustation with those who focused on a fair trial for the defendants rather than on the survivor, or both, is unclear. Nevertheless, the image of circus animals was imprinted on fair-trial advocates, irrespective of their stances on sexual violence.

African American males charged in interracial rape cases do not inspire much credibility, even among nonwhites. In fact, historically, African American communities were initially reluctant to support defendants in the Scottsboro case in the 1930s and the Harlem Six case in the 1960s, in which black defendants were falsely accused of assaulting white females. (After years of imprisonment and political agitation for justice, the defendants were eventually released.) In the Central Park case, the majority of blacks, like their white counterparts, likely considered the youths guilty of attacking the survivor. But African Americans were more inclined to believe that the black and Latino youths would not get a fair trial.

Although mainstream media frequently reported the misogynist statements of blacks who insisted on the youths' innocence, much of the media censured and censored those who spoke against both racial and sexual violence. For the most part, feminist fair-trial advocacy as well as multiracial women's coalitions went unrecognized.

Women and Fair-Trial Activism in the Central Park Case

During the first collective trial, the problematic aspects of the state's case did indeed motivate women into fair-trial activism. The following narrative may, or may not, explain why some women publicly took such an unpopular and controversial stance. On April 20, 1989, at 1:30 A.M. two men found a brutally beaten, unconscious woman in a muddy ravine in Central Park. The two collective trials in 1990 for the assault ended with the convictions of six African American and Latino youths. After the first collective trial in August 1990, Antron McCray (sixteen years old), Yusef Salaam (sixteen), and Raymond Santana (fifteen) received and began to serve the maximum youth sentence for rape and assault, five to ten years in prison. Their appeal attorneys included William Kunstler (for Salaam) and Vernon Mason (for McCray).

During the night of April 19, the woman was violently assaulted while jogging in Central Park. That same night approximately fifty African American and Puerto Rican youths had assembled around 9 P.M. and entered the park, scattering in groups of various sizes. Some African American and Latino youths assaulted several men in the park and threatened others. Youths who were detained while exiting the park around 10 P.M. and those picked up for questioning in the following days became suspects in whatever crimes had occurred in Central Park that night. Those detained had been dispersed earlier throughout the park. These youths were with other males who entered the park that night and moved about at different locations and exited at different times.³ Within several days, the *New York Times* and other mainstream media sources dubbed the survivor, an upper-class European American woman who worked as an investment banker for Salomon Brothers, the "investment banker" or "the jogger"; the detained African American and Latino male teens became known as the "wolfpack." Many of these sources at this point also denounced the suspects as guilty. The first *New York Times* article to cover the assault appeared on April 21. Written by Craig Wolff and relying on uncorroborated police statements for its information, it ran under the headline "Youths Rape and Beat Central Park Jogger."⁴ All subsequent *Times* coverage was consistent with the tone of this first article. In this climate, the claims made by New York City's African American press and some activists that these premature "convictions" had turned the case into a legal lynching were dismissed as misogynist or racist.

Because the case had already assumed the mythic proportions of a morality play, police officials and assistant district attorneys involved in the case played up racial and sexual myths and imagery. European American journalist Michelle Hammer describes the "callousness" of the mythology that objectified the survivor:

> How many times have we heard the word miraculous, as though the gods themselves were on her side? This miraculous recovery has been expressed as a triumph of good over evil, her extraordinarily good attitude—the result, as the myth would have it, of good breeding, good family, good schools, a good job—has made medicine itself seem almost superfluous. Her good attitude has prevailed over bad boys, from bad families, who do bad things (including live) in that bad part of town where the good jogger somehow strayed. In the stiff

and demanding morality of this myth, only a miraculous recovery will do, because her recovery is not only her reward for being good, but also proof that she is good. As an '80s morality tale this made perfect sense, since having the goods in the '80s made you good. Hence, the apotheosis came when Salomon [Brothers] named her a vice president. It was as if to say, not only had she not lost ground, she had gained. And gains could be made only by getting ahead, not by wavering.[5]

By promoting and then appending themselves to the reconstruction of the survivor as an icon, police and legal officials came to represent all that was good (or at least safe), while the youths represented a *Clockwork Orange* type of criminality (symbolized in the violent rape scenes that open and close that film). Assistant district attorneys Elizabeth Lederer and Linda Fairstein, as white women, became simultaneously the avengers and symbols of victimized (white) women—avengers by assuming the male roles of state prosecutors, and symbols by appropriating the body and voice of the survivor. Their highly visible presence in turn feminized the state's role in the case.

When the survivor testified for fifteen minutes during the August 1990 trial, it was to detail her recovery from the brutal beating. This account was used as testimony against the youths, whom she could not identify as her assailants. Lederer and Fairstein were the only women who claimed in court that the youths had sexually and physically assaulted anyone. With repeated displays of medical photographs (taken soon after the assault) of the survivor's battered and partially nude body, the state introduced the woman's body as evidence of the youths' guilt. In fact, however, only words—those of Lederer, Fairstein, and the police, and the teens' (except Salaam) own incriminating, contradictory, and repudiated statements—connected the youths to the body. The Manhattan district attorney's office lists the file of the Central Park case as closed, although Lederer publicly acknowledges that there is still a "rapist out there" connected to the assault; even though physical evidence existed, police never attempted to find the male(s) whose semen matched that found on the survivor.[6]

Generally, the issue of a fair trial appeared newsworthy only to African American media and individuals skeptical of most other reports. Not surprisingly, arguments for presuming innocence until the youths were proven guilty contained information largely unknown or ignored; popular sources tended to present accounts critical of the prosecution sporadically or only within narratives of conviction. Details that challenged the indictments disturbed a social equilibrium poised on the image of the youths' savagery. Given the absence of evidence and the sensationalist pretrial judgments, progressive activists argued that critically reexamining the Central Park case would help to demystify the racial and sexual stereotypes that shaped most media representations of it. Such a critique would also address critics' suspicion of media, police, and court activity surrounding the trial. Some argued that the media and the police traded a just judicial process for a cloak of chivalry, citing those officials' racist, rhetorical, and selectively sincere opposition to the epidemic of sexual violence and abuse of women. This chivalry was apparently reserved for upper-class, white women: the white media paid little attention to the rapes, brutal beatings, or murders of twenty-five women of color reported the same week of the assault. (The police's concerned response to the September 1995 murder of a Brazilian woman who had also been jogging in the park was a marked departure from earlier reactions to assaults against women of color in the late 1980s.)

The reluctance of some women and men to accept the prosecution's narrative stemmed in part from questionable aspects of police activity on the case. Most media sources, even those whose pretrial judgments greatly threatened the possibility of a fair trial, observed that convictions would be difficult in the absence of a physical case against the youths. Police had obtained neither witnesses nor evidence (blood, semen, hair, soil, fingerprints, footprints, or skin tissue) to connect any of the defendants in the first trial to the scene of the crime. Still, in the spring of 1989, without corroborating physical evidence or witnesses, mainstream media sources essentially convicted the youths. The basis of those and later jury convictions rested on so-called confessions, the videotaped and written statements taken from the young men during police interrogations. Some defense attorneys maintained that police officers intimidated or assaulted several of the youths during these sessions and detained others for long hours without food or sleep. Timothy Sullivan describes troubling aspects of jury deliberations as well. Jurors who already believed that the youths were guilty reconstructed reality: "[Juror] Brueland . . . believed he could read the lips of one defendant on videotape [tapes were redacted] and discern Salaam's name. . . . In fact, neither McCray nor Santana names Salaam anyplace on the tapes."[7] The continuous pretrial replaying and rehashing of the videotapes on television and in print gave them a reality independent of their correspondence to fact: in some videotaped statements, the young men spoke of the wrong location of the assault, described holding down the arms of the survivor who was found bound and gagged, and misidentified her attire.

Inconsistencies in the prosecution's case were reported in various smaller journals. Elombe Brath's "The Media, Rape and Race: The Central Park Jogger Case" argued that it was more accurate to refer to these depositions as "self-incriminating statements" rather than confessions, given their contradictions and the questionable conditions under which they were taken.[8] Along with the video statements, the youths' inconsistent and factually incorrect written accounts were conveyed in a language that was unbelievable to some. *Newsday*, which among the predominantly white New York dailies was the most critical of the prosecution, ran several stories questioning the validity of a case built on these statements. In "Salaam's Mom Also Waits for Evidence," Carole Agus wrote:

> [A] detective read a supposed "confession" of Raymond Santana. . . . it sounded like coptalk in its purest form. There never was a 14-year-old working-class kid that ever talked the way Santana is supposed to have talked to the police that night: "We met up with an additional group of approximately 15 other males who also entered Central Park with us. . . . We all walked southbound in the park in the vicinity of 105th Street."
>
> We who are watching this trial all have more than we think in common with [Ms.] Salaam. We are waiting to see if there is any believable evidence that will connect these kids to the crime. So far, we haven't heard any.[9]

Unlike Santana and McCray, Sharomme Salaam's son, Yusef, gave no statement. He also passed a lie-detector test soon after the assault supporting his assertions that he was never at the scene of the crime. The collective trial proved particularly disadvantageous for him. Some argue that in such trials a defendant risks being assumed guilty by association with his or her codefendants. The presiding judge Thomas B. Galligan, whom some blacks and white progressives referred to as a hanging judge, was allegedly selected for the case by district attorney Robert Morgenthau. Galligan mandated collective trials. (The *New York Times* reported in 1990 that Morgenthau's offices were charged with antiblack bias by NAACP legal counsel on issues unrelated to this case.)[10] An unsigned confession attributed to Salaam was written by detective Thomas McKenna two days after his interrogation and included more information than was found in McKenna's notes taken on April 20, the night Salaam was detained by the police. In fact, McKenna admitted that in order to induce Salaam to confess, he lied to him during the session, telling Yusef that his fingerprints had been found on the survivor's clothing. Although Salaam told McKenna he had not been at the scene of the crime and knew nothing of the assault, most media sources condoned McKenna's actions: because the detective publicly confessed to lying to the fifteen-year-old, he retained his integrity and credibility as a cop. Without eyewitnesses or corroborating witnesses to testify that the young men on trial attacked the survivor, the prosecution team could only call on themselves and the police to testify to the validity of the incriminating statements obtained during the interrogations. In fact, the district attorneys had a stronger case against other youths implicated in attacks against male joggers and cyclists in the park that night.

Detailing how police admitted to breaking the law in order to obtain incriminating accounts, *Village Voice* writer Rick Hornung predicted that they "engaged in . . . conduct so improper that it . . . will undoubtedly be the grounds of a strong appeal even if the defendants are found guilty."[11] According to Hornung, the pretrial hearings revealed that police violated all of the following: state laws protecting juvenile rights, for separating all the children from their parents; Fifth Amendment and Sixth Amendment rights of at least three defendants, by failing to inform them of their rights to remain silent and to consult an attorney; the Fifth Amendment right against compelled self-incrimination. Regarding this last-mentioned violation, police officials (with Linda Fairstein) transported several of the youths involved in the second trial (without defense lawyers or parents) to the scene of the crime in order to have them "put themselves in it" more convincingly (32). The refusal to accept statements from the police or prosecution team led to progressive fair-trial activism. I distinguish here between progressive fair-trial activism, which critiqued sexual violence and researched specific facts concerning the case, and reactionary fair-trial activism, which presented a misogynist defense of the youths or denied the reality of the assault; both types of activism emerged during the case although the latter was usually privileged in mainstream media accounts.

During the first collective trial, women in Mother Love and the International Working Women's Day Committee (IWWDC) called a citywide meeting of antisexist and antiracist activists advocating for a fair trial. Mother Love, a small Harlem-based women's group created to support the mothers of the defendants, had organized forums in the Harlem community. The IWWDC, a group of African, Latina, and European American women activists, had held educational events on March 8 celebrating women's contributions to liberation movements. At the suggestion of Mother Love, IWWDC issued an open letter to the community. Through progressive media channels such as African American journalist Rosemari Mealy's WBAI radio show, the group invited representatives from women's and social-justice organizations to attend an educational forum on the case on July 19, 1990, at the Martin Luther King Labor Center (Local 1199) in Manhattan. That night, lawyers, journalists, and activists (all representing different political views), spoke to the packed meeting room, mostly filled with African American, Latina, and European American women.

The key presentation came from IWWDC. Citing the tradition of legal lynchings carried out in U.S. courts, group members linked the Central Park case to the Scottsboro case in the 1930s, the Harlem Six and George Whitmore cases in the 1960s, and, more recently, the Carol Stuart case in Boston.[12] In all these cases innocent African American men were imprisoned for violent crimes against white women. Because the innocence of the Central Park case defendants could not be proven beyond a reasonable doubt, these previous cases were used by IWWDC speakers to emphasize the flaws and racial and sexual biases of the judicial system. The need to prove innocence in order to mobilize for a fair trial is in fact an inversion of the U.S. legal system where, in theory, only those proven guilty beyond a reasonable doubt can be convicted. Without proof of the youths' innocence, many acquiesced to police malfeasance and unfair legal proceedings; as one African American male colleague put it, "they railroaded the right guys." Such views were shaped by the media.

Village Voice reporter Erica Munk's "Body Politics at Its Worst" described the July 19 organizing session as an antisurvivor event.[13] Although present at the forum, Munk focused on black women who were minor speakers and depicted them as major spokespersons. (In addition, she attacked one woman journalist who was a forum organizer but not a featured speaker.) Munk also described the black women as uniformly hostile to the survivor and to white women in general. And yet, Munk's report did not reflect the reality of the forum. For example, one African American woman, who worked on a city task force on sexual violence and abuse, strongly criticized a black male lawyer who condemned the defense lawyers' refusal to cross-examine the survivor with harsh rhetoric about her.[14] Black women at the forum generally focused their comments on the police, the perceived malfeasance, and the defendants' rights to a fair trial; few if any made reference to the survivor. White women were not identified by name in this article; in fact, Munk failed to note the presence of any white women at the forum or to state that the key address was given by a white woman, Suzanne Ross; a reader might easily assume that the forum was a black women's rather than a multiracial women's gathering.

Consequently, *Voice* readers were led to believe that the worst "body politics" were espoused by black women who were both hostile to white women and sympathetic to black rapists. This biased reporting polarized black and white women in its inaccurate portrayal of the forum's black women as antifeminist and antiwhite; it also likely influenced black women who felt pressured to prove where they stood on the issue of sexual violence—that is, to prove that they did not sympathize with rapists. Munk's racially divisive politics also made it to the airwaves. As an authority on the case by virtue of her *Voice* articles, she was interviewed by the leftist WBAI, commenting on the anti-sexual-violence work of all women, including black women, in coalition. Within the week, on another radio program at a more mainstream liberal station with a smaller black audience, however, she reportedly asked rhetorically and impatiently, "Where are the black women?" Clearly, she was implying that African American women had made no efforts to condemn the violence. (Munk resigned from the *Voice* that summer after participants in the forum presented *Voice* editors with a detailed account that contradicted her report.)

Because more people read the *Voice* than attended the forum at Local 1199, the perception of fair-trial activism as politically retrogressive dominated. Those present, however, encountered another form of politics. In her keynote address, Suzanne Ross used Angela Davis's essay "Rape, Racism and the Myth of the Black Rapist" to analyze the historical and political aspects of press coverage and the exploitation of the survivor as a racial and sexual icon by the white press.[15] Ross connected Davis's critique of the white obsession with African American men as rapists with an analysis of how this mythology rendered the prosecution of sexual violence against women of color a legal aberration and downplayed sexual violence in white women's lives and their complicity in this obscurantism. Just as antilynching activists had done in the nineteenth century, IWWDC members argued that these unexamined racial and sexual mythologies, providing the cultural and social backdrop for interracial rape cases, increased the likelihood of lynching and the social indifference to it. Forum leaders also maintained that legal lynchings legitimize violence and the state's refusal to prosecute sexual crimes seriously. Finally, forum organizers urged audience members to investigate for themselves the legitimacy of the prosecution's case by attending the trial; to join antiracist and antisexist coalitions; and to recognize that the denial of the democratic right to a fair trial would set a dangerous precedent for everyone.

Demands for justice in the Central Park case were often condemned for mitigating and condoning sexual violence. Activists who argued that racism and classism created an unfair judicial process and that violence against women was unacceptable were criticized by media sources that depicted all fair-trial organizing as antiwhite and antifemale. African Americans who made misogynist and sexist statements throughout the case were portrayed by the mainstream press as representative of the reactionary politics of African Americans in general and fair-trial activists in particular. This selective focus on misogyny, and the general social outrage that accompanied such reports, enabled these conviction narratives to ignore or obscure the weaknesses of the prosecution's case, thus erasing the distinction between the brutal assault, on the one hand, and the prosecution of the youths, on the other. Without that critical distinction, given the emotionalism and media hype surrounding the case, criticism of the prosecution was portrayed uniformly as criticism of the survivor; support for the youths' right to a fair trial then appeared as sympathy for rapists. The possibility of being outraged by both the violent assault against the survivor and the mishandling of the case became a public anomaly. As it had a century ago, the dominant media sources mandated that no context existed for simultaneous organizing against sexual and racist violence, ensuring that most of the public equated progressive organizing with reactionary denial—denial that the attack was horrific, that African American men assault white women, and that sexual violence is a deadly epidemic.

Stigmatized as counterfeminist, fair-trial activism was rarely recognized as part of a discernible, radical African American tradition of antiviolence organizing. Even black feminists writing for predominantly white publications obscured the complexities of the case, allowing only narratives of conviction to bear the respectability of feminism and moralism. As legitimacy became based on one's distance from fair-trial activism, criticism of the state's prosecution was transformed into an indifference to sexual violence. The desire to remain distant from such a critique stemmed from the unpopularity of the stance, given the pretrial publicity that depicted the youths as guilty; this aloofness also was connected to another desire—not to be identified with the misogynist or antisurvivor statements made by African Americans. Both desires worked to discourage investigative research and critical thinking. The multiplicity of responses among African Americans to this interracial rape case ranged from an inflexible certainty of the youths' guilt (which precluded any critical study of the prosecution's arguments) to a considerable hostility toward the courts, police, and white media (an antagonism that for some extended to the survivor as well). Although some African Americans vilified the survivor, others, specifically those engaged in progressive politics, expressed their concern for her as well as their general abhorrence of sexual violence. For instance, East Harlem district leader William Perkins and activist Reverend Herbert Daughtery questioned the legitimacy of media narratives of conviction and organized a prayer vigil for the survivor soon after the attack; New York City leaders, including white feminists, spoke at this vigil. In general, however, most progressive arguments for critically rethinking the case, particularly political efforts by African American women, were minimized, ignored, or derided in mainstream media sources.

Conclusion

Most media sources described coalitions that denounced the state's prosecution as indifferent to sexual violence. Depictions of fair-trial activists as mostly disgruntled blacks, motivated by racial paranoia and antiwhite sentiments, disqualified such activism as a legitimate choice for anyone in the political mainstream. Only those (whether conservative or liberal) who supported state prosecution could convincingly call sexual violence abhorrent. Although *pro-prosecution* is not synonymous with *pro-feminism,* the terms were constructed and worn as such in the Central Park case. Individuals strongly advocating prosecution, such as conservative commentator Patrick J. Buchanan, were free to express misogynist and racist views. Women and men, including those not noted for their progressive gender politics, chastised women (including feminist activists) who advocated fair-trial proceedings for being antifeminist. This condemnation was often customized to fit the ethnicity of the woman. If the fair-trial activist was black or Latina, she was accused of being antiwhite and sympathetic to rapists. (Valerie Smith uses this argument against Ida B. Wells.)[16] If she was white, she was accused of being a race traitor, bleeding heart, and sympathetic to rapists because of her racial guilt. Any woman, regardless of her ethnicity, who criticized the state's procedures was susceptible to the charge that she had subordinated sexual politics to racial politics. The stigma of these accusations produced two types of obscurantism. First, the charges erased the prominent role of multiethnic coalitions that included a considerable number of radical white women and lesbians who did not consider the state their natural protector in the face of sexual violence. Second, such charges discouraged investigation into the specifics of the case, portraying all state critics as sharing the widely publicized misogyny of angry blacks.

When I initially wrote about the first collective trial of the 1989 case (I made no study of the second trial), focusing on the media coverage, women's fair-trial forums, and my court attendance during Salaam's testimony and cross-examination, I was warned to limit my observations to critiques of the racist representations underscoring the youths' guilt rather than the assumption of their guilt. Questioning the validity of any of the convictions was considered a breech of civility and morality and, as such, the cause for more of an outrage than the incarceration of defendants who had been denied due process. In 1993 a white female junior professor at Amherst College gave a talk on representation and the Central Park case. A senior white male professor responded to her report of inconsistencies in the prosecution's case by bluntly asking whether she was saying that the youths were innocent. By evading the question—perhaps because the only logical response would have been "yes, they're innocent," given her arguments—she retained her mark of civility and sexual respectability. She remained neutral by severing her speech about racist representations from political or ethical stances that directly challenged the incarceration of the convicted. To suggest the possibility that some of the defendants might have been convicted on the basis of representation rather than evidence was viewed as crossing over the threshold of respectable discourse. Few intellectuals would take that step. Those who did, from the status of social pariah, continued to write and organize to demystify the case as well as the perception that black women are generally indifferent to sexual violence.

Although there was more physical evidence introduced in the trial of O. J. Simpson for the murders of Nicole Brown Simpson and Ronald Goldman, in that case most commentators refrained from making pretrial judgments. During the Simpson case, more than a few African Americans would see institutional racism as the primary issue rather than the sexism and misogyny of the assault. Because the black and Latino youths in the Central Park case lacked Simpson's wealth and popularity as a transracial entertainer, the early declaration of their guilt was predictable. Any state wrongdoing in the Central Park case would go relatively unchallenged except by some marginalized critics, whereas in the Simpson case malfeasance along with inconclusive evidence became the cornerstone of his defense and acquittal. In the aftermath of Simpson's acquittal, however, the diatribes against black women jurors and blacks in general became so extreme that they marked a new turn in American racism and sexual politics.[17]

In a culture profoundly ignorant of racist mythologies, state violence, and women's radicalism, black women's politics on racial and sexual violence are easily misrepresented as uniformly counterprogressive. Historically, in interracial rape cases, radical women activists have worked to determine the facts of the case, independent of information and narratives of the dominant media and have refused to validate uncritically the notion of state prosecution as protection. Women have also dialogued with other organizers and writers cognizant of local street politics, progressive activism, and repressive policing. The presence (or absence) of similar strategies in contemporary responses to racialized sexual violence determines the schism between antiracist and feminist progressive politics regarding interracial sexual assault.

IV

Teaching, Community, and Political Activism

9 / "Discredited Knowledge" in the Nonfiction of Toni Morrison

African American Intellectuals and Academic Questions

The education of the next generation of black intellectuals is something that is terrifically important to me. But the questions black intellectuals put to themselves, and to African American students, are not limited and confined to our own community. For the major crises in politics, in government, in practically any social issue in this country, the axis turns on issues of race. Is this country willing to sabotage its cities and school systems if they're occupied mostly by black people? It seems so. When we take on these issues and problems as black intellectuals, what we are doing is not merely the primary work of enlightening and producing a generation of young black intellectuals. Whatever the flash points are, they frequently have to do with amelioration, enhancement or identification of the problems of the entire country. So this is not parochial; it is not marginal; it is not even primarily self-interest.

— Toni Morrison, "African American Intellectual
Life at Princeton: A Conversation," *Princeton Today*

In her nonfiction essays, Toni Morrison's dissection of racist paradigms is framed by a worldview that testifies to African American ancestral spirits, the centrality of transcendent community, and her faith in the abilities of African American intellectuals to critique and civilize a racist society.[1] Reading Morrison as a cultural observer and practitioner, I share a sensibility that privileges community and ancestors while confronting dehumanizing cultural representations and practices. I quote from Morrison's nonfiction to sketch a frame for viewing her observations on racist stereotypes and black resistance. Even in its incompleteness, a sketch reveals clues for deciphering how Morrison uncovers and recovers ground for "discredited knowledge" in which traditional and contemporary cultural beliefs held among African Americans are connected to political struggles.[2] The outline of a conceptual site or worldview is not an argument for black essentialism; recognizing the political place of African American cultural views, which manifest and mutate through time and location, constructs these views neither as quintessential nor universal to everyone of African descent. Likewise, a passionate interest in African American intellectual and political resistance to antiblack racism is not synonymous with an indifference to non-African Americans or to accommodations to Eurocentrism and white supremacy.

Morrison explores the intellectual service of African American educators in ways compatible to the role of the African philosopher, as development within and through service is described by Tsenay Serequeberhan: "The calling of the African philosopher . . . comes to us from a lived history whose endurance and sacrifice—against slavery and colonialism—has made our present and future existence in freedom possible. The reflective explorations of African philosophy are thus aimed at further enhancing and expanding this freedom."[3] This call of the African philosopher or theorist, shared by the African American intellectual, predates imperialism, enslavement, and racism. If, as Morrison argues, the questions that African American intellectuals raise for and among themselves reverberate beyond black communities, then exploring a worldview that presents service and community as indispensable, time and space as expansive, knowledge as intergenerational and responsive to the conditions of people, and community as a changing, transcendent but nevertheless shared and thorny tie, would frame responses to state violence and resistance to oppressive cultural practices.

Morrison's essays raise a number of questions about the possibilities for critiquing and developing curricular paradigms that acknowledge realities greater than those recognized by conventional academia. Worldviews contextualize educators' lives and shape how they develop curricula, pedagogy, and scholarship to talk about, or silence talk about, critical theory and racialized knowledge. Educators can challenge or reinforce academic relationships to the worldviews of alternative thinkers such as Morrison. For instance, teaching her writings without a critical discussion of racism and slavery is a perhaps not uncommon, appropriative act that reproduces racial dominance. In Morrison's work discussed below, one finds the demystification of racism tied to a deep commitment to the well-being of African Americans. Educators who unravel these ties depoliticize the radical nature of her writings, and, in effect, repoliticize the work as compatible with intellectual paradigms that are indifferent to the racist practices of American society.

In the classroom, expanding the intellectual canon to include Morrison and other Others—people of color, women, poor and working-class people, gay, lesbian, and bisexual people—for more inclusive and representative curricula does not subvert racialized hierarchies. Additive curricula do not inherently democratize education: in integrative reforms, the axis of the universe remains the same. For instance, bell hooks notes:

> A white woman professor teaching a novel by a black woman writer (Toni Morrison's *Sula*) who never acknowledges the "race" of the characters is not including works by "different" writers in a manner that challenges ways we have been traditionally taught as English majors to look at literature. The political standpoint of any professor engaged with the development of cultural studies will determine whether issues of difference and otherness will be discussed in new ways or in ways that reinforce domination.[4]

At best, additive curricula that offer no critique of the dominant worldview civilize racist practices; at worst, they function as decorative shields against critiques of Eurocentrism. Where analyses of whiteness as a metaparadigm are absent, critiques of racialized oppression are insufficient to create a learning environment in which teaching critical work maintains rather than dismantles communal ties and subversive insights. More accurate representation of the diversity of intellectual life and work of transgressive African American intellectuals requires a context greater than the traditional academic paradigm. Perhaps the only way to attain greater accuracy and honesty is to stand on some terrain, within some worldview other than that legitimized by Eurocentric academe. Engaging in this "dangerous, solitary, radical work," we might finally confront the academic penchant for playing in the dark.[5]

Traditional Worldviews

[In Song of Solomon*] I could blend the acceptance of the supernatural and a profound rootedness in the real world at the same time with neither taking precedence over the other. It is indicative of the cosmology, the way in which Black people looked at the world. We are very practical people, very down-to-earth, even shrewd people. But within that practicality we also accepted what I suppose could be called superstition and magic, which is another way of knowing things. But to blend those two worlds together at the same time was enhancing, not limiting. And some of those things were "discredited knowledge" that Black people had; discredited only because Black people were discredited therefore what they knew was "discredited." And also because the press toward upward social mobility would mean to get as far away from that kind of knowledge as possible. That kind of knowledge has a very strong place in my work.*
—Toni Morrison, "Rootedness"

Distinguishing worldview from superstition requires sketching the cosmology that grounds Morrison's work. Some black writers posit a non-hegemonic perspective in which (1) community or the collective is central rather than individual achievement or individualism; (2) the transcendent or spiritual is inseparable from the mundane or secular; (3) "nature" is a force essential to humanity; and (4) feminine and masculine are complementary rather than contradictory components of identity and culture. These beliefs (considered illogical in conventional U.S. culture) are not exclusive to an "African-centered" viewpoint. There are similarities between traditional African cosmology and other cosmologies. For instance, in some traditional Native American worldviews, the concept of community also extends through time, for example, in Native American discussions of the seven generations.

What some call superstition or magic, John Mbiti describes as aspects of a cultural worldview in his book *Traditional African Religions and Philosophies:*

> Most [traditional] peoples . . . believe that the spirits are what remains of human beings when they die physically. This then becomes the ultimate status . . . the point of change or development beyond which [one] cannot go apart from a few national heroes who might become deified. . . . Man [or Woman] does not, and need not, hope to become a spirit: [s]he is inevitably to become one, just as a child will automatically grow to become an adult.[6]

Mbiti notes that historically African worldviews have maintained nonlinear time in which the past, present, and future coexist and overlap. (This view is also held in other cultures and in some scientific communities.) Traditional African cosmology sees the nonduality of time and space. Rather than suggest a monolithic Africa, Mbiti's work describes the diversity of religions throughout the continent. Yet he maintains that various organizing principles are prevalent despite ethnic and societal differences. The cosmology he documents rejects the socially constructed dichotomies between sacred and secular, spiritual and political, the individual and community that are characteristic of Western culture. This perspective reappears in African American culture.

Worldviews or values are not deterministic. One may choose. In fact, Mbiti, an African theologian trained in European universities, selects Christianity, depicting it as superior to traditional African religions, which he notes share Christianity's monotheism. We may elect to reject the traditional worldviews that shape African cultures, as Mbiti does. Or we may reaffirm these values, as Morrison does. Stating that "discredited knowledge" has "a very strong place" in her work, Morrison refuses to distance herself from a traditional African and African American cultural worldview, despite the fact that academic or social assimilation and advancement "would mean to get as far away from that kind of knowledge as possible." Without considering the validity of this discredited knowledge or academically marginalized belief system, some may portray Morrison's work as romantic, ungrounded mysticism. Outside of a worldview that recognizes the values mirrored in her work, it is difficult to perceive of Morrison as anything other than exotic. Her fiction is not mere phantasm. As her nonfiction explains, she writes within the framework of African American cultural values and political and spiritual perspectives.

Morrison's work clearly relies on African-centered cultural paradigms that are documented by anthropologists, theologians, philosophers, and sociologists. For centuries, these paradigms have been derided by Eurocentric thought and dismissed as primitive superstition. The invalidation of these frameworks is traceable to European colonization on several continents for several centuries. Historically, European racial mythology determined whether people whose physiology and ancestry were strikingly different were capable of creating theory, philosophy, and cosmology or were merely able to ape superstition. Today, the rejection of discredited knowledge, held by not-fully-assimilated African Americans, branches from this disparagement of the African origins of these views. As Congolese philosopher K. Kia Bunseki Fu-Kiau notes in *The African Book without Title*:

> Africa was invaded . . . to civilize its people. . . . [Civilization] having "accomplished" her "noble" mission . . . African people are still known as people without logic, people without systems, people without concepts. . . . African wisdom hidden in proverbs, the old way of theorizing among people of oral literature [cannot be] seen and understood in the way [the] western world sees and understands [a proverb]. . . . For us . . . proverbs are principles, theories, warehouses of knowledge . . . they have "force de loi," [the] force of law.[7]

People whose traditional culture is supposedly known to be illogical, without complex belief systems, are generally received in racialized societies as dubious contributors to intellectual life or theory. Spoken and unspoken debates about their epistemic subculture range ideologically from reactionary conservatism to progressive radicalism.

Morrison's writings are radical precisely because they reject the Eurocentric labels of primitive for African cosmology and the epistemological aspects of African American culture (all the while cognizant of the value of parts of European culture). Critiquing the racial stereotypes of white supremacy, she asserts the presence of traditional, communal culture as connected to black and African ancestors. Challenging hegemonic paradigms, Morrison delineates and deconstructs the European American muse's addiction to ethnic notions. She issues two complementary calls that politicize the spirit: to resist the racial mythology embodied in the white European American imagination and to reconnect with the values rooted in traditional African American culture. Of these values, the one that provides the foundation for her work is that of African American community: in her writings, Morrison draws down the spirit to house it in community.

The Centrality of Community

Perhaps one of the most debated concepts is the viability of an autonomous African American cultural community. Irrespective of the arguments that discredit this concept, Morrison expresses a personal sense of responsibility to community, making it a cornerstone in her work. The individual's salvation, her or his sanity, comes through relationship to others.

This knowledge resonates in Morrison's work, and it inspires and informs her political risk-taking and daring. The community she explores is neither a global nor a nation-state one, yet she does not deny the existence or significance of either. The vibrant collection of people that engages her is the African American community. And it is its synthesis of seeming polarities—maleness and femaleness, ugliness and beauty, good and evil, the spiritual and the mundane—that intrigues her.

In "Unspeakable Things Unspoken: The Afro-American Presence in American Literature," Morrison's analysis of her novels, particularly her comments on *Beloved* and *Song of Solomon*, illustrates her emphasis on community and the individual's relationship to it. In this essay, Morrison examines how language "activates" and is activated by outlining the context for the first sentences of each of her novels. She reminds us that this exploration into how she "practice[s] language" seeks and presents a "posture of vulnerability to those aspects of Afro-American culture" that shape her novels.[8]

Of those novels, *Beloved* is a striking example of her awareness of the destructive impact of unbalanced spiritual and political worlds on community. According to Morrison, *Beloved* is haunting because it works in part "to keep the reader preoccupied with the nature of the incredible spirit world while being supplied a controlled diet of the incredible political world."[9] An aspect of this incredible political world is this novel's inspiration in a specific historical tragedy, the story of an African American woman, Margaret Garner, who tried to flee slavery with her children in the nineteenth century.[10] After she was captured in Cincinnati, Garner killed her daughter to save her from slavery and then attempted to take her own life. In a videotaped interview with the BBC, Morrison describes how her own haunting by Garner's life and death ended when she wrote *Beloved*. The context for community and the resistance to oppression is the groundwork for Garner's story of the "unnatural" mother who may or may not have demonstrated the incredible depths of maternal love and political resistance, as fictionalized in *Beloved*. In life and in death, individuals remain connected to and grow within the life of the community.

This is true as well in *Song of Solomon*, where the essence of community directs Morrison's discussion of freedom and grace. In her essay she describes the insurance agent whose suicide fulfills his promise to fly from (no-)Mercy Hospital:

> The agent's flight, like that of the Solomon in the title, although
> toward asylum (Canada, or freedom, or home, or the company of
> the welcoming dead), and although it carries the possibility of failure
> and the certainty of danger, is toward change, an alternative way, a
> cessation of things—as—they—are. It should not be understood as a
> simple desperate act . . . but as obedience to a deeper contract with
> his people. (28)

Morrison explains: "The insurance agent does not declare, announce, or
threaten his act. He promises, as though a contract is being executed faithfully between himself and others. Promises broken, or kept; the difficulty
of ferreting out loyalties and ties that bind or bruise wend their way
throughout the action and the shifting relationships" (28). Dangerous but
not desperate, the insurance agent embraces rather than flees his community. His notion of a contract is connected to a cultural understanding of
community as transcendent; his flight transcends dualities that posit a divide between life and death. Morrison relates how his not-fully-compre-
hensible gift is acknowledged and received:

> It is his commitment to them, regardless of whether, in all its details,
> they understand it. There is, however, in their response to his action,
> a tenderness, some contrition and mounting respect ("They didn't
> know he had it in him.") and an awareness that the gesture enclosed
> rather than repudiated themselves. The note he leaves asks for for-
> giveness. . . . an almost Christian declaration of love as well as hu-
> mility of one who was not able to do more. (28)

Exploring the relationship between community and individual, Morrison suggests that her novels involve the reader and narrator in communal
ties. In the worldview of her literature, knowledge emerges from connection to rather than alienation from other people. Wisdom arises within
community, in spite of the flawed character of its constituents:

> That egalitarianism which places us all (reader, the novel's popula-
> tion, the narrator's voice) on the same footing, reflected for me the
> force of flight and mercy, and the precious, imaginative yet realistic
> gaze of black people who (at one time, anyway) did not mythologize
> what or whom it mythologized. The "song" itself contains this un-
> blinking evaluation of the miraculous and heroic flight of the leg-
> endary Solomon, an unblinking gaze which is lurking in the tender
> but amused choral-community response to the agent's flight. (29)

Morrison's own unblinking gaze fosters critical self-reflection in regard to African American communities. It would be simple yet simplistic to idealize the African American community as a haven of safety and harmony against dehumanizing racism. Nowhere do Morrison's essays argue for this perfected black bliss. Everywhere in her literature there exists the reality of the grim, bizarre, and determined struggle in community that embodies both the rotting and the purifying. Rather than succumb to romantic idealism, Morrison admits that her "vulnerability would lie in romanticizing blackness rather than demonizing it; vilifying whiteness rather than reifying it."[11] Her deconstruction of Eurocentrism and Africanisms coexists with a critique of the limitations of black community. Those limitations partly stem from African Americans' stunted group abilities and our refusal to recognize and honor the ancestors and each other. For example, Morrison details how in *Song of Solomon,* the ancestral figure represented by Solomon, who embodies the African ancestors' flight toward freedom, is not readily recognized by community members: "The African myth is also contaminated. Unprogressive, unreconstructed, self-born Pilate [the female protagonist] is unimpressed by Solomon's flight" (29).

Rejection, alienation, and violence toward self, others, or the ancestors, however, do not negate the reality of these ties. Relationships are determinant. One cannot erase community. One decides only how to relate to the community, which includes self, others, ancestors, and future born. Morrison's commentary on *Beloved* and *Song of Solomon* suggests that our ancestors are indispensable to community. Through them, the past sits in the present and future, guiding descendants. The writings suggest that to the extent that we recognize our ancestors, seeking their advice and spiritual power, we deepen our ability to grow in community with them.

The Role of African Ancestors

When you kill the ancestor you kill yourself. . . . nice things don't always happen to the totally self-reliant. —Toni Morrison, "Rootedness"

For some worldviews, the greatest spiritual development is tied to service to the community; in fact, in time through such work one will likely evolve into an elder and later an ancestor. Ancestors are communal mem-

bers in these traditional worldviews.[12] The practice of honoring or wor-
shiping ancestors is prevalent worldwide. The symbols of European American cultural icons are both physical and literary. For example, the ancestral spirits of Confederate soldiers and slaveholders, in iconic statues in
Memphis, Jackson, or Birmingham parks, inspire devoted visitors. The
fervor of canonical reverence in universities belies the disdain that many
European-descended Americans feel for ancestral worship. Popularized
ancestors such as George Washington, Thomas Jefferson, and Elvis evince
complex relationships to and facile representations of white American freedom and civilization that are dependent on enslaved or exploited African
Americans. Increasingly, since the civil-rights movement, American culture has jumbled the contradictory values embodied in ancestors who
manifest oppositional worldviews: holidays, coins, and postage stamps pay
tribute to Washington and Jefferson as well as Ida B. Wells and Martin
Luther King Jr. (although John Brown is rarely memorialized). All collectively comprise community. Extending through time and space to include
our predecessors, contemporaries, and future generations, community
here is not bound by physical or temporal limits; its relationships are transcendent. This transcendence is marked by the presence of ancestors.

Morrison uses the term *ancestor* to refer to living elders and ancestral
spirits. (I reserve the term for historical figures.) Arguing that "there is always an elder" in black literature, Morrison maintains that a distinctive
characteristic of African American writing is its focus on the ancestors:
"These ancestors are not just parents, they are sort of timeless people whose
relationships to the characters are benevolent, instructive, and protective,
and they provide a certain kind of wisdom."[13] For Morrison, studying how
African American writers relate to the ancestor(s) is revealing:

> Some of them, such as Richard Wright, had great difficulty with that
> ancestor. Some of them, like James Baldwin, were confounded and
> disturbed by the presence or absence of an ancestor. What struck me
> in looking at some contemporary fiction was that whether the novel
> took place in the city or in the country, the presence or absence of
> that figure determined the success or the happiness of the character.
> It was the absence of an ancestor that was frightening, that was
> threatening, and it caused huge destruction and disarray in the work
> itself. That the solace comes, not from the contemplation of serene
> nature as in a lot of mainstream white literature, nor from the regard

in which the city was held as a kind of corrupt place to be. Whether the character was in Harlem or Arkansas, the point was there, this timelessness was there, this person who represented this ancestor.[14]

Speech about the ancestors not only enables critiques of historical oppression (such as the references to slavery made in *Beloved* and *Song of Solomon*), but it also establishes communal realities to support and reflect political-spiritual and secular-sacred traditions. Within this worldview, ancestors illuminate an avenue for liberation: listen, and you learn from them; acknowledge their contributions and legacies, and you share their power (which does not necessarily promise redemption). In their physical lives, our predecessors who attained the stature of elders helped others to develop as free human beings. As spiritual forces after death, they continue to guide human development. In this worldview, according to Congolese philosophy, knowledge is "the experience of that deepest reality found between the spiritualized ancestors and the physically living thinkers."[15]

As a living thinker, Toni Morrison is a mapper of recollection sites. Instructional and often inspirational calls to expansive community come from various locations of memory, which despite cultural variances point to unifying elements that are based on shared values. In my own recollection sites, I remember the values of family, peers, and teachers. I recall the political work in the 1980s of friends and activists countering apartheid and U.S. imperialism in the Caribbean and Latin America, where Nicaraguans and El Salvadorans, fighting United States-funded contras and death squads, honored their dead by calling "Presente!" after their names were read in roll calls. I remember the teachings of activist elders and ancestors, the technique of seminary, and the spirit of African-based religious houses in Brooklyn and the Bronx. All these experiences politicized me and now remind me of the futility of traveling without faith or ancestral hope, and the liabilities of academic training that encourages ignorance of communal culture.

Morrison's writings present us with the knower who reaches beyond the straitjacket of Africanisms into the past, which is the present and future, to pull out both the African presence and the European American imagining of that presence. Morrison is only one of many African Americans following liberating traditions that acknowledge the ancestors as part of a spiritual and political place and practice. Calls to the ancestral presence and the primacy of historical African American figures appear in African American religion, politics, and art. This recognition is also in written (literary) and oral culture. For instance, the African American women's vocal group Sweet Honey in the Rock consistently honors the ancestors in song. Their "Ella's Song," dedicated to civil-rights activist Ella Josephine Baker, uses excerpts from Baker's speeches: "We who believe in freedom cannot rest, until the killing of black men, black mothers' sons, is as important as the killing of white men, white mothers' sons."[16] In their introduction to the song "Fannie Lou Hamer," the group and its founder, Bernice Johnson Reagon, former Student Nonviolent Coordinating Committee activist and now director of African American culture at the Smithsonian, explicates their worldview:

> During the civil rights movement of the 1960s . . . Fannie Lou Hamer . . . became a symbol of the strength and power of resistance. . . .We call her name today in the tradition of African libation. By pouring libation we honor those who provide the ground we stand on. We acknowledge that we are here today because of something someone did before we came.[17]

In the academic works of African American intellectuals, the ancestral spirits also appear. Angela Davis speaks of the ancestors in *The Autobiography of Angela Davis* and *Women, Race and Class*.[18] Historian Vincent Harding pays tribute to the ancestors in *There Is a River: The Black Struggle for Freedom in America*.[19] Using "we" throughout his narrative history of African American resistance to enslavement over centuries, Harding merges past, present, and future. With the pronoun "we" he includes himself in the historical telling of our liberation struggles. Finding the historical accounts of black radicalism in the United States to be limited by their abstractness, scope, and Eurocentrism, Harding's narrative both analyzes and celebrates the history of the African American freedom struggles. Using the metaphor of a river and the imagery of a poem by Langston Hughes, he describes as mentacide the dehumanizing practices that turned Africans into slaves, arguing that to enslave a people, one must first destroy their belief systems, their knowledge in themselves, and their understandings of physical and metaphysical power.

Morrison's work is very familiar within this worldview, framing the vision of African American artists and writers who assert that invoking the spirit honors the memories of ancestors. This act of conjuring also testifies to the prevailing wisdom that we, as a people, resist enslavement and genocide because of the spirits that politicize our lives. Reading as strangers in strange sites can politicize the spirit of our societies and instill some honest vigor in our intellectual and moral life. What prevents new, critical, and antiracist readings are the racist stereotypes that have been imprinted on American literary and academic minds.

American Africanisms

My work requires me to think about how free I can be as an African-American woman writer in my genderized, sexualized, wholly racialized world. To think about (and wrestle with) the full implications of my situation leads me to consider what happens when other writers work in a highly and historically racialized society. —Toni Morrison, *Playing in the Dark*

Writers working in a highly racialized society often express fascination with blackness that is both overt and covert. In *Playing in the Dark: Whiteness and the Literary Imagination,* Morrison maintains that Europeans and European Americans "choose to talk about themselves through and within a sometimes allegorical, sometimes metaphorical, but always choked representation of an Africanist presence."[20] She labels this practice and its arsenal "American Africanisms," which mirror European Africanisms. The term *Africanism* represents for Morrison

> the denotative and connotative blackness that African peoples have come to signify, as well as the entire range of views, assumptions, readings, and misreadings that accompany Eurocentric learning about these people. . . . As a disabling virus within literary discourse, Africanism has become, in the Eurocentric tradition that American education favors, both a way of talking about and a way of policing matters of class, sexual license, and repression, formations and exercises of power, and meditations on ethics and accountability. (6–7)

As a literary and political tool, Africanism "provides a way of contemplating chaos and civilization, desire and fear, and a mechanism for testing the problems and blessings of freedom"(7). The distinctive difference of the New World, she writes, is that its claim to freedom coexisted with "the presence of the unfree within the heart of the democratic experiment"

(48). It is arguably still the same. Morrison advises that we investigate "the Africanist character as surrogate and enabler" and the use of the "Africanist idiom" to mark difference or the "hip, sophisticated, ultra-urbane." Her own explorations inform us that within the "construction of blackness and enslavement" existed

> not only the not-free but also, with the dramatic polarity created by skin color, the projection of the not-me. The result was a playground for the imagination. What rose up out of collective needs to allay internal fears and to rationalize external exploitation was a [European] American Africanism—a fabricated brew of darkness, otherness, alarm, and desire that is uniquely American. (38)

Newly constructed beings and inhumanities, such as the white male as both exalted demigod and brutish enslaver, were sanctioned by literature. Morrison emphasizes the cultural aspects of dominance in order to critique the European American literary imagination: "Cultural identities are formed and informed by a nation's literature. . . . what seemed to be on the 'mind' of the literature of the United States was the self-conscious but highly problematic construction of the American as a new white man" (39). In the formation of this new American identity, blackness as embodied in the African was indispensable to elevating whiteness. In this exaltation of whiteness, the Africanist other became the device for "thinking about body, mind, chaos, kindness, and love; [and] provided the occasion for exercises in the absence of restraint, the presence of restraint, the contemplation of freedom and of aggression (47–48). Within this framework, the boundaries of the conventional literary imagination were set to ignore or rationalize enslavement and freedom that was based on enslavement. Transgressing such boundaries is rarely encouraged. Those determined to see themselves without mystification, however, do cross these borders.

According to Morrison, an exceptional few and brave European American writers attempted to free themselves of their entrapment in whiteness. She describes the courage in Herman Melville's tormented struggle to demystify whiteness in *Moby Dick:*

> To question the very notion of white progress, the very idea of racial superiority, of whiteness as privileged place in the evolutionary ladder of humankind, and to meditate on the fraudulent, self-destroying philosophy of that superiority, to "pluck it out from under the robes

of Senators and Judges," to drag the "judge himself to the bar,"—
that was dangerous, solitary, radical work. Especially then. Especially
now.[21]

Today, this "dangerous, solitary, radical work" is discouraged by claims
that race or discussions of racism politicize and so pollute literary work:

> When matters of race are located and called attention to in American
> literature, critical response has tended to be on the order of a hu-
> manistic nostrum—or a dismissal mandated by the label "political."
> Excising the political from the life of the mind is a sacrifice that has
> proven costly. I think of this erasure as a kind of trembling
> hypochondria always curing itself with unnecessary surgery.[22]

This surgery is also selective, usually performed only on those deviating
from the dominant ideologies. Literary works derive their meaning from
worldviews that intend political consequences. Worldviews carry cultural
values as well as political agendas. Only by replicating or naturalizing the
dominant political ideologies—in effect, reproducing the racialized hegemony—can writers claim to be apolitical. Morrison clearly identifies her
work as a practical art with a political focus, writing in "Rootedness: The
Ancestor as Foundation":

> I am not interested in indulging myself in some private, closed exer-
> cise of my imagination that fulfills only the obligation of my per-
> sonal dreams—which is to say, yes, the work must be political. It
> must have that as its thrust. That's a pejorative term in critical circles
> now: if a work of art has any political influence in it, somehow it's
> tainted. My feeling is just the opposite; if it has none, it is tainted.
> (344–45)

These writings enable discussions in a society guarded against analyses of
white supremacy. Her critical thought, despite increasing calls for the irrelevance of race, is particularly important in a society that routinely rejects
such commentary as politically uncivil. Racial discourse seems to be pulled
by marionette strings that work to curtail antiracist critiques. As Morrison
notes in "Unspeakable Things Unspoken":

> For three hundred years black Americans insisted that "race" was no
> usefully distinguishing factor in human relationships. During those
> same three centuries every academic discipline, including theology,
> history and natural science, insisted "race" was *the* determining fac-

tor in human development. When blacks discovered they had shaped or become a culturally formed race, and that it had specific and revered difference, suddenly they were told there is no such thing as "race," biological or cultural, that matters and that genuinely intellectual exchange cannot accommodate it. In trying to come to some terms about "race" and writing, I am tempted to throw my hands up. It always seemed to me that the people who invented the hierarchy of "race" when it was convenient for them ought not to be the ones to explain it away, now that it does not suit their purposes for it to exist. But there is culture and both gender and "race" inform and are informed by it. Afro-American culture exists and though it is clear (and becoming clearer) how it has responded to Western culture, the instances where and means by which it has shaped Western culture are poorly recognized or understood. (3)

African American culture exists within the worldviews that shape and inform it. This culture and its practices reappear in Morrison's work. For instance, typical of the African and African American call-and-response tradition, she receives the call to testify to worldviews that are greater than white myths and to demystify, and thereby resist, a Frankensteinian blackness. Politicized by and politicizing the spirit, she issues her own charge to intellectuals and educators. This spirit is one of black resistance to oppression, a resistance historically rooted in the African American community, its elders, and its ancestors. This spirit fuels current social debates. The worldview that shapes her politics is rooted to traditional African culture. This worldview coexists with and influences other perspectives within the dominant culture.

Conclusion

The ability to distinguish between humane culture and dehumanizing, racialized mythology presupposes critical thinking that is grounded someplace other than in the conventional academic mind. Because critical race thinking is rarely encouraged in racialized settings, we seldom ask how a people, manufacturing and depending on racist myths and ghosts in order to see their reflections in the world, lose more than they gain. It seems that hauntings cannot be restricted. Inevitably, the racially privileged caste and its entourage find themselves marked and demarcated, more obsessed and possessed than their demonized Africanist inferiors. Morrison's work clinically and coolly dissects this production and possession. It calls us to witness a literacy that predates and overcomes Africanism, individualism, and materialism. With this literacy, we read about spirit and power through time and space. This knowledge is made meaningful—or meaningless—by the worldviews we embrace, viewpoints that credit—or discredit—the questions raised by the nonfiction of Toni Morrison.

All educators reflect and articulate worldviews in which they reveal themselves as compromised or uncompromisable knowers, either reproducing or resisting dominance. (There seem to be at least three types of compromised knowers connected to academe—the unwittingly, the voluntarily, and the forcibly compromised.) Bernice Johnson Reagon maintains that the uncompromisable knower is the one who straddles, standing with a foot in both worlds, unsplit by dualities and unhampered by a toxic imagination.[23] As I straddle and sometimes seem to fall from places in which an African American spirit world and European American racial mythology converge, I marvel at Morrison's grace, her ability to call out both the reactionary—the Africanisms of the racist mind—and the revolutionary—the African ancestors and communal commitments.

Whether it is reactionary, reformist, or revolutionary, movement for curricular change entails a spirit of political struggle. Three oppositional tendencies generally appear: advocacy for a romanticized past as intellectually civilized; acquiescence to hierarchical but relatively stable structures; and visionary projections toward the unknowable known as the promise and risk of future justice. Those of us who straddle walk between worlds, in a space where insight and agency arise from community. Between, in, and within these worlds, some intellectuals respond when called. Morrison is such a traditionalist, an uncompromisable knower, a straddler with deep communal ties. How else could she blend two worlds to stand, rooted as she is, politicized by and politicizing the spirit? In that rootedness she writes:

> There must have been a time when an artist could be genuinely representative of the tribe and in it; when an artist could have a tribal or racial sensibility and an individual expression of it. There were spaces and places in which a single person could enter and behave as an individual within the context of the community. A small remnant of that you can see sometimes in Black churches where people shout. It is a very personal grief and a personal statement done among people

you trust. Done within the context of the community, therefore safe. And while the shouter is performing some rite that is extremely sub- jective, the other people are performing as a community in protect- ing that person.[24]

Because cultural remnants are markers for realities denied or suppressed in a racialized society, African American subjective and communal rites reveal the immeasurable distance between African ancestors and European/ American Africanisms. Through her essays, which are unique and repre- sentative, political and spirit-filled, Toni Morrison invites us to struggle with these distinctions and differences in a polarized world.

10 / Teaching, Intersections, and the Integration of Multiculturalism

Integrating Analyses: Pedagogy, Epistemology, and Ethics in the Interdisciplinary Classroom

The phrase *gender, race, and class* has become a litany in some educators' attempts to democratize Eurocentric, male-focused studies with gender-progressive multiculturalism.[1] I first tried to put the litany into practice academically while team teaching as a visiting scholar at a white, Midwestern, so-called public ivy school. The first-year required class, Gender, Race, and Class: Perspectives on Oppression, Power, and Liberation, used multicultural and interdisciplinary approaches. Its four professors (three African American women and one European American man with degrees in social geography, political philosophy, art/architecture, and psychology) sought to teach one hundred students (in five seminars of twenty students each) to analyze racism, heterosexism, sexism, and classism and to integrate their analyses of society and themselves in society. With considerable ambition, the course encouraged students to question the foundations of their schooling and culture.

My only other teaching experience had been as an instructor of ethics at a New York City seminary to black and Latino working-class church activists, and it did not prepare me for this new experience. Perhaps even less prepared were our students—a population of white, upper-middle-class youths, whose privileges seemed clearly tied to the exploitation of or indifference to the experiences of others. Cautious, if not pessimistic, about my own grim expectations of class receptivity to integrative analysis, I needed to avoid the contempt I had seen directed at white students at a recent women's studies conference, where two white professors as panelists ridiculed the students in their classes for racism and sexism in their (mis)reading of Toni Morrison's *The Bluest Eye*. I agreed with the black woman in the audience who pointed out that students, like faculty, reflect socialized cultural biases, poorly developed analytical skills, and a general ignorance of antiblack racism and black peoples.

Unskilled in what Paulo Freire calls critical consciousness, most schooled by years of rote learning and cultural biases have few resources for an alternative approach to learning. Patricia Hill Collins critiques a form of this schooling that leaves much untaught:

> Several requirements typify positivist methodological approaches. First, research methods generally require a distancing of the researcher from her/his "object" of study by defining the researcher as a "subject" with full human subjectivity and objectifying the "object" of study. A second requirement is the absence of emotions from the research process. Third, ethics and values are deemed inappropriate in the research process, either as the reason for scientific inquiry or as part of the research process itself. Finally, adversarial debates, whether written or oral, become the preferred method of ascertaining truth—the arguments that can withstand the greatest assault and survive intact become the strongest truths.[2]

Engaging Collins's argument in our classroom, my colleagues and I critiqued the claims of an "apolitical" social science as well as Peter Berger and Thomas Luckmann's argument on social construction and knowledge.[3] Rejecting the view that education is value-neutral, we employed a theory of knowing and extracurricular activities to promote interdisciplinary study and critical thinking that challenge racist, sexist, classist, and nationalist biases. We also encouraged students to be active rather than passive in what we hoped would be a humane learning process.

Where class, race, and gender biases were often stumbling blocks, the debate on ethics emerged as a cornerstone of our epistemological assumptions. We presented an ethical paradigm to the class, suggesting that knowledge exists for the sake of communal good and human liberation. One of the most academically controversial proposals we put to the class was that they consider the political and ethical implications of worldviews that hold each individual accountable to her or his community, ancestors, and future generations. Examples given for reflection included African philosopher John Mbiti's *Traditional African Religions and Philosophies,* which outlines a worldview in which the individual, while sacred, cannot exist outside or alienated from the development of the whole community. Similarly, Paula Gunn Allen's *The Sacred Hoop: Recovering the Feminine in American Indian Traditions* describes the North American indigenous concepts of seven generations and the sacred hoop as guides for ethical action and right relationships with self, society, and nature.[4]

The epistemology of our course rejected the dichotomy between knowing and doing. Students were asked to approach learning with a critical mind and an activist outlook, with the belief that only when one acts on the material studied does one know it and so becomes Freire's integrated person. In Freire's concept of adaptive versus integrative persons, the adaptive person is defined as a conformist determined by socialization, with limited choices and capacity for critical thought; the integrative person is defined as someone who works to transcend such limitations and to act in the world to free up possibilities for change. Using Bernard Lonergan's concept of human knowing as a four-part process—experience, reflection, judgment, and action—the class evaluated action as indispensable to the learning process.[5] For example, we argued that one knows how to ride a bicycle not from merely reading books about bicycles but from riding one; more in-depth knowledge would enable one to construct a bike. Consequently, society learns how to live, learn, and teach without elitist assumptions by doing activities that confront and diminish oppression.

Lonergan's four-part process organized the assignments for the course: readings to stimulate and challenge students to expand their experiences in race, class, and gender relations; reflections recorded in journals; judgment; and participation in "active engagements" by implementing social-justice projects. Thus the course's approach to learning incorporated experience, reflection, judgment of personal and cultural values, and collective and individual action. In their active-engagement assignments, students designed their own "direct actions" that included a video in which students were asked whether they thought racism existed on campus; a poster critiquing sexist advertisements that use images of women; a letter petitioning the university to change the name of its athletics teams from Redskins to something else; and organizational meetings to counter an impending Ku Klux Klan and neo-Nazi skinhead rally in the local town.

In theory, these were laudatory ethical concepts. In practice, students rebelled against them often during the semester. In fact, the team-teachers did not uniformly accept such approaches to knowledge, including the interrelatedness of doing and knowing. In particular, the white male professor felt that students should not be required to participate in antiracist and antisexist research activities because such actions might contradict their political beliefs. In his seminar sections, which included only white students, youths felt more comfortable expressing hostility toward the antiracist course work, while they remained silent about these feelings with the black women professors. For instance, when one group of his students was asked what community action it would undertake for course credit, one person responded, "Does this mean that we can join the KKK?"

In terms of appropriate pedagogy, it became apparent that faculty who unquestioningly accepted the beneficial role of activity outside the classroom in chemistry, physics, or architecture (as a method to deepen students' understanding of theoretical models) resisted applying the same reasoning to this course. (Such pedagogy is considered less controversial if it reflects value neutrality or conventional values—for instance, African American political scientists at George Mason University assigning voter-registration projects to their students.) In private interviews, students explained that what they resented was not the request to act outside the classroom (which they did in other classes), but the request to engage in antiracist or antisexist actions. Academically, they believed that value-laden commitments were inappropriate in the learning process. Such requests, as our white male colleague had argued, were perceived as infringing on their rights.

These differences in pedagogy were exaggerated by the fact that not only did we have diverse backgrounds, critiques, and expectations, but we also shared little in our ability to communicate political differences. Early in the semester the difficulties in discussing pervasive practices of institutionalized oppression without a shared, supportive language became apparent. Students acknowledged the need for a common political vocabu-

lary in their group work. We began searching for such a language by examining definitions of political terms central in discussions of oppression
and liberation. The class was given handouts with definitions of the terms
paradigm, power, hegemony, and *ideology.* Because these were working definitions rather than comprehensive or fixed ones, students were encouraged
to read works in which these terms were discussed.

Thomas Kuhn's term *paradigm,* for example, used in reference to personal and cultural mind-sets, became central.[6] We discussed Kuhn's representation of paradigms as worldviews—self-contained systems of social
meanings that explain and provide guidelines for thinking and acting.
Judged by their abilities to explain reality and allow integrated action, paradigms fail when they no longer offer adequate explanations or facilitate
problem solving. When the faltering worldview is replaced by a more capable, conceptual, or intellectual view, a scientific revolution or "paradigm
shift" occurs. This shift is also consistent with Freire's notion of epochs of
change or epochral crises based on social upheavals; the need for new social meanings and worldviews comes through a crisis that engenders critical and creative thought.

In our discussions, we then linked this concept of a paradigm as a socially constructed worldview to Antonio Gramsci's notion of *hegemony,*
defined as domination through institutions and therefore the control over
social meanings in a state or society.[7] Because it is institutional and systemic, hegemonic control is pervasive and usually is not attributed to a
controlling group but is perceived as the nature of society. In the construction and dissemination of information (that is, education), whoever con-
trols text, media, and language has hegemony. Shaping the collective
worldview and perceptions of freedom, hegemonies legitimize or delegitimize hierarchies, systems, and relationships of domination. The vehicles
through which this control is made to appear normal and valued are but-
tressed by compatible ideologies or systems of beliefs. Critical theory promoting questions, exploration, and problem solving leads to revolutioniz-
ing worldviews. Ideology, however, can also function as dogma—a closed,
reified set of beliefs. In forming a common language in the context of our
class, students eventually labeled ideologies that legitimate oppression as
closed (rather than open), static (rather than dynamic), and authoritarian
(rather than egalitarian).

In constructing their common political language, most students disagreed on the meaning of the word *power*. Assigned texts did not clearly distinguish between two contradictory notions of power: power as control or domination (the most common understanding), and power as democratic, noncoercive action. My colleagues and I advocated a definition of power as collective or communal action dedicated to achieving a common good, for example, democracy, using Hannah Arendt's constructions; power here becomes "power to" (empowerment) rather than "power over" (domination).[8] The latter as coercive and controlling was viewed as a corruption of democratic power, tending toward violence. Having formed a common vocabulary and a deeper understanding of political language, the students familiarized themselves with the implicit and explicit use of these concepts by feminist writers Audre Lorde, Peggy McIntosh, Angela Davis, Maria Mies, and bell hooks. Hooks's definition of feminism, which implicitly critiques individualism as an ideological pillar in U.S. society, served as one model of a theory of liberation. For hooks, feminism embodies "a commitment to eradicating the ideology of domination . . . and a commitment to reorganizing society so that the self-development of people can take precedence over imperialism, economic expansion, and material desires."[9]

Before midterm, the uniqueness of the course, its unsettling content and pedagogy, and the complexities of theory for first-year students created new forms of resistance. To break the intellectual impasse in their encounters with critical theory and integrative analyses focused on activism, the architecture professor (one of the African American women) suggested that we bring sugar cubes for students to build models of their theories of oppression and liberation. Her idea led to several small groups in each class in which students played and created nonlinear, multilayered depictions of the intersections of gender, race, and class in society. We had already scheduled play or creative interaction for the end of the semester when students would be asked to create a wall mural incorporating the themes studied as part of their final grades. This earlier exercise in tactile work with peers diffused tension while still allowing students to focus on theoretical and political concerns.

Before constructing their models, students were asked to restudy assigned readings and fill in a grid that listed authors' names under the headings Gender, Race, Class, and Power. Using this grid as a memory aid, they summarized the writers' definitions of the four categories (G, R, C, and

P); the grid became a learning tool. Students identified power as the energy flowing throughout the model and as the necessary requisite for change. Whenever possible, they designated terms to synthesize progressive theories; without necessarily agreeing with the writers, students classified, documented, and analyzed their positions. Next, they constructed models by arranging the sugar cubes they had color-coded: blue = gender; black = power; red = class; green = race. Black arrows were drawn to denote the flow of power from different cubes. Once G, R, and C cubes were identified, they were related to each other by P cubes. Some students chose to mark cubes with several variables: for example, a cube that was half-red and half-green represented sexualized racism. Relations of power in the model changed as students' definitions of power evolved. One section chose to represent two types of power: a negative power for relationships of domination and a positive power for democratic relationships. Finally, students sketched their models (on their study sheets containing the grid of feminist theorists) and translated the images into language or theories that retained the various dimensions of their cube models. Asked to examine existing relations of dominance and oppression and emerging relations of liberation, students identified both actuality and potentiality in the model, following the Aristotelian concept that embedded in an acorn is simultaneously actuality (the seed) and potentiality (the oak tree).

Most students were able to construct physical models and translate these into theoretical language. As expected by this time, however, there was a backlash. Describing her group's initial response, one student called the construction of the model dumb and complained of being tired of feminist theory: "Okay, so black women are oppressed. So what?" Few seemed to respond to the request that they place themselves in their work and identify the ways in which their actions supported or challenged the models of power and dominance that they explored. Their reluctance to critique themselves, coupled with a desire to distance themselves from the issues, signaled both student and faculty fatigue and frustrations.

At the end of the semester, more students were able to engage more fully with the final project. Each seminar group of twenty students painted a wall mural reflecting themes explored. The course culminated in this group activity, in which students drew and painted images and, following a public reception, displayed their murals on the ground floor of their residential and classroom buildings. During the semester, students had written reflective and analytical papers, and sketched, drawn, or constructed images of the social and political relationships they were studying, thus expressing themselves and their worldviews through verbal, written, and visual skills.

Paradigm shifts became discernible. The most difficult critique, however, centered on racism. Responses to racism were resisted at a much higher level than those concerning sexism or classism. In their seminars, most of the students agreed that there was a dominant gender and class in the United States but rejected the concept of a dominant or colonizing race. Rutledge M. Dennis states that for the white population, racism breeds irrationality, inhibited intellectual growth, and negated democracy.[10] We teachers of Gender, Race, and Class sought to counter such irrational denials by nurturing our students in critical thought, analytical skills, community, and democratic values. Yet the stress, anxiety, and anger in a learning process largely shaped by African American women faculty that established ethical, antiracist, and antisexist action as normative proved that this nurturing would be perceived as torture by the white, middle-class youths.

Take, for instance, the students' emotional responses to the readings and film viewings (particularly Marlon Riggs's video *Ethnic Notions*). Hostility (reserved for the black women faculty) grew in proportion to the severity of the critique. White students, primarily female, retreated into a form of passivity—silence followed by complaints of being asked to "save the world" or "shoulder the weight of oppression." A significant number of the one hundred students poorly grasped the assigned readings, misrepresenting authors' positions or reducing them to superficialities. Students had difficulty reading and retaining information that was critical rather than merely repetitive of their previous schooling. Enrollment in a special program (a liberal college within a conservative university) created an additional pressure on those who sought to conform to their image of the enlightened young adult.

As faculty, we encouraged the students to struggle with their feelings of unfamiliarity and dissonance. In the opening lecture we pointed out that few, if any, had ever been taught by one African American woman (let alone three). While cautioned not to let their feelings become a retreat from critical analysis, students were repeatedly asked to explore their anger against the writers and African American women professors through discussion, drawing, and writing. Recognizing that relationships are instrumental in the learning process, we also met with students individually to discuss their attitudes toward the class and their first year at college. These personal interactions with faculty, along with play and creative space in constructing the mural, helped to allay their defenses.

It was really only toward the end of the semester that the paradigm shifts became clear. Student responses to the class went from rebellion to ambivalent acceptance to transformation and back to opposition. Transformation does not imply that students accepted the social critiques presented; rather, many became less dependent on their socialized biases toward class, race, and gender and more willing to think critically. In their end-of-the-term course evaluations, most students gave Gender, Race, and Class: Perspectives on Oppression, Power, and Liberation high ratings. Although ambivalent about the course, students still used it as ground for future development. Despite their flaws, courses such as this one promote critical, community-focused education, notwithstanding their susceptibility to repeating a catchall litany for every oppression.

When too ambitious, such courses lose focus, becoming merely crash courses in humanity and sensitivity training. When forced to function as correctives for entire programs that offer little critical race or feminist theory in other courses, they remain isolated with little reinforcement in or support from upper-division classes. The ghettoization of these courses burdens their instructors to provide a permanent intellectual and ethical base for students compelled to take one so-called diversity course, which becomes an aberration in their schooling. (The disparate interests and commitments of faculty in team-taught courses further compounds such problems.) Classroom challenges to the academic penchant for separating critical consciousness and political activism from education require teaching critical theory about the interrelatedness of gender, race, class, and sexuality—and a politics of liberation that is unapologetic about confrontations with oppression.

Integrating Multiculturalism

As part of my own unapologetic political commitments, I argue that in expanding democratic reforms—or better, radical transformations—one is invariably confronted with the claims by privileged sectors that they are victimized by ethnic, antiracist, feminist, queer, and Marxist studies. Those who argue that these courses, and the values they embody, disenfranchise whites, males, heterosexuals, and the affluent bring a perverse twist to the term used to disparage critics of the traditional canon, *victim studies*. Within and outside the walls of academe, reverse-victimization calls are made by the propertied against the poor; heterosexuals (with "straight pride") against gays, lesbians, and bisexuals; whites against people of color. Where critiques of domination are labeled assaults, the chastisement of critical thinkers seems compulsory—in other words, only uncivil women and men point out that the emperor has no clothes. In this breech in civility, such "abuse" warrants punishment for uncivil antiracism. (The notion of an uncivil antiracism outside of respectable society is tied to the notion of a civil racism within the boundaries of respectable society.) Allowing the most privileged citizens to make their status and discomfort the central issue—and so their maintenance the primary goal—rationalizes opposition to democratic reforms. Attention is redirected from constructive criticism to the personal grievances of the powerful who confront change they cannot fully control.

The claim that multiculturalism oppresses members of the dominant culture is echoed by the belief that multiculturalism is also irrelevant. In "Trends of Opposition to Multiculturalism," Jon Michael Spencer maintains that to argue the irrelevance of race in contemporary society is to acquiesce to "the postmodern conspiracy to explode racial identity . . . when the quest for racial equity [as] a central motivating factor in multiculturalism . . . undermine[s] this historical movement."[11] It is debatable whether racial equity remains a "central motivating factor" in contemporary multiculturalism, given its tendencies to produce literary commodities in the form of ethnic texts available for consumption and its appropriation by those who may not place antiracism as a priority.

It is unclear, and unlikely, that postmodernists have intentionally constructed a "conspiracy to explode racial identity," although their deradicalizing, not necessarily antiracist, politics are noted by writers such as Aijaz Ahmad, who critiques postcolonialism, and Lewis Gordon, who critiques postmodernism.[12] Spencer's conspiracy theory gains more credence if one notes the role of Eurocentrism in postmodernism. Samir Amin describes Eurocentrism as "antiuniversalist, since it is not interested in seeking possible general laws of human evolution. . . . [Yet] it does present itself as universalist, for it claims that imitation of the Western model by all peoples is the only solution to the challenges of our time."[13] In a hierarchical society built on racial conquest, all cultures are neither considered nor treated as equal, even if they are created so. European or white culture is not just one of many cultures under Eurocentrism; neither is African or black culture, which has been historically constructed as the antithesis of European culture under Eurocentrism.

The conservative backlash against multiculturalism is tied to an attempt to salvage Eurocentrism's hegemony as part of the general campaign against antiracist and multicultural education (which are not synonymous). Sara Diamond's "Endowing the Right-wing Academic Agenda" documents the role of corporations that have financed counterprogressive university organizing.[14] Illustrating the role of rightists in education, Margaret Cerullo, at a 1992 OUT/Write conference, also noted the Heritage Foundation's role in the conservative backlash.[15] Identifying the rhetoric surrounding political correctness as the third (and only successful) rightwing attempt to maintain hegemony, Cerullo cited conservative organizing by the groups Accuracy in Academia and Tenured Radicals as the preceding two waves. The fact that rightist organizations also critique postmodernists does not negate their similar motivations in discrediting leftist politics and radical engagement.

Cultural studies scholars and postmodernists point out the multiplicity and pervasiveness of racial identity filtered through gender, class, and sexuality. Race, like other social constructions such as gender, class, and sexuality, cannot be understood without analyzing its manifestations in hierarchies and social roles. (The difficulty in advocating multicultural and *antiracist* studies is that often those marginalized and on the backlash defensive may imitate conservatives by ignoring or dismissing diversities within race as irrelevant or divisive.) The assertion that race is nonexistent brings no inherent progress to antiracist discourse, as race is a construct that has been critiqued and repudiated in previous eras. Racism is less idiosyncratic and more fixed than racial identity.

"Exploding" racial identity, to use Spencer's phrase, does not erase the real and morbid scenarios in political, economic, and cultural policies that are shaped by racism. Projecting identity beyond race without first dismantling racist structures suggests that one has managed to stand outside of race as a social construction, that is, to stand outside of society. Such a move might be more an accomplishment of flight and fancy than one of intellectual resistance. To imagine this transcendent racial identity as a political reality (rather than a personal, spiritual, or religious advocacy) requires an ideology of romantic individualism that obscures the real failure to transcend race in a racialized, sexualized, and class-stratified world. Transgressing racist taboos in one's personal life can allow one to cross the cultural limitations of racial construction and division, yet this does not constitute social or political transcendence. Transgressing race, like transgender practices, creates the possibility of drag, which is not necessarily subversive: one may invert and appropriate rather than subvert old paradigms of oppression. The jet-set futurology of deracialized and deracinated intellectuals seems strangely compatible with the anachronistic nostalgia for the good old days expressed by neoconservatives. Both transport us beyond contemporary oppressive realities and material struggles in increasingly polarized and impoverished societies to romanticize and posit a brave (old) new world order, where the ethical project of dismantling social hierarchies becomes irrelevant.

Educational strategies that integrate critiques of the old paradigms may also emphasize the relevancy of addressing state violence. Integrative analysis that stresses complex, overlapping commonalities is not necessarily compatible with concepts of hybridity, which in discrediting notions of conformity, totalizing similarity, or unity seem more linked to dispersal than to integration. Paradigms of exclusion are practiced by both opponents and advocates of multiculturalism. Defenders of multiculturalism may fail to include the work of radical activists, women, working and poorer classes, gays, lesbians, and bisexuals in challenging Eurocentric monoculturalism, erasure, and marginalization. The rich intersections of African American/black studies and ethnic studies; women's studies, multiculturalism, and cultural studies; academic and social-justice programs; and conservative, liberal, and radical ideologies must not be ignored in the name of a unifying multicultural agenda. Diversity is not inherently progressive; some advocates of multicultural studies may reproduce patterns of dominance and appropriation. Countering paradigms of exclusion within multiculturalism promotes integration or synthesis that may build on emancipatory theories.

Black feminist E. Frances White challenges paradigms of exclusion to emphasize multi- rather than bicultural relations and to critique frameworks that seek black unity through homophobia, sexism, and the segregation of other disenfranchised ethnic groups.[16] Exploring the meanings of expanded cultural studies includes examining the chauvinistic paradigms inherent in concepts of the traditional black family. For White, problematizing the African American heterosexual family is a discursive tact shared by black nationalist, Afrocentric, as well as liberal and conservative writers:

> You can read anyone from Ron Karenga to Patrick Moynihan, from Haki Madhubuti to Bill Moyers, and you will find that the problem with the Black community is that we have weak heterosexual bonds. Thus, the building blocks for a strong community don't include welfare dependent families, single-parent female-headed households, and especially they don't include gay, lesbian and bisexual family members. (36)

According to White, "students who are militant about being queer *and* people of color" rejected that discourse during a performance piece by rap singer and author Sister Souljah at Hampshire College in 1992 (36).

White and other lesbian and gay African American writers and theorists such as Audre Lorde, James Baldwin, Essex Hemphill, Marlon Riggs, and Barbara Smith deconstruct the intersections of racism and homophobia in an effort to expand the scope of multicultural studies. These theorists seek to locate "the place of lesbian and gay literature" in debates about multiculturalism. In his contribution to "Multi/Queer/Culture," Phillip Harper identifies the use of the term *multiculturalism* to designate (1) a remedy for the "cultural myopia" that obscures and invalidates the cultures of other societies; and (2) the demystification of an official mainstream culture by acknowledging the contributions of African, Native, Asian, and Latin Americans to what passes for (whitened) U.S. culture.[17] Harper defines the second practice as more radical, given that the remedies for exclusion largely focus on cultural tourism that commodifies Third World cultures as exotic. Applying this dual model of multiculturalism in gay and lesbian studies, he posits two trends of advocacy: lesbian and gay culture alongside other so-called minority cultures in the formation of mainstream culture; and the acknowledgment of the multiplicity of lesbian and gay culture itself. Harper argues that because the most popularized and marketed gay male literature minimizes ethnicity and race the second trend can be considered more radical (29). But what constitutes a radical approach to multiculturalism? How is that radicalism shaped by a discourse reproducing exclusion? Ethnic queer theory may ignore class as a category for analysis (as Harper does in this piece) just as some race-centered advocacy for multiculturalism is silent about gender and sexuality. Although ideologically diverse, opponents and advocates of multiculturalism share common myopic tendencies.

Radical approaches to multiculturalism go beyond the struggle for recognition and diversity (and the demystification of a monocultural society) to include strategies for dismantling the oppression of culturally subordinated peoples. An educator's radicalism is inevitably shaped by her or his self-critical awareness of economic positions. The middle- or upper-class caste of most academics encourages them to ignore how their economic status frames their intellectual debates. Bell hooks's description of the competitive tension between Third World and African American scholars is also applicable to indigenous, home-grown elites:

> Third World nationals who are, for diverse reasons, engaged in scholarship on African-American culture . . . may be non-white, but they may not necessarily have a radical politic or be at all concerned about challenging racial hierarchies. They may choose instead to exploit the privileged location already allotted them in the existing structure.[18]

Being part of that "privileged location" may entail limiting one's academic forays into achievement and recognition. Because racial hierarchies are reflected in economic and sexual exploitation, however, this strategy would have a limited effect; for this reason, activist-intellectuals have set higher standards for engagement. In academic classrooms, one may try to bring learners and educators closer to integrating their analyses for social justice; yet in the absence of political activism outside of academic enclaves, it is difficult to travel beyond merely rhetorical radicalism to confront the structures of dominance.

Conclusion

Alongside the interrogation of texts and analyses of political struggles, classroom teaching ranks high in importance. Teachers can encourage students to study activism and to develop an experiential base that is often critiqued but uncircumscribed by textual studies. Teachers active in communities also find that experiences and relationships broader than the academy can provide a foundation for assessing and reinterpreting texts. Grappling with the issues of domination and distortion in education, one all too often finds support from faculty and administrators for maintaining racial, sexual, and class biases. Passive reinforcement of biases, particularly racial bias, persists, despite inclusive syllabi and educators who assert different ways of knowing. Yet increasingly integrative analyses and progressive pedagogy contribute to social-justice-based education.

11 / Gender, Race, and Radicalism: Reading the Autobiographies of Native and African American Women Activists

The 1992 Post-Columbus Classroom: Women's Resistance to American Racism

In American society where indigenous and African Americans signify the primitive and exotic (often dangerous) other, antiblack and anti-Indian racism coexists within a larger context of political opposition to radicalism.[1] Antiradicalism often appears in reactionary or conservative politics. At other times, radicalism is depoliticized and co-opted by rhetorical trends and fashion: for instance, television commercials explain that the soft drink Mountain Dew is "radical" and that Revlon makes "revolutionary cosmetics for revolutionary women." Within academe, as in pop culture, radical and antiracist politics are usually distorted if not denigrated. Dominant trends in academic studies seem to either denounce radicalism and antiracism as misguided approaches to redress injustices (that are increasingly denied)—even the liberal remedy of affirmative action is now considered reverse racism or sexism—or reduce them to a surrogate liberalism or literary insurgency. Obviously, there are exceptions: those who most often go beyond rhetorical antiracism and radicalism are student and faculty activists engaged in organizing for social justice.

Many teachers who were student activists have experiences that illustrate how academic sites tend to silence or marginalize radicalism. The meanings of radicalism in my past days as a nonacademic activist encompassed not only political ideas (or rhetoric about such ideas) but also strategies for uprooting oppressive structures rather than assimilating into or reforming them. After several years as a full-time academic in western Massachusetts, estranged from the urban activism I had known in New York City, I was unsure about the nature of progressive politics and race discourse. Most of what I had known as radical from organizing and teaching ethics with religious leaders in the city was generally received by more seasoned academics as inappropriately political (polemical) or academically uncivilized in a university setting. As an assistant professor in women's studies engaged in antiracist education, I focused primarily on marginalized black and indigenous women. Both groups of women figured prominently in my courses as I argued that material and existential wealth in the Americas is accumulated through systemic exploitation or expropriation of these women and their peoples.

While teaching, I often wondered pessimistically how students perceive women of color whom they encounter as "texts," particularly those activists who critique the American state. I imagined that it was difficult for academics to conceptualize such women as anything other than fashionable literary commodities—colorful accessories to Eurocentric and transethnic paradigms. With the ascendency of postcolonial, postmodern, and postracial discourses, I was also curious whether students considered antiracist, radical activists as politically antiquated, cultural throwbacks or ethnocentric oddities. My pessimism about the academic reception of the worldviews and politics of Native and African Americans who actively confront genocide was also related to my general reading of dominant academic politics: that most teaching (conservative, liberal, or postmodern/postcolonial) privileges Eurocentric or multicultural paradigms over antiracist frameworks, with little juxtaposition to radical critiques from nonacademics or nonelites.

The year 1992 was a watershed for educational analyses of structural violence and genocide. That fall, community, student, and faculty intellectuals worked together to examine the quincentennial celebrations of the supposed discovery of the Americas. In Amherst, faculty, staff, and students initiated curriculum changes, held campus forums, and promoted recent publications by Native Americans and others on contemporary indigenous oppression and resistance. This call issued by progressive academics elicited various responses. Mine was to develop and teach a first-time course at the University of Massachusetts at Amherst the following semester—Gender, Race, and Radicalism: Native and African American Women Activists, which was open to students in the local five-college system (the university and Amherst, Smith, Mount Holyoke, and Hampshire Colleges). I had taught the autobiographies of black women active in the civil-rights and black-liberation movements of the '50s, '60s, and '70s in other courses. Over several years, Mohawk scholar-activist Donna Goodleaf, who colectured in this course, had introduced me to the writings of contemporary Native American women in resistance to state domination and colonization. Gender, Race, and Radicalism seemed an ideal opportunity to synthesize research on women from two marginalized ethnic groups into a unique, comparative women's studies class. The fact that the women to be studied were also radical activists brought added significance: more than marginalizing conservative and liberal women of color, the academy had virtually erased radical women of color from curricula.

Comparative women studies courses often define women of European descent and liberal or conservative women as normative. Most scholarship on radicalism emphasizes men, as does the comparative literature on black or red-black Indians and Native and African Americans. (An estimated one-third to one-fourth of African Americans have Native American ancestry.) Departing from those norms, my course centered on writings by Native and African American women radicals from so-called captive communities, which I presented within nonconventional analytical frameworks. As an upper-level elective, it brought together approximately twenty students, mostly juniors and seniors interested in not only women of color but also Native and African American women radicals engaged in liberation movements.

Classroom Encounters

As an experimental, one-time course aimed to expand the context(s) for progressive politics by encouraging the study of women's radical antiracist activism, Gender, Race, and Radicalism was atypical in subject matter, texts, and pedagogy. We examined recent indigenous and African American social movements from the perspectives of their women leaders; the assigned texts were by academic or activist women engaged in red and/or black liberation. Course requirements included journals for individual reflection, comparative essays, and group presentations on paired auto-biographies. Occasionally, I asked students to participate in on-campus cultural and political events organized by women of color; in spring of 1993 these events included a performance by the Native American Spider-Women Theater collective and a conference on women and organizing that featured a keynote address by Angela Davis. Exposed to social issues in personal narratives and asked to share their own reflections and experi-ences, students were confronted with ethical questions. The autobiograph-ical accounts that students both read and composed encouraged them to depart from the traditional genre of explorer-colonizer encounters. Not every student was willing to engage in such a journey: some failed to sub-mit the journals that were to focus on students' relationships to text, class, pedagogy, instructor, and women's radical antiracist politics.

On the first day of teaching, I was pleased to encounter a fairly diverse women's studies class. Two-thirds of the students were female; nearly half were of African, Latino, or Asian descent; the remaining half were Euro-pean American. The students held a variety of political views as well, al-though all generally considered themselves progressives. A quarter or more of the class identified themselves as community activists. Most of those with extensive organizing experience in nonacademic and middle-class communities were themselves middle- and upper-middle-class white women in their third year at Hampshire College, a nearby alternative liberal-arts institution. As self-identified activists, these European and Jewish Ameri-can women had experience countering sexual and racial violence that in-creased their receptivity to developing critical perspectives on the connec-tions among women's struggles, antiracism, and genocide. A small number of these women activists provided the student comments reprinted below.[2] The political experiences of these students shaped their ethnic and gen-der identities so that they tended to disengage more quickly from self-absorbed reflections or narrowly defined identity politics.

During the semester, other students—white and nonwhite, male and female—who had little or no experience in political organizing more often strayed from structural analyses to emphasize their personal anxieties about race and critiques of racism and genocide. Perhaps because they had a pragmatic approach that connected critiques with practical applications, the women student activists tended to advocate classroom attempts to build useful critical analyses:

> Both of us came into "Gender, Race, and Radicalism" with a commitment to playing an active role in bringing about social justice in the world, and with experience in attempting to act on this commitment in coalition with other people. We lacked, however, a political analysis which dealt explicitly with genocide and colonialism. Without this analysis, our political actions in the past have often felt incomplete or misguided. (JM and JL)

Not only the students felt their past and present political actions to be incomplete. Early on, I had shared with the class my view that the life stories of indigenous and African American women—who survive and resist the most intensive forms of state violence—reveal their tenacious faith and fierce love in confronting oppression. Suggesting that we encounter these women as conduits for reviewing our own political commitments rather than models to be emulated, I did not share with the class my personal search: that working with students to analyze the autobiographies of Native and African American women activists might help me, as an academic, find my own answers about political integrity and social justice. Looking in these works for answers to the questions I silently asked myself, I asked the class: "What does it mean to be a woman in a captive community in resistance? And what is your relationship to such political actors and actions?" I could not and did not assert what those meanings or relationships were or should be—only that these questions had to be addressed. Throughout that semester, we all struggled with our spoken and unspoken questions. Often these questions crystallized around the issue of genocide in America.

Questioning Genocide: Building Frameworks for Studying Women and State Racism

During the first class, I lectured on the conditions of Native and African Americans, who have been historically devastated by state policies; I explained that they suffer greater discrimination and higher infant and adult mortality rates in the United States than the rest of the population. My lecture referenced that for decades African and Native American activists have organized around racism and human-rights violations. The African-

American-led Civil Rights Congress of 1951 petitioned the United Nations with *We Charge Genocide: The Crime of Government against the Negro People*; more recently, the International Indian Treaty Council appended the 1948 United Nations Convention on the Prevention and Punishment of the Crime of Genocide to U.S. domestic policies. The editor of *We Charge Genocide,* William Patterson, explains that the UN Convention defines genocide as "any intent to destroy, *in whole or in part,* a national, racial, ethnic or religious group" or kill or inflict "serious bodily or mental harm to members of the group."[3]

Stressing that struggles around law and (legal) language also shape consciousness and activism around racism, I raised in our first sessions the role of conventional speech in obscuring critical thinking about genocidal racism in U.S. domestic and foreign policies. For most, racism in America is conceptually severed from genocide. This detachment obstructs a national common language for analyzing genocide against indigenous and African American peoples. I maintained that it was important for the class to discuss contemporary genocide critically in order to construct a lens for viewing women's autobiographies that refer to cultural and/or physical genocide as a by-product of state racism. For examples of women seeking to develop a common language about racism and genocide, I referred to Native American scholar Paula Gunn Allen's critique of America's moral amnesia concerning its anti-Indian wars:

> We are horrified by South African apartheid and the removal of millions of indigenous African black natives to what is there called "homelands"—but this is simply a replay of the nineteenth-century U.S. government removal of American Indians to reservations. Nor do many even notice the parallel or fight South African apartheid by demanding an end to its counterpart within the borders of the United States. The American Indian people are in a situation comparable to . . . genocide in many parts of the world today. . . . deliberately, as a matter of national policy, or accidentally as a matter of "fate," every single government, right, left, or centrist in the western hemisphere is consciously or subconsciously dedicated to the extinction of those tribal people who live within its borders.[4]

The familiar context for linking South African apartheid to genocide, or even Nazi anti-Semitism to genocide in Germany, has no counterpart in the United States connecting racism to genocide. Annette Jaimes's comparison of U.S. political ideology in historical wars against Native Americans to the campaigns of Nazi Germany was a part of course readings that offered a similar argument.[5]

These discussions of language, meaning, and violence were not purely theoretical. The issue of relationships (of student readers to the political struggles of women and oppressed and colonized peoples) and ethics continuously circulated. Exploring the meanings of genocide and Native and African American women's resistance, I asked the class how our speech about and conceptions of racism determine what we say and do about genocide. In their writings, some students said that they felt inadequately prepared to analyze genocide as a contemporary phenomenon:

> It is not often in academia (even at oh so liberal . . . college) that we talk about genocide, as a political reality, not off in the past somewhere, but here and now. in attempting to do so, i feel at loss for language. the tools i have been taught to use in writing analytical papers seem insufficient. this seems to be the case more and more as i have made the decision to no longer detach myself from what i write. at the same time, developing a stronger analysis of how systematic oppression/genocide has worked and works in the united states is an incredibly important part of working to end them. (JM)

Emphasizing the moral dimensions of words and acts, students became more engaged in personal reflections. Considering their thoughts as responses to women's lives committed to resisting racist state oppression, students initially showed discomfort; this dissipated for some but continued throughout the course for others. There would be no way around feeling uncomfortable if grappling with ethics was to be critical to our study of the autobiographies. Ethics, a sense of personal responsibility and moral accountability, was central in the works we read by Native and African American women activists. I also incorporated ethical response into course pedagogy: reflection summaries concluded each analytical paper; student journals provided the space for less-structured thinking; in class and small-group discussions, students were encouraged to explore their relationships to the writings studied. These discussions sparked ethical debates that were then developed in student writings. Again, the point was not to dictate to students an appropriate response but to provide them with the space to incorporate those ideas into their institutional education.

Frameworks for Reading Women's Political Autobiographies

In academic settings, whites study people of color; the middle class investigates the lives of poor and working-class peoples; and conservatives and liberals critique radicals. In such contexts, constructing a framework or narrative lens for reading autobiographies of radical activist women is crucial to deconstructing the other. Consequently, I divided the course into two sections. In the first section, students were to quilt a framework for critical reading in their studies of women struggling against genocide. The class spent the first third of the semester building rudimentary frames, which students would continuously reevaluate and refine later in their papers and oral presentations. With references to Thomas Kuhn's *The Structure of Scientific Revolutions*, we discussed paradigmatic shifts, evaluating political ideologies for their ability to address the crises of oppression and to point toward possible strategies for just resolutions.[6]

Building interdisciplinary frameworks based on course readings and discussions, students outlined key themes—agency, systemic oppression, genocide and autogenocide, ethnic and gender identity—to explore within the paradigms of the autobiographer as well as the worldview of the student-writer. Most had never been asked to explicate the belief systems that shape their political and social ideas and found constructing such models difficult. Many had naturalized the prevailing assumptions of their academic experiences, which were largely silent about antiracist radicalism. In these assignments I asked the class to push the parameters of these conventional frameworks in which whiteness, conservatism, and liberalism constituted the norm. Giving an example of naturalizing whiteness, I recalled the commercials of my childhood that marketed "flesh-colored" bandages—in one color.

Identifying racism in political, economic, and cultural practices, not only as self-contained acts but as reflective of structures of thought and policy, proved very difficult. In order to develop useful paradigms in this first section, we read selections from Manning Marable's *How Capitalism Underdeveloped Black America* and Jaimes's *The State of Native America*.[7] We also used visual resources: Marlon Riggs's *Ethnic Notions* allowed us to examine dehumanizing antiblack icons and racial and sexual stereotypes of African Americans; the PBS documentary *In the Image of the White Man* analyzed the U.S. government's quest to "de-Indianize" indigenous children through residential schools.[8] Using these videos, students examined the images of cultural representations that have historically legitimized violence against blackness (Africanness) and redness (Indianness). Through the readings of Marable and Jaimes, we examined strategies for resisting dehumanizing images and practices.

During the remaining two-thirds of the semester, using their frameworks and selective themes, students wrote comparative papers for each set of autobiographies. I had grouped the texts into pairs of Native and African American women authors. Although the course title identified the autobiographers collectively as radicals, their political ideologies could not be reduced to a monolithic concept. The autobiographies were paired based on possible similarities between the women's political views. The order in which they were read reflected my perception of increasing radicalism among the women's strategies to counter state domination. Curious to see if students identified variations in radicalism, I asked about the differences between revolutionary, radical, liberal, and conservative politics. Our imprecise answers—I refused to provide a fixed definition—reflected the general imprecision of political references and labels for political phenomena. Students who felt confident in distinguishing between conservatism, liberalism, and radicalism were nonplussed when asked to differentiate between radical and revolutionary: revolutionary was either indistinguishable from radical or, as irrelevant terminology, was absent from their view of the political continuum.

The African American autobiographies were restricted to those written by activists in the civil-rights and black-liberation movements. Given the smaller number of published narratives by U.S. Native American women radicals, I included works by American indigenous activists, Guatemalan Rigoberta Menchú, and Bolivian Domitila Chungara, who link their liberation struggles to U.S. foreign policy. Most students knew of Angela Davis and 1992 Nobel Peace Prize laureate Menchú. Through women's studies courses, some had heard of Mary Crow Dog and Anne Moody, whose autobiography is also studied in courses on the civil-rights movement; few had heard of Chungara or Assata Shakur.

With visual resources, students could see images of these women in their roles as activists. Crow Dog's *Lakota Woman* was read alongside the film *Bravehearted Woman: Annie Mae*, which portrayed Annie Mae Aquash, the assassinated indigenous leader who had organized with Crow Dog on the Pine Ridge reservation; segments from the PBS series *Eyes on the Prize* on the Student Nonviolent Coordinating Committee framed Moody's *Coming of Age in Mississippi*. Reading the second set, Davis's *Autobiography of Angela Davis* and Menchú's *I, Rigoberta Menchú: An Indian Woman in Guatemala*, students viewed *A Nation of Law?*, the *Eyes on the Prize* segment on COINTELPRO and prison conditions, in which Davis is interviewed on the violent suppression of the Attica uprising. Students also screened *When the Mountains Tremble;* this film, narrated by Menchú, examines the Guatemalan war against indigenous Americans in the 1980s and the funding of the Guatemalan military and death squads during the Reagan administration. Along with Amnesty International reports on Guatemala, the film provided a context for Menchú's book. After reading the last pair, Shakur's *Assata: An Autobiography* and Chungara's *Let Me Speak!*, we watched *Interview with Assata* and researched Bolivian workers and peasants.[9]

Gender and Race: Student Critiques of Native and African American Racial and Sexual Politics

As useful as their frameworks proved in expanding their existing paradigms, students were reluctant to critique the writers' racial and ethnic politics and chauvinism. For instance, the class was silent about the absence of black Indians as either contributors or subject matter, as well as any discussion of color prejudice among Native Americans in Jaimes's anthology. When I asked about their perceptions of a passage in which Mary Crow Dog refers to an African American man who assists her as her "slave," they were noncommittal. They were also quiet about Marable's distorted portrait of African Americans as the most oppressed ethnic population and his disregard of ample documentation that Native Americans suffer the most depressed conditions in the United States. When offered, student criticisms of black or Indian bias were usually directed at African Americans. Students tended to romanticize and identify with Native Americans more than with African Americans. Interestingly, all students had personal interactions with African Americans, including with those who were in the class. On the other hand, class members knew virtually no Native Americans, especially those represented in the autobiographies—Native Americans living on reservations or Latin Americans. Class participants (regardless of their own ethnicity) almost uniformly idealized Native Americans as sacrosanct in terms of ethnic and racial politics and attitudes.

The uneasiness and reluctance with which students addressed classism, (internalized) racism, and the interrelatedness of gender, race, and class among Native and African American communities disappeared in their discussions about sexism. Unsurprisingly in a women's studies course, students focused on gender; in this focus, however, they tended to isolate gender from class and race, ignoring its intersections with other variables. I cited examples of sexism and misogyny among each peoples, including the Indigenous Women's Network, which faced criticism from some Native American men in the International Indian Treaty Council and American Indian Movement who argued that women alienate themselves from their men and community; I also described similar accusations from African American males against African American feminists and women's organizations. Pointing to examples of patriarchy, however, does not provide a sufficient critique of gender and power relations in antiracist struggles for ethnic sovereignty and independence.

One of the greatest challenges posed by Gender, Race, and Radicalism was that it prodded students to maintain the specificity of gender as a category in critical analysis. It encouraged students to reexamine gender analysis by expanding their definition of *gender-progressive* to include women who may not identify as feminists and/or those who emphasize the concerns of their disenfranchised ethnic communities. The gender perspectives of these Native and African American activists from the sixties and seventies could not be easily dismissed as prefeminist or part of a primitive feminism, even if they contradicted feminist ideologies that treat women as a class (one that often universalizes privileged women). On the question of nationalism, students were initially inclined to view the activists as retrogressive in terms of gender and race. Many considered nationalism as uniformly misogynist and counterrevolutionary. Largely ignorant of the works of gender-progressive women (and men) who identified with national-liberation struggles, some students considered nationalist women as unenlightened or counterfeminist. Most generally failed to consider the nonessentialism of nationalism; that is, the diversities of nationalism(s) encompass a range of ideologies spanning from the reactionary to the progressive revolutionary.

The women's memoirs studied highlight a progressive, revolutionary nationalism. Nearly all the autobiographers strongly identify with their ethnicity, with some positing their ethnic group as a nation. Among Native Americans, for instance, this nation status is recognized by U.S. law. At the same time, each writer acknowledges the importance of friendships and alliances beyond her own ethnic group. Moody's and Crow Dog's narratives depict how each woman worked with progressive whites. Other autobiographers explicate their liberation struggles within international politics; for instance, Davis describes multiracial, transnational struggle:

> [Through] political repression . . . racism, poverty, police brutal-
> ity . . . Black, Brown, Red, Yellow, and white working people are
> kept chained to misery and despair. And it was not only within the
> United States of America, but in countries like Vietnam, with the
> bombs falling like rain from U.S. B52's, burning and dismembering
> innocent children. (382)

For Davis, to address white supremacy one must address capitalism and economic exploitation: "When white people are indiscriminately viewed as the enemy, it is virtually impossible to develop a political solution" (150). Menchú also asserts the need for the development of oppressed ethnic communities within a just international world order.

Shakur, the most nationalist of the African American autobiographers, advocates internationalism as a balance to nationalist commitments:

> It was also clear to me that without a truly internationalist compo-
> nent nationalism was reactionary. There was nothing revolutionary
> about nationalism by itself—Hitler and Mussolini were nationalists.
> Any community seriously concerned with its own freedom has to be
> concerned about other people's freedom as well. The victory of op-
> pressed people anywhere in the world is a victory for Black peo-
> ple. . . . Imperialism is an international system of exploitation, and
> we, as revolutionaries, need to be internationalists to defeat it. (267)

One student wrote that Shakur's autobiography "illustrates the integration of multiple elements: art, music, poetry, history, education, armed struggle, day to day survival, and flexibility, which are necessary for a revolution." Still others described Domitila Chungara's autobiography as less engaging, partly because of its lack of creative style and partly because of its silence about racism, ethnicity, and traditional indigenous values. Of the six works, Chungara's pays the least attention to ethnicity and race. Unlike Crow Dog, who emphasizes traditional religions, or Menchú who seeks a return to ancestral ways and traditional indigenous culture and economic justice, Chungara focuses nearly exclusively on the Bolivian working class. An advocate for exploited miners, she emphasizes the importance of class, socialism, and especially internationalism: "Many other countries suffer persecutions, outrages, murders, massacres, like Bolivia. And how beautiful it is to feel that in other peoples we have brothers and sisters who support us, who are in solidarity with us, and make us understand that our struggles aren't isolated from one another" (37). It is resistance to international solidarity for workers among some feminists that leads to Chungara's strong critique of feminism. *Let Me Speak!* recounts Chungara's disappointment in an international women's conference after participants, most of whom were economically privileged or European or American, rejected her plea for assistance to independence movements and exploited laborers:

> Our position is not like the feminists' position. We think our liberation consists primarily in our country being freed forever from the yoke of imperialism and we want a worker like us to be in power and the laws, education, everything, to be controlled by this person. Then yes, we'll have better conditions for reaching a complete liberation, including our liberation as women. (41)

The autobiographies challenge the construction of monolithic or essentialist approaches to nationalism as universally parochial, chauvinistic, and misogynist. In their generalizations of the black-liberation and Indian movements as uniformly shaped by patriarchal nationalism, students dissociated any gender-progressive politics from men or women in liberation movements in the United States in the 1970s. Their assumptions were reflected in Manning Marable's essay "Groundings with My Sisters," which describes patriarchy in the black-liberation movements: "Every Black male leader of the 1960's accepted and perpetuated the idea of Black Macho, the notion that all political and social power was somehow sexual, and that the possession of a penis was the symbol of revolution."[10] In a passage that cannot be easily applied to women, who formed a good part of the civil-rights leadership, Marable's language denounces black leaders' male chauvinism. A number of students referred to this passage as profeminist, uncritical of its divergence from the women's own accounts of the complexity of gender struggles within the movement; the women's narratives, in contrast, did not erase the sexist and abusive practices of indigenous or African American males. As accurate as Marable's statement is concerning tendencies and trends—patriarchy and misogyny obviously existed within the black and American Indian movements—it is unclear whether this machismo can be generalized to all male leaders. For instance, Assata Shakur, a leader in the black-liberation movements who describes how sexism and elitism led her to leave the Black Panther Party (BPP), writes of her coactivist Zayd Shakur: "I also respected him because he refused to become part of the macho cult that was an official body in the BPP. He never voted on issues or took a position just to be one of the boys" (223).

Despite the constraints of reactionary gender politics, women's radical independence and interdependency shaped resistance movements and provided national leadership. According to Jaimes and Theresa Halsey,

> Contrary to those images of meekness, docility and subordination to males with which we women typically have been portrayed by the dominant culture's books and movies, anthropology and political ideologues of both rightist and leftist persuasions, it is women who have formed the very core of indigenous resistance to genocide and colonization since the first . . . conflict between Indians and invaders.[11]

Alongside Jaimes's anthology, the autobiographical writings exhibit an awareness of gender oppression that coexists with other injustices and inequalities. Their concepts of liberation pursued women's equality through the liberation of a people, not merely a gender within a people. This, of course, meant that the goals of liberation could not be set by masculinist standards, a fact that women activists recognized with the various constituencies to be freed from oppression. As Rigoberta Menchú observes, "we have to erase the barriers which exist between ethnic groups, between Indians and ladinos, between men and women, between intellectuals and non-intellectuals, and between all the linguistic areas" (223). Erasing barriers and hierarchies in the pursuit of social justice, however, has proved extremely dangerous.

Repression and Women's Resistance

The memoirs describe how organizing for social justice was met by a backlash of repression. All the writers were politically targeted for imprisonment and/or violence. Anne Moody, who was placed on a local Ku Klux Klan's hit list because of her civil-rights activism, describes the use of lynchings or "terror killings" in the 1960s to intimidate whole communities involved in human-rights work. In the 1970s, the Black Panther Party and the American Indian Movement were infiltrated by government informers, some of whom incited violent behavior within these organizations. The FBI and police were also instrumental in assaulting indigenous and African American leaders in the 1970s, incarcerating some as political prisoners such as Angela Davis, Leonard Peltier (who remains imprisoned), and Assata Shakur (in political exile in Cuba), and harassing countless others in order to destabilize progressive movements.

The autobiographical accounts of violence are grimly shocking for most students unfamiliar with the police brutality and police-state measures employed during that era. Shakur recounts how New Jersey police repeatedly obstructed her ambulance transport after she was severely wounded by state troopers' gunfire. Crow Dog describes her own violent arrest on the Pine Ridge Reservation, where from 1973 to 1975, she reports, as many as twenty-five of the eight thousand tribe members were killed for their political activities or associations with progressives; Crow Dog also links Bureau of Indian Affairs agent and tribal leader Dick Wilson and the FBI to those deaths, including the assassination and mutilation of Annie Mae Aquash (193, 195, 218–19). Beatings, torture, and the deaths of friends and loved ones marked and marred the lives of these radical women in the United States.

Political violence against indigenous peoples and activists in Latin America has been even more brutish and pervasive. Menchú and Chungara offer first-person accounts of systemic, devastating brutality. Distinguishing assimilation from acculturation, Menchú presents Ladinized Indians who joined the Guatemalan army and killed indigenous people as having adopted the genocidal values of the dominant culture; she depicts those who learned the language, trades, and technology of Guatemalans to serve oppressed people as acculturated. Menchú's family was massacred by the military. While pregnant, Chungara was detained in jail and tortured until she gave birth to her dead child; she identified CIA agents as present during her interrogation.

Despite their experiences of state-directed atrocities, each woman disapproves of the vanguard militarism among activists confronting state violence. Shakur, who argues for political strategies that mobilize large numbers of people, criticizes the obsessive, romantic militarism within sections of the Black Panther Party. A founder of the Housewives Committee for peasant mining communities, Chungara maintained that Che Guevara's failure to organize an international liberation movement, and his capture and execution by the Bolivian military, were due in part to the revolutionaries' alienation from poor people who were not necessarily supporters of armed struggle: "It seems to me that that was the mistake these guerrillas made: they didn't get close enough to the people. No one can get anywhere if they aren't in tight with the people" (67).

Internal violence has also undermined Native and African American communities. In the class's definition, external genocidal violence included systemic poverty; the suppression of traditional cultural practices and languages through church and educational systems; repression enforced by the police, army, and right-wing vigilantes. Using a term from Jaimes's *The State of Native America,* the class referred to violence among Native and African Americans as *autogenocide.* We understood autogenocidal violence as a result of community-generated violence. Expanding the definition of *autogenocide* to include the failure to resist oppression, assimilation, and inhumane working conditions, students blurred the distinctions between passivity, opportunism, and complicity. By doing so, they set very high standards for judging Native and African Americans. Paradoxically, they also relied uncritically on a presentation at a women's conference that had described "horizontal violence" (autogenocide) as stemming from "vertical violence" (genocide). Some used this construct to absolve oppressed peoples of any responsibility for destructive behavior. This vindication extended to Native and African American men's sexual assaults and domestic violence (other forms of autogenocide); such abuses were excused because the males were seen to be oppressed by vertical or state violence.

Examples of African or Native American autogenocide appear in each woman's autobiography. Angela Davis writes of her childhood classmates who "fought the meanness of Birmingham while they sliced the air with knives and punched black faces because they could not reach white ones"

(94). Anne Moody describes her father's depression from his inability to provide for the family and his emotional violence inside the family. Her mother—pregnant with her seventh child by Moody's unemployed stepfather Raymond—cried so much that "she almost drove us all crazy. Every evening I came home from work, she was beating on the children making them cry too" (113). This violence, which Moody describes as based on racial and economic oppression, erupted in the streets as well as in their homes: "Some Negroes would come to town on Saturday night just to pick a fight with another negro. Once the fight was over, they were satisfied. They beat their frustrations and discontent out on each other."

Drug abuse and domestic violence were also identified as aspects of autogenocide. In Native American communities the inability of Native males to function in untraditional roles as the head of the household or breadwinner, according to Annette Jaimes, "led to a perpetual spiral of internalized violence in which Indian men engage in brutal (and all too often lethal) bar fights with one another, or turn their angry attentions on their wives and children" (325). She explains that colonization "has manifested itself in the most pronounced incidence of alcoholism of any ethnic group in the United States," resulting in fetal alcohol syndrome, higher death rates from drunk driving, and higher rates of "child abuse and abandonment, [both] unknown in traditional native societies" (325). "Colonially induced despair" also created a wave of teen suicide in Native American communities in the 1980s, which had run several times higher than the national average (325).

Despite violence, betrayal, and massive fissures in community foundations, the autobiographies portray each ethnic group as a people with shared interests, values, and culture—that is, as a community. The women's affirmation of the ability to build community irrespective of genocidal and autogenocidal violence challenged students' perceptions of agency and power that focused on the isolated individual. Students found commonalities in the women's resistance to violence and abuse. For instance, Shakur and Moody both write about their teenage experiences with sexual violence and harassment inside the African American community: Moody was sexually harassed by her stepfather and forced to leave home; Shakur, a runaway, escaped a "train" or gang rape by black male teens. Moody's accounts of sexual abuse, family rejection, and extreme poverty as a girl and young adult resonated with the women students. Although overwhelmed by racist violence, political repression, a nonsupportive family, and the financial burdens of attending and graduating from college, she continued to grow as a woman in the movement, through her own struggles. Several student papers quoted this passage from Moody's book: "Something happened to me as I got more and more involved in the Movement. . . . It no longer seemed important to prove anything. I had found something outside myself that gave meaning to my life."

Moody's and Crow Dog's coming-of-age stories, detailing adolescent alienation and abuse, were especially compelling for students who were in their late teens or early- to mid-twenties. Young people struggling with racial identity, some with mixed parentage, noted how both autobiographies refer to racism and colorism, revealing painful experiences of rejection or acceptance; the terms *light-skinned* or *high yellow* were constructed in opposition to *dark-skinned* blacks, or *full blood* versus *half-breed* Indians. Observing that white teachers and administrators favored lighter-skinned Indians in the residential schools, some students compared the attempts to de-Indianize indigenous peoples with the dependency fostered on African American schools and education. The cultural genocide and violence of the residential schools, however, is unique to Native Americans. *Lakota Woman* describes this particularly violent assimilation through institutional education:

> The kids were taken away from their villages and pueblos, in their blankets and moccasins, kept completely isolated from their families—sometimes for as long as ten years—suddenly coming back, their short hair slick with pomade, their necks raw from stiff, high collars, their thick jackets always short in the sleeves and pinching under the arms, their tight patent leather shoes giving them corns, the girls in starched white blouses and clumsy, high-buttoned boots—caricatures of white people. When they found out—and they found out quickly—that they were neither wanted by whites nor by Indians, they got good and drunk, many of them staying drunk for the rest of their lives. (30)

Regardless of repression and internal domestic violence, Native and African American women activists consistently advocated a democratic concept of power. In these writings, power stemmed from the people as a collective; it was not reducible to military or intellectual vanguards and elites. The autobiographers criticized centralized, autocratic leadership, arguing instead for a concept of shared, nonhierarchical guidance. As Rigoberta Menchú maintains, "we have understood that each one of us is responsible for the struggle and we don't need leaders who only shuffle paper. We need leaders who are in danger, who run the same risks as the people. When there are many companeros with equal abilities, they must all have the opportunity to lead their struggle" (228). Nonelitist notions of leadership recognize the role of culture in the identity, spirituality, and resistance of a community. Moody describes the inspirational role of music in black-liberation movements: "Listening to those old negroes sing freedom songs was like listening to music from heaven. They sang them as though they were singing away the chains of slavery" (303). Traditional forms of singing and dancing by enslaved Africans and African Americans were banned just as the religious singing and dancing of Native Americans had been; in *Lakota Woman*, Mary Crow Dog recounts indigenous efforts to revive the sun dance (253). Collective leadership and culture, tenaciously shared and renewed, were cementing bonds for women and communities in crisis and resistance.

Radical Visionaries: Building on Community Foundations and Fissures

The concept of community was the most problematic and contentious for the class. Students frequently used the existence of violence within peoples or intraethnic relations to argue the nonexistence of community. Interestingly, student alienation from emotional, physical, and sexual abuse within their families and society (some students volunteered accounts of surviving rape and other abuse) did not lead them to assert the nonexistence of family or society. Yet community in its ideal form supplanted community in its imperfect form. Using the faults of a community as ample reason to negate the possibility of community, class members courted nihilistic pessimism. They argued that in the absence of a realizable ideal, there was nothing for which to strive: struggling to transform flawed communities became unrealistic. Students resigned themselves to viewing social injustices as unchangeable realities. Without the courageous optimism of Moody's struggles found in most of her book, they echoed the pessimism of *Coming of Age in Mississippi*'s concluding paragraphs, which question the efficacy of communal power in the face of state violence and family betrayal.

When students stated that they had no community, belonged to and identified with none, their understanding of past, present, and future relationships were shaped by personal experiences of isolation as well as by a social ideology of individualism. Detailing violence and betrayal in community, the autobiographies presented democratic society as the fundamental task, describing it not only as objective but also vehicle for social transformation: liberation emerged from the unified efforts of people with common, progressive goals. Reflecting on the Native and African American women's perceptions of liberation as a collective enterprise, students worked hard to comprehend the claims made by Davis (and echoed by others) that "individual activity—sporadic and disconnected—is not revolutionary work" (162). In the process, class members began to reexamine their individualism as neither universally applicable to the women activists nor as even uniformly fitting to their own lives: "Many of my attempts to understand and name my community have been frustrated by my individualist education. my tendency has been to try and 'figure out' where i 'fit in,' rather than recognizing that i am already a part of a community, and in actuality, many communities" (JM).

The concept of many communities rather than one exclusive community is also found in the autobiographies. As members of multiethnic political groups, most of the writers present community as expansive and international. At times their political affiliations, such as Davis's (former) membership in the Communist Party USA and Menchú's connection to Comité de Unidad Campesina, did not necessarily embody the cultural and spiritual values of the cultures of their youths. Davis describes an "overwhelming sense of belonging to a community of humans—a community of struggle against poverty and racism" (xvi). Menchú explains that "the important thing is that what has happened to me has happened to many other people too: my story is the story of all poor Guatemalans. My personal experience is the reality of a whole people" (1). For the autobiographers, community is transcendent, unrestricted by color, language, gender, or even conventional time and space. For some such as Davis, it includes ancestors:

> There were visions in my head of my grandmother going to join Harriet Tubman, where she would look down peacefully upon the happenings in this world. Wasn't she being lowered into the same soil where our ancestors had fought so passionately for freedom?

> After her burial the old country lands took on for me an ineffable, awe-inspiring dimension: they became the stage on which the history of my people had been acted out. And my grandmother, in death, became more heroic. I felt a strange kind of unbreakable bond, vaguely religious, with her in that new world that she entered. (82)

A sense of community, independent of oppression, is reflected in Menchú's descriptions of traditional customs:

> So, a mother on her first day of pregnancy goes with her husband to tell these elected leaders that she's going to have a child, because the child will not only belong to them, but to the whole community, and must follow as far as he can our ancestors' traditions. The leaders then pledge the support of the community and say: "We will help you, we will be the child's second parents." (7)

These understandings of community, as well as the sense of accountability to community, called women to and sustained them in political activism. In turn, they became the conduit for students' rethinking their own perceptions of communal relations.

Conclusion

In Gender, Race, and Radicalism, the initial student frustration with unconventional topics, texts, and pedagogy were predictable. Classroom uneasiness, however, gave way to introspection and insight in papers and journal entries. Only the following summer while reading anonymous course evaluations did I find out that most students were deeply affected by our study of the autobiographies of red and black women activists.

Many students were and are survivors of racism, sexism, homophobia, anti-Semitism, and classism. Social violence and/or family abuse had led them to see and represent themselves as victims powerless to effect social change. Initially, students were baffled by the way that women activists kept faith and agency amid oppression. Gradually, through their reflections on the political and spiritual values and collective struggles revealed in the autobiographies, students began to respond to narratives of resistance. Relatively privileged ones had been moved to write:

> Reflecting on the tremendous fears that festered in these communities and served as a constant barrier to [unified resistance] . . . I began

to analyze my own fears which keep me from truly dedicating myself to the struggle against racism. . . . There are two primary fears which I find myself faced with as I work through and analyze my own racism and white privilege. The first is the fear of isolation, of losing support from family and friends for having ideas which are "too radical." The second [is] the fear of moving down the class system. . . . All my life I have been prepared by my family, friends, and a white education system, to stay in the same class level or move up through individual achievement in high school and college in order to *succeed* in a well-paying job. (RG)

Using the course as a channel for examining political commitments that they felt would socially marginalize them, class members who saw themselves as engagé were empowered by the Native and African American women radicals they studied. Without sharing the experiences or political ideologies of the autobiographers, students reaffirmed their commitments to actively and, for some, radically counter racism, heterosexism, sexism, and economic poverty, irrespective of the unpopularity of these politics in the general society. Displaying a resiliency for critical inquiry and self-reflection, some confronted their fears with a resolve to continue their investigations and commitments:

So severe is the reality of political repression, that we at times find ourselves paralyzed by fear and overwhelmed by feelings of hopelessness and grief. the emphasis so often placed on the realities of the oppressions we act to counter can sometimes obscure the fact that the history of oppression is also a history of resistance. it is our connection to this history of resistance, to this history of pain, joy, struggle, strength and freedom, which brings guidance and sustenance to our work. (JM)

Students were not the only ones who found at least partial answers to spoken and unspoken questions. Over the years, I had repeatedly read the autobiographies as well as taught the African American autobiographers in other classes. In the past, I had found these texts to be the most thought-provoking component in courses. In Gender, Race, and Radicalism, however, rather than the literature itself, it was students' use of the memoirs to decipher their own life stories and strengthen a resolve for ethical practice that called me closer to my own beliefs about radicalism. Focusing on the developing critical consciousness of my students, my own vision and paradigm became less cloudy. I was better able to see that in a one-semester journey, student struggles for self and community transformation radicalized the course and shaped our relationships in an academic setting. Although students had repoliticized the classroom, critical questions about radicalism and academic intellectuals remained.

Earlier in the semester when I had encouraged students to differentiate between the radicalisms of the women's autobiographies, they responded by pressing me to give my own political identification: was I a radical or a revolutionary? if so, in what ways? At the time I was unable and unwilling to answer these naming questions, which I had never put to them. In one of our last classes, I finally stated that as an academic I had removed myself from a revolutionary praxis to work within a corporate setting that modifies radical notions of social transformation. Several of my students, disagreeing with my refusal to place myself—as a teacher— on a radical continuum, offered their own assessment of teachers and students who struggle in academic sites:

> There needs to be some criteria for the evaluation of political action that claims to be revolutionary. . . . a revolutionary agenda is one which is able to adequately confront [neo]colonialism and genocide [and one] which can not be co-opted by the oppressive dominant society. We feel however that actions in themselves are not inherently "revolutionary" or "nonrevolutionary"; it is the context in which they occur and their connection to a larger movement for change that determines their revolutionary status. In order for one's action[s] to be revolutionary, they must be consciously connected to a larger movement for revolutionary change. Under this definition, it is possible for even the University professor who makes concessions in order to remain in an academic institution to be contributing to a revolutionary process. (JM and JL)

Conclusion / United Nations Conventions, Antiracist Feminisms, and Coalition Politics

We have had to fight, and still do, for that very visibility which also renders us most vulnerable, our Blackness. For to survive in the mouth of this dragon we call america, we have had to learn this first and most vital lesson—that we were never meant to survive. Not as human beings. And neither were most of you here today, Black or not. And that visibility which makes us most vulnerable is that which also is the source of our greatest strength.
— Audre Lorde, *Sister Outsider*

It is possible to create multi-racial or interracial organizations even in a racist society, but most of the ones I know started that way, with much dialogue between whites and people of color at the outset and a shared commitment to building that kind of group. . . . We struggled as we organized it, and we struggle constantly to insure that it continues as an interracial entity.
— Anne Braden, "Un-Doing Racism: Lessons for the Peace Movement"

Banking on the United Nations

The prognosis for international human rights was grim in 1988, although many felt that the United Nations' covenants and goals for humanity posed an alternative vision and site for creating a just and peaceful society.[1] Understanding that the UN is not a panacea, the supportive critics gave voice to pressing concerns on its fortieth anniversary:

> The call for a new international economic order has not proved to be successful, the terms of trade are constantly deteriorating, the gap between rich and poor countries is growing, we are rapidly destroying our environment and the biologic foundations for our own survival, and millions of human beings die every year from hunger, starvation and warfare. The 40th anniversary of the Universal Declaration should be more a reminder of these facts than a cause for celebration. Otherwise, the international human-rights movement will run the risk of avoiding to tackle the major contemporary threats to human dignity.[2]

Six years later, the tragic, ongoing debacle in Bosnia and Herzegovina, as well as other sites under UN jurisdiction, exemplify its ineffectiveness and either the renegade status or passivity of individual nations.

Human-rights activists have found ample opportunities to be skeptical about the UN's dominant parties. For instance, the unanimous vote on January 24, 1989, by the five permanent members of the security council (the United States, the former Soviet Union, China, Great Britain, and France) to reduce funding for the UN peacekeeping force in Namibia alerted many to the UN's Janus-like characteristics. The council's vote saved millions of dollars but cost a number of lives: cutting the allocation of 7,500 troops at a cost of $700 million to 4,650 troops at $416 million hindered the peaceful transition of Namibia to self-rule and independence from its colonial status as South West Africa. The vote also violated UN Resolution 435, which mandated provisions for UN-protected free elections in Namibia. As a result, scores of Namibians, organizing for the elections or attempting to vote in the transition period, were killed by South African troops or proxies. Namibians died because no one held the UN accountable to its own human-rights covenants and doctrines. One of the greatest stumbling blocks for the UN is its economic dependency on wealthier nations and its relationships with international economic structures such as the World Bank and the International Monetary Fund (IMF).

With 184 member nations, representing over 90 percent of the world population, the UN sponsors anticolonial and progressive politics that are most often traceable to the leadership of the nonaligned nations of the Third World. In the past, the Non Aligned Movement actively called for a New International Economic Order as well as a New International Information Order, positions generally opposed by the United States yet supported by the former Eastern European Socialist bloc as well as the Scandinavian countries. A key contributor to a substantial part of the UN budget (although in arrears for years), the United States carries undue influence within the UN and its security council. By 1989, the United States owed the deficit-ridden UN $401.8 million in back dues. In 1995, it owed $1 billion. A strategy of both the Reagan and Bush administrations was to withhold financial commitments to an international body that, through the Non Aligned Movement and its supporters, routinely condemned American foreign policy for human-rights violations and military and economic aggression.

In the global order, there are ample reasons for censuring the United States, other developed countries, and international economic institutions for their financial dealings in the Third World. Throughout the 1980s, Western underdevelopment and IMF austerity programs worldwide pushed women and children of color deeper into poverty. The Environmental Defense Fund in 1994 cited the World Bank and the debt crisis as largely responsible for income disparities between the richest and poorest nations, which were at a ratio of ten to one in 1948, grew to thirty to one in 1960, and exploded to sixty to one in 1989.[3] UNICEF's 1988 *Report on the State of the World's Children* described how Third World nations were in debt to American and Western European banks for over $1 trillion (U.S. currency), paying to the West more in interest and capital than they received in new aid and loans; these debt repayments comprised about 25 percent of export revenues.[4] African, Caribbean, and Latin American nations annually transfer more than $20 billion to their former colonizers. The growing impoverishment of Africa and Latin America is tied to their underdevelopment maintained by Western nations. According to the UNICEF report, nearly 900 million people, one-sixth of humanity, had sunk deeper into poverty by 1988. These increasing rates of impoverishment, disease, and death occur mostly in Africa and Latin America, where average incomes declined 10 percent to 25 percent in the 1980s, and spending on health and education were reduced 50 percent and 25 percent, respectively. At least half a million young children die each year from debt-induced poverty in these two regions.

The foreign debt, created by national and international elites, is paid predominantly by the poor, working, and middle classes. (For example, as a debtor nation, Haiti allowed U.S. corporations to pay Haitian women $2.40 a day to sew dresses in sweatshops for the Kenwood Corporation, a wholesale distributor to Sears department stores.) Militarism is another integral factor in the foreign debt. In "Defusing the Debt Bomb," Barbara Wein maintains that IMF austerity programs dictate spending cuts in social services but never cuts in military spending; she cites such measures as interference in internal security matters. Wein describes the "Third World debt and its U.S. counterpart" potentially as destabilizing as the arms race; in the 1980s, "world military spending and the Third World debt each total[ed] over $900 billion a year. . . . the global arms build up and the entire international debt are inextricably linked."[5] With unprecedented military spending in the 1980s, the United States became the world's most militarized nation as well as its greatest debtor nation. On November 27, 1994, *Sixty Minutes* reported that with the collapse of the Soviet Union, the United States gained control of 72 percent of the international arms industry—a $22 billion annual trade. Throughout the 1980s, the U.S. government spent approximately $1 billion a year on defense and the military. State officials and commentators warned of the demoralizing effects on U.S. military personnel stationed abroad if military foreign aid were reduced. The deficit-reduction arguments of the neoconservatives and Republicans elected to Congress in 1994 echo Henry Kissinger and Cyrus Vance's pronouncement in 1988 that military spending was sacrosanct and that the domestic sector must tighten its belt: "We must face the fact that our economy and consumption have become so overextended in recent years that the remedies will involve sacrifice and slower growth in our standard of living."[6] These sacrifices, however, were not uniformly shouldered; government policies in the 1980s and early 1990s enriched the wealthy, burdened the middle classes, and constituted a staggering weight for working class and poor people. The portion of the debt financed by the public sector was escalated further by the Pentagon's contract overruns and by financial investors in the savings and loan scandals. Public lands and resources such as housing have been sold, unions broken, and industries deregulated. Austerity programs implemented in the United States have mirrored their international counterparts, resulting in spending cuts in education, housing, health, and job training.

Global and Antiracist Feminisms

Global feminism, a phrase popularized during the UN Decade for Women's Equality (1975-1985), focuses on economic exploitation, racism, sexism, and imperialism, defining each as a women's issue. Women for Racial and Economic Equality (WREE) is a U.S. affiliate of the UN nongovernmental organization (NGO), the Women's International Democratic Federation (WIDF). The WIDF was formed in 1948 by women in the Socialist Bloc to support liberation movements, organize for peace, and work for women's rights. Its sister organizations included the women's groups affiliated with national liberation movements such as the ANC and SWAPO, as well as AMNLAE, the Sandinista Women's organization, El Salvador's FMLN, and Cuba's FMC. For several decades, WREE organized for international human-rights conventions in respect to women's struggles, focusing on U.S. domestic and foreign policy. It played a key role in radical politics at the UN Conferences on the Decade for Women's Equality. The organization's participation in the 1985 conference on women in Kenya was coordinated through the Women's Coalition for Nairobi (WCN), an ad hoc group that WREE had helped to create. At the conference, the WCN organized a petition, eventually obtaining the signatures of the overwhelming majority of U.S. women attendees; more than two thousand U.S. delegates signed a document calling for the American government to support UN resolutions on behalf of women and to end racist and classist practices.

Organizing for human rights, the women delegates faced contradictory reactions to their presence at the 1985 conference. International delegates, walking downtown on the first day of the conference, were greeted by calls from Kenyan women, who thrust their hands and arms from behind barred windows at the women passing by. Someone later explained that the imprisoned women were yelling because they blamed their incarceration on the NGO women's delegations. President Daniel arap Moi ordered the military and police to make sweeps of all women sex workers, including any women working the streets in whatever capacity thought suspicious and even some who were merely walking down the street during the raids. Later, to minimize the embarrassment of the government and the "discomfort" of the international visitors, the Kenyan women who were picked up were transported to detention camps in the countryside until the end of the conference.

There was also ambivalence expressed about coalition politics and critiques of state violence. At two simultaneous rallies, held yards apart in the same outdoor quad, women speakers competed to be heard above each other's amplified speeches. The rally organized by Latina and African American women of the Third World Women's Alliance criticized the economic devastation and physical violence that victimizes women in Latin America, particularly in countries where the United States funds low-intensity conflicts. In the same courtyard, a women-of-color rally sponsored by the National Organization for Women (NOW) focused on a feminist agenda that included more ethnic and racial integration. After the conference, NOW created a position in its national office in Washington, D.C., for women of color, which was headed by an African American woman who participated in both the conference and rally. The differences between these two agendas, however, became increasingly clear.

Toward the close of the conference, the petition was developed and circulated in the Peace Tent. This was a large canvas tent with literature tables and a speaking area with microphone and chairs; it had been funded by wealthy American women as an alternative site to the classrooms and buildings that were occasionally guarded by the Kenyan military. Inside the tent, women described the conditions of their struggles for liberation to various audiences. One day, while members of the WCN and WREE circulated their petition, I watched as an older Argentine woman rose and spoke about the "disappeared" in her community, the death squads, and the kidnapping and possible murder of her granddaughter. As she began to plead with American women to return to their country and work to end U.S. support of terrorist regimes, she was brusquely cut off by the prominent American lesbian feminist Sonia Johnson. Johnson informed the Argentine woman that the point of the Peace Tent was not to hear anti-U.S. propaganda—in other words, critiques of U.S. funding for death squads in El Salvador, contras in Nicaragua and Angola, apartheid in South Africa, and the Israeli occupation of the West Bank and Gaza Strip. When Johnson stated that the "real struggle" was around who "scrubbed the toilets," young white U.S. women (likely the same age of the Argentine woman's granddaughter) applauded and cheered. Ironically, the young women's neophyte state nationalism and patriotism resembled that of Jeane Kirkpatrick, the Reagan administration's delegate to the UN.

Signatures from women in the Peace Tent and at other conference sites were gathered and presented to the U.S. official delegation. Printed in its entirety below, the WCN's petition reflected a radical stance on state violence that is rare in most feminist organizations:

PETITION TO THE U.S. DELEGATION

As U.S. women living in the world's wealthiest industrial-capitalist country, we have an obligation to analyze our conditions of inequality, to single out the obstacles to our progress and chart necessary strategies to insure the implementation of the goals of the Decade—Equality, Development and Peace.

Therefore, we call on the U.S. delegation to the UN Decade For Women Conference, Nairobi, 1985, to support the following positions and demands, as proposed in the document, "The Effects of Racism and Militarization on Women's Equality" (UN Document A/Conf.116/NGO12):

1. SUPPORT all United Nations' initiatives, resolutions and conventions on behalf of women. These include the *Convention on the Elimination of Discrimination Against Women* (to be ratified by the U.S.) and the *Declaration on the Participation of Women in Promoting International Peace and Cooperation.* It is important that the U.S. remain in the UN and participate in the work toward world peace.

2. REDUCE the U.S. military budget and use the released funds for the overall development of society and the equality of women.

3. CURB the activities of the transnational corporations which adversely affect women's employment and conditions of work.

4. RECOGNIZE the key to women's equality as our ability to be economically independent and to be organized into trade unions. Guarantee the basic right of women to equal pay for work of comparable value as well as the right to full employment and a guaranteed income.

5. ELIMINATE all forms of racial oppression and discrimination against women. Support full economic, social and political rights for foreign and undocumented workers.

6. SUPPORT all measures to improve the quality of life for all women, such as the control of police brutality and the right to decent housing, health care and quality education.

7. ELIMINATE sexual violence and insure women's right to choose in matters of sexuality. Create economic, social and legislative guarantees for full reproductive rights, including abortion, freedom from forced sterilization, access to birth control, childbearing, primary

health care, infant care, child care, paid maternity leave, and job and pension guarantees.

8. PROVIDE moral and material aid to women struggling for their democratic and economic rights and national independence in Southern Africa, the Middle East and throughout the world.

9. WORK toward international peace by halting intervention and aggression, withdrawing all nuclear missiles, negotiating bilateral arms control agreements, including stopping the militarization of outer space.[7]

The issues argued in the WCN petition, however, were not always easily sustained as the focal point in multiethnic women's coalitions that followed the UN conference.

It took days to arrange a meeting with the U.S. delegation, headed by Maureen Reagan and Linda Chavez, to present the petition. Negotiating for that meeting, Chavez's entourage had sent a message stating that Maureen Reagan refused to meet with Angela Davis, a WCN member. As governor of California, Ronald Reagan had campaigned to have Davis fired from her teaching position at UCLA and had promised that she would never teach again in a California university, given her affiliations with the Soledad Brothers Defense Committee and the Communist Party. (Reagan had also called for Davis's execution while she was on trial.) After negotiating the composition of the group, date, and time of the meeting, a WCN committee, minus Davis, presented the petition to the U.S. delegation, headed by the president's daughter. Following recommendations from the Heritage Foundation, the Reagan delegation opposed all nine points of the petition.[8]

Women of Color and Black Women's Coalitions

Challenging racial and sexual stereotypes and oppressive structures, people of color have organized collectively as *blacks,* employing this designation as a political term and not as reference to race or skin color. In this context, *black* denotes a multiethnic people in antiracist decolonization struggles. In South African antiapartheid organizations, Africans, Coloreds, and Indians have identified themselves as such; in Britain's antiracism organizations, African Caribbeans and Pakistanis share the same self-designation; and in progressive U.S. academic-activist groups such as the international

Cross-Cultural Institute for Black Women's Studies, Native American, African, Latin, Asian, and Middle Eastern women all identify as black. This political designation neither denies nor minimizes cultural and caste differences, which are usually exacerbated by a reactionary state. Nor can such political language erase ethnic chauvinism or antipathy for blackness.

Crossing color lines for black alliances is fairly tricky. All people of color do not experience racism in the same manner. If the quintessential object of racist hatred under American white supremacy is its antithesis— the black—then clearly not every person of color can share in this blackness and its social denigration. A flight from blackness for nonwhites might be seen as a strategy for establishing their humanity—that is, proving that they are not black. Bridging the gap between polarized subaltern ethnic groups seems to be secondary to black and white or colored and white alliances. Because women generally share the race thinking of their ethnic brothers and are pressured or elect to reproduce racial hierarchies in homes, schools, and communities, alliance building is extremely difficult. Countering state violence requires political language and coalition work that go beyond difference and multiculturalism. Such efforts are embodied in the activism of racially and politically marginalized women who are engaged in transnational organizing.

The Cross-Cultural Institute for Black Women's Studies housed at Medgar Evers College in Brooklyn, New York, is one such group of women. Its sixth international summer institute, held in Caracas, Venezuela, in August 1993 with the theme "The Black Woman: Five Centuries of Resistance and Cultural Affirmation in the Americas," was hosted by La Unión de Mujeres Negras de Venezuela, Cáritas de Panamá, El Movimiento para la Identidad de la Mujer Negra, República Dominicana, and Gelede's Instituto da Mulher Negra, Brasil. The conference, which received funding from UN nongovernmental organizations, offered resolutions advocating positions for black women (defined by the institute as women of Asian, African, indigenous, Latin, and Arab descent) and state politics in the international arena. Conference participants urged women to confront racial discrimination and neoliberalism by focusing on the global economic crisis, capitalist accumulation, and the impoverishment of women, and to condemn genocide, including the medical dangers associated with some UN-sponsored birth-control measures. They also offered expressions of solidarity to women suffering the effects of war; women refugees; the self-

determination struggles of Cuba and Haiti; the Maori nation, which is petitioning the New Zealand government to honor the Treaty of Waitangi
for the Maori nation of Aoetearoa; women in resistance in South Africa;
Hawaiian initiatives for self-governance; and Nigeria's self-determination.

The recognition of the importance of spirituality and religion and the
difference between the two was considered pressing, as was the "urgent
need for information on indigenous spirituality as a source of empowerment" and the need to document and educate about African religions during the era of American slavery. The institute also recommended that all
black women's organizations facilitate the development of spirituality, recognizing both the role that traditional belief systems played in resistance to
enslavement and the sexist and racist structures within contemporary religions. It also addressed the issue of education and culture, denouncing
racist and sexist language and advocating alternative teaching through
storytelling, informal schools, and home schools. The institute's position
paper argued for black women's resistance to oppression that encompassed
developing strategies to deal with contemporary economic and cultural
imperialism; redefining spirituality as part of black women's feminism;
linking self-empowerment with community well-being rather than individualism; and organizing educational projects about violence and sexual
trafficking. In advocating human rights and coalitions, the institute denounced the U.S. blockade against Cuba and urged solidarity between
Africans and indigenous people in the Americas, particularly in respect to
struggles to regain indigenous control of native lands.

The following year at MIT in January 1994, participants in a conference titled "Black Women in the Academy: Defending Our Name, 1894–
1994," issued a petition to President Clinton, stating that "86 percent of
black women who voted, voted for the Democratic Party ticket which
brought you and Hillary Rodham Clinton to the White House and a
Democratic Congress to Washington in 1992."[9] As the conference women
and men noted, this "was the largest proportion of any constituency to
vote for your administration." With copies sent to the black, women's, and
Hispanic caucuses of the Congress, attendees urged the Clinton administration to commission a blue-ribbon panel on race relations, based on the
1968 Kerner report and its 1988 review of a polarized society. Leaders of the
conference maintained that the "new panel must be cognizant of the myriad new realities of race in America, and must present recommendations to

alleviate the continuing injuries of racism, sexism and homophobia." The administration was asked to promote research on black women for "the well-being of African American communities" and to extend the mandate of the "Glass-Ceiling Commission to explore issues of career advancement for women of color in higher education." Increased funding for community-based service organizations for poor black families was also requested: "We stress the need to extend economic empowerment and development programs, support services, health care, housing, child care and education. Women in prison, those with AIDS, and in crisis need special attention." Concerning U.S. foreign policy, calls to end antidemocratic covert actions against Haiti and restore Jean-Bertrand Aristide to the presidency; to lift the embargo against Cuba; to support the democratic process in South and southern Africa; and to continue aid for Somalia, completed the petition endorsed by the more than two thousand mostly black women (and some men) who attended the conference.

Like the Cross-Cultural Institute for Black Women's Studies and the Black Women in the Academy conference, the Empowering Women of Color Conference in California advocated new domestic and foreign policies with objectives specified by antiracist and antisexist organizing. One keynote speaker for the MIT conference, Angela Davis (others were Lani Guinier and Johnnetta B. Cole), also spoke at the 1995 conference, "Reaping Fruit, Throwing Seed," held at the University of California at Berkeley in April. In her 1995 address, Davis urged activists to expand the possibilities of coalitions, particularly those between welfare-rights and lesbian, gay, and bisexual organizations, given that conservatives have targeted such types of groups as antithetical to so-called family values. She also suggested that because California's anti-immigrant Proposition 187 demands strict documentation that turns colleges and universities into "sites of surveillance," coalitions between teachers, students, immigrants, and immigrant-rights advocates were necessary. Likewise, Davis identified the need for partnerships between prisoners and students because California's leadership has begun to channel funds from education to prison construction and incarceration. In 1995, California had twenty-nine prisons (twenty of which were constructed in the past ten years); the state now boasts the world's third-largest prison industry, after two nations, the United States and China. Women (predominately poor Native, African, Latina, Pacific Islander, and Chicana) are entering prisons at twice the rate of men. The inequities in sentencing and the privatization and exploitation of prison labor for corporate industries, therefore, provide central issues for both feminists and antiracists to address.

Countering Violence with UN *Human-Rights Conventions*

The U.S. government is clearly drifting from the progressivism of international covenants opposing genocide, racism, and sexism. The majority of Supreme Court justices, particularly the Reagan and Bush appointees, predictably have restricted privacy and abortion rights, the Bill of Rights, and civil-rights legislation. Before the Court's unprecedented 1995 rulings that struck down key legislative acts mostly dealing with civil rights, there had been considerable speculation on the conservative activism of a court hostile to liberalism, one that some argued also showed hostility to racial equality.

On January 23, 1989, the Supreme Court voted down the city of Richmond, Virginia's plan to award 30 percent of its public contracts to people of color. Contending that "racial classifications are suspect," Justice Sandra Day O'Connor wrote the majority opinion, proclaiming that Richmond's affirmative-action program discriminates against whites. ("Sexual classifications" or "set asides" for women to redress past sexist discrimination in hiring or promotion have not been condemned as "suspect" as have "racial classifications.") Responding to the majority, Justice Thurgood Marshall issued the dissenting opinion:

> Today's decision marks a deliberate and giant step backward in this Court's affirmative action jurisprudence. . . . [the] majority of this Court signals that it regards racial discrimination as largely a phenomenon of the past, and that government bodies need no longer preoccupy themselves with rectifying racial injustice. I, however, do not believe this nation is anywhere close to eradicating racial discrimination or its vestiges. In constitutionalizing its wishful thinking, the majority today does a grave disservice not only to those victims of past and present racial discrimination in this nation whom government has sought to assist, but also to this Court's long tradition of approaching issues of race with the utmost sensitivity.[10]

But the Court's "long tradition of approaching issues of race with the utmost sensitivity" had been broken several years prior. The most notable departure from the progressivism of the Warren Court was the reinstitution of the death penalty despite its often racist applications.

Political observers in the late 1980s had cautioned progressives to seek other vehicles besides federal law to guarantee civil and human rights. In a January 16, 1989, interview on WBAI, District of Columbia Congresswoman Eleanor Holmes Norton stated that, given the conservative composition of the federal judiciary, women and African Americans should turn to state and local laws to secure rights.[11] In the states-rights movement and the so-called new federalism, however, which in 1995 turned over Medicare and welfare supervision to local state governments, neoconservatives and rightists have sought to repeal civil-rights legislation, ban abortion, limit federal jurisdiction over the environment, as well as eviscerate standards of economic decency for the poor and labor practices.

Irrespective of the difficulties in politically conservative times, progressives continue to advocate a literacy in political and moral language based on human-rights conventions. Organizations such as the Center for Constitutional Rights provide pamphlets such as "An Activist's Guide: Bringing International Human Rights Claims in United States Courts." Organizations and NGOs, including the League of Women Voters, the National Council of Churches, and approximately one thousand consultant groups continue to lobby UN representatives for humanitarian projects and policies. For instance, the NGO Human Rights Advocates sponsored the first gay and lesbian group as consultants to the UN. Both the National Conference of Black Lawyers and the International Indian Treaty Council have petitioned the UN on human-rights violations. In 1986, Mayor Marcia Walker and city clerk Kathleen P. Salisbury signed Ordinance 2807 of the Burlington, Iowa City Council, effecting the Convention on the Elimination of Racial Discrimination as law. The city council amended its human-rights ordinance, with the assistance of law professors Francis Boyle and Burns H. Weston, to bring it into compliance with the convention, believing that ratification by cities and towns supports a base for the eventual passage of UN conventions in state assemblies and the U.S. Senate.[12]

Various organizations seek the enforcement of the UN conventions and charter as *the* language of rights in the United States. In January 1989, four years after the Women's Coalition for Nairobi and WREE presented their petition to the U.S. government, WREE, through its WIDF international affiliate, petitioned the UN Commission on Human Rights in Geneva on violations against American women of color. In their testimony to the commission, members of WREE and WIDF argued that the United States violates Articles 2 and 25 of the Universal Declaration of Human Rights and Article 55 of the UN charter "as regards the institutionalized racism against women, children and families of the national and ethnic minorities" in America:

> Black, Latin, Asian, Native American and women workers suffer a disproportionately higher loss of jobs in the higher-wage basic industries and face more intense discrimination in hiring for new jobs as well as systematic exclusion from skilled positions. Union-busting is common practice by corporate America and federal equal pay provisions are violated with impunity. The corporations establish unequal pay for the same position, pay minimum wages for extended periods of time by demanding longer probationary periods. They lay off at will in order to deny benefits to experienced workers, who are then readmitted as "new hires" at the lowest, starting wage.[13]

The rights of U.S. prisoners have also been raised in the international forum. Amnesty International documents more than one hundred political prisoners incarcerated in the United States. Two of the longest held are Native American Leonard Peltier and African American Elmer "Geronimo" Pratt, activists in the American Indian Movement and the Black Panther Party, respectively. Their imprisonments' link to COINTELPRO suggests the continuity of a police policy. Having prosecuted and convicted such prisoners on criminal charges, the U.S. government denies that it has political prisoners. By criminalizing political resistance, the U.S. government can continue to delegitimize radicalism, shifting the focus away from state-mandated violence. In February 1989 and 1990, members of Freedom Now: National Campaign for Amnesty and Human Rights for Political Prisoners, accredited through the Indigenous World Organization, traveled to Geneva to petition the UN Commission under Article 10, which concerns the human rights of detained or imprisoned persons. Freedom Now testimony to the commission stated that more than "150 persons [are] . . . incarcerated in U.S. prisons because of their exercise of the rights to freedom of expression and association, and to self-determination and freedom from racial oppression and alien domination."[14] Spokespersons also contended that "once incarcerated, virtually every political activist in the U.S. is subjected to extremely harsh conditions of confinement, including designation to 'behavior modification' units employing sensory deprivation techniques, such as those at Marion, Illinois, Shawangunk, New York, Marianna, Florida and Lexington, Kentucky." Although some control units have been closed, activists maintain that new units have been opened at other prisons. According to Freedom Now representatives, in 1989 the U.S. delegation walked out during testimony excerpted below:

> Phenomenal material progress has been built upon three gross and well-documented violations of human rights: the dispossession and disenfranchisement of Indigenous Peoples, the kidnapping and enslavement of Africans and their transportation to the United States, and the imposition of United States rule in Puerto Rico. This material progress has produced two U.S. societies, separate but connected, yet drifting ever further apart. One society is overwhelmingly white, collectively possessed of great wealth, with few restrictions on political, economic and social opportunity. The second group, disproportionately peopled by those of color, face tremendous barriers to political, economic and social development.[15]

Coalitions such as that between Freedom Now and the Indigenous World Organization are not unusual, although they are not often documented or discussed outside the circles of activists directly engaged in human-rights organizing.

Activism in New York, for example, shows how UN human-rights efforts have trickled down to the local government level. In the 1990s an alternative high school, Brooklyn's El Puente School, was developed as a human-rights theme school. In 1993, New York Assemblyman Roger Greene formed an independent party, the Children First Party, based on UN conventions on the rights of children (which the United States has not yet ratified), to focus on legislation dealing with children's needs and rights. Also in 1993, the New York-based Center for Constitutional Rights used statutes of international law in arguing its case for Dianna Ortiz, the American nun who was tortured and raped by Guatemalan death squads reportedly funded by the United States.

In addition, there are coalitions between women's groups and the U.S. government concerning UN conventions on women. For example, in October 1994 the Assistant Secretary of Human Rights reported at a national conference covered by C-SPAN that the Clinton administration is working to ratify the Convention on the Elimination of All Forms of Discrimination against Women (CEDAW) in the U.S. Senate. According to Margaret Wadstein, a former rapporteur of the UN Committee on the Elimination of Discrimination Against Women, the convention was adopted by the General Assembly in December 1979, implemented in September 1981, and is one of the most widely ratified international conventions.[16] The committee staff in Vienna, which supports and monitors states in their enforcement of the convention, however, is hampered by insufficient time and persons to review reports and make recommendations (21). States also make reservations contradictory to the intent of the convention and file incomplete and untimely reports. Article 2 of the convention mandates that states, through legislation countering discrimination, "embody the principle of equality between women and men in their national constitution," offer legal protection to women, and "modify or abolish existing laws, regulations, customs, and practices discriminating against women" (10). The convention was created to cover direct and indirect discrimination, yet its enforcement is tenuous, according to Wadstein, who notes that CEDAW does not make obligatory "positive action, preferential treatment, or quota systems for women," unlike the UN Convention on the Elimination of Racial Discrimination (9). In the absence of a timetable and obligatory positive action, states are free to set their own standards for progress (9). Introduced into the U.S. Congress on November 12, 1980, CEDAW surpasses the ill-fated Equal Rights Amendment of the 1970s in its guarantees to poor and working-class women and women of color. It defines and prohibits discrimination while guaranteeing basic human rights and freedom; it prohibits trafficking in women through prostitution; it guarantees the right to nationality (which conceivably applies to language and culture, criminalizing the English Only movement). Its provisions for equal-employment rights include pay equity, health protection and safety, social security, and prohibition against dismissal for pregnancy or marital status. The convention also guarantees the right to vote. Finally, CEDAW challenges the Supreme Court's ruling on affirmative action because it grants "temporary special measures to accelerate women's equity"; in other words, affirmative-action programs are not reverse discrimination under this international law.

Conclusion: Instrumental Politics—Power to the Community

In expanding the focus of progressive coalitions toward communities, the practice of power is key. Resistance presupposes power, just as domination presupposes violence. If power is not a synonym for domination, then there are possibilities for social transformation without violence. Those who differentiate between power and domination in order to link power to communal goals for social and cultural freedoms, economic sufficiency, and radical democracy posit a vision of political community as the context for human development. Recognizing the diverse experiences and powers of oppressed peoples is essential in order to challenge subordination and exploitation. Viable political communities reflect the diversity and plurality of humanity. With foundations in justice and equity, a law of human rights posits one humanity: the right to participate in self-governance, to experience freedom, to live without violence and economic degradation. The ideals of freedom and community contribute to political power as an expression of humanity. Relationships are determinant; our common need for others means that it is in our interest to collectively carry on the seemingly endless struggle for justice and antiviolence measures.

Civil-rights activist Ella Baker's pronouncement that "strong people don't need a strong leader" speaks to our obvious need for each other as leaders, learners, and activists. Struggle for more than survival in sites where we are disciplined and discipline ourselves in conformity requires nonconventional education, political formations, and critiques for democratic community. The quality of political community and democracy depends on resistance to violence and state malfeasance. Resistance means that we must confront our fear. The fear of being perceived as and punished for ideological radicalism and nonpatriotism leads to a choreography of conventionality in which one sidesteps the labels of militant, communist, feminist (particularly *radical* feminist), queer, polemical, or ethnic nationalist. Despite the intimidations of political marginalization, despair, and the factionalism of coalition cross fire, many choose to organize for democratic policies and politically and economically egalitarian communities. And in their movements, which become resistance, they see and create beauty that merits risk-taking commitments.

Notes

Introduction

1. Aijaz Ahmad, *In Theory: Classes, Nations and Literatures* (London: Verso, 1992), 2.
2. Barbara Christian, "A Race for Theory," *Cultural Critique* 6 (Spring 1987): 51–63.
3. Ralph Miliband, *The State in Capitalist Society* (New York: Basic Books, 1969).
4. For the debates on state power between Miliband, who emphasizes state elites and a ruling class, and Nicos Poulantzas, who focuses on systems and structures of domination, see Nicos Poulantzas, "The Problem of the Capitalist State," *New Left Review* 58 (November-December 1969): 67–78; Ralph Miliband, "The Capitalist State: Reply to Nicos Poulantzas," *New Left Review* 59 (January-February 1970): 53–60; Ralph Miliband, "Poulantzas and the Capitalist State," *New Left Review* 62 (November-December 1973): 83–92.

Catharine MacKinnon's *Toward a Feminist Theory of the State* (Cambridge, Mass.: Harvard University Press, 1989) offers a feminist analysis missing from the above works; MacKinnon, however, makes little use of critical race theory. Presentations by black feminists at the "Race, the State, and Creating the National Subject" panel at the April 1994 Race Matters conference, Princeton University, raised issues of control, repression, and democracy that are often left unaddressed: in particular, see Kimberle Crenshaw, "Doctrine, Distribution, and Determinations: The Problem of Race Blindness and Social Vision on the Supreme Court"; Angela Davis, "Race and Criminalization: Black Americans and the Punishment Industry"; and Patricia Williams, "The Rooster's Egg."

5. See, e.g., Bread for the World, *Hunger in America* (Washington, D.C.: Bread for the World, 1985).
6. National Public Radio, 21 November 1994.
7. Thomas Edsall and Mary Edsall, *Chain Reaction* (New York: W. W. Norton, 1991), 119–220.
8. Jason DeParle, "Census Report Sees Incomes in Decline and More Poverty," *New York Times*, 7 October 1994, A1.
9. Quoted in Edsall and Edsall, *Chain Reaction*, 221.
10. An African American serving a life sentence without parole for murder in Massachusetts, Horton disappeared on a weekend work furlough in 1986. In 1987 he was recaptured and tried for breaking into the home of Clifford Barnes and Angela Miller, binding and cutting Barnes multiple times and raping Miller several times. Barnes later escaped from his assailant and contacted the police. Horton's rape of Miller, a white woman, was easily sensationalized for electoral gains given its fit with old mythology; if Horton had been accused of victimizing a black woman, the outrage over the violence would likely not have been so pronounced.
11. Marlon Riggs, "Meet the New Willie Horton," *New York Times*, 6 March 1992.
12. Cited in Steven Greenhouse, "Helms Takes New Swipe at Clinton, Then Calls It Mistake," *New York Times*, 23 November 1994, A19.
13. From January 1992 to December 1994, there were 151 homophobia-motivated murders in twenty-nine states and the District of Columbia. These killings, like racist killings, were usually marked by "overkill," defined as four or more gunshots or stab wounds or the repeated use of

blunt objects. The racial breakdown of the overkilled victims was 71 percent of "Hispanics," 63 percent of blacks, 52 percent of whites. The Federal Bureau of Investigation (FBI) lists these motivations for hate-crime victims in 1993: 62 percent racial bias; 18 percent religious bias; 12 percent sexual-orientation bias; 8 percent ethnic bias. David W. Dunlap, "Survey on Slayings of Homosexuals Finds High Violence and Low Arrest Rate," *New York Times,* 21 December 1994, A10. By 1995, according to the National Abortion Rights Action League (NARAL), five physicians or staff members were killed and seven wounded in abortion clinics.

14. Derrick Z. Jackson, "The Wrong Face on Crime," *Boston Globe,* 19 August 1994, 19.

15. Reported by the Baltimore Metropolitan Chapter of the National Black Women's Health Project (NBWHP) and the Maryland Physicians' Campaign against Family Violence in their domestic-violence brochure distributed at the June 1995 NBWHP conference in Baltimore.

16. Statistics are reported in Emilie Buchwald, Pamela R. Fletcher, and Martha Roth, eds., *Transforming a Rape Culture* (Minneapolis: Milkweed Editions, 1993).

17. Film critic Armond White notes in a 1991 *City Sun* article that "the black" is often synonymous with the corporeal body: in a review of *Ferris Bueller's Day Off* and *Houseparty I,* he writes that the films respectively depict how white youth control property whereas black youth control their bodies.

18. John T. McQuiston, "Colin Ferguson Convicted of L.I.R.R. Train Massacre," *New York Times,* 18 February 1995, A1, A10.

19. "Under Scrutiny with Jane Wallace," televised 27 April 1995.

20. See Clayborne Carson's foreword to Philip S. Foner, ed., *Black Panthers Speak* (New York: Da Capo Press, 1995).

21. National Public Radio, 6 July 1995.

22. David M. Shoup's remarks were taken from a poster displayed at the United Methodist Seminars on International and National Affairs, New York City.

23. From Gertrude Stein, *How Writing Is Written* (1935), quoted in Sara Halpirn, *Look at My Ugly Face* (New York: Viking Press, 1995).

1 / Erasing the Spectacle of Racialized State Violence

1. Michel Foucault, *Discipline and Punish: The Birth of the Prison* (New York: Vintage Press, 1979), 7.

2. A 1994 television documentary by Michael Moore, producer of *Roger and Me,* illustrated how in the American mind criminality is constructed as a racial marker. The producers videotaped an African American middle-class man attempting to hail a taxicab while a block behind him a European American man, an ex-convict who had served lengthy jail sentences for violent crimes, also tried to hail the same cabs. Overwhelmingly, the taxi drivers bypassed the black man to pick up the white man. In this racialized society, white convicts (and ex-convicts) exhibit a higher social status than black noncriminals and criminals. Whiteness exculpates and signifies the "normal," just as blackness implicates and marks deviance. In addition, individual whites who depart from the legal norm still retain normative standing through their group status.

3. Frantz Fanon, "The Negro and Psychopathology," in his *Black Skins, White Masks,* trans. Charles Lam Markmann (New York: Grove Press, 1967), 170.

4. See, e.g., Frantz Fanon, *Black Skins, White Masks;* Sander Gilman, *Difference and Pathology: Stereotypes of Sexuality, Race, and Madness* (Ithaca, N.Y.: Cornell University Press, 1985).

5. Paula Giddings, *When and Where I Enter: The Impact of Black Women on Race in America* (New York: Vintage, 1986), 79.

6. Center for Law and Social Justice, "Black Women under Siege by New York City Police" (Brooklyn, N.Y.: Medgar Evers College Center for Law and Justice, 1988).

7. Ward Churchill and Jim Vander Wall, *Agents of Repression: The FBI's Secret Wars against the Black Panther Party and the American Indian Movement* (Boston: South End Press, 1988).

8. Peter Breggin, "The 'Violence Initiative'—A Racist Biomedical Program for Social Control," *Rights Tenet* (Summer 1992): 3–8.

9. Mumia Abu-Jamal, *Live from Death Row* (Reading, Mass.: Addison-Wesley, 1995), 3; Abu-Jamal quotes Camus's *Reflections on the Guillotine.*

10. Convicted of killing a white man, Alpha Otis Stephens was executed in Georgia in December 1984 during a Federal Appeals Court review of cases alleging racism in Georgia's application of the death-penalty statute. Stephens had made appeals to the U.S. Supreme Court in 1983 for a stay of execution pending the resolution of one of the race cases before the appeals court. Suddenly and without explanation, the Supreme Court lifted the stay in November 1984. Stephens's lawyers believe that the decision was due to a technicality and that Stephens should have raised the racial-bias issue earlier in his appeals process. Amnesty International, *USA: The Death Penalty Briefing* (London: Amnesty International, 1988).

11. Representative Joseph Kennedy (Dem., Mass.) has introduced HR 2652 to close SOA and convert it to an academy for democracy and civil-military relations.

12. Gerald M. Boyd, "Reagan Terms Nicaraguan Rebels 'Moral Equal of Founding Fathers,'" *New York Times,* 2 March 1985, A1, A4; Joel Brinkley, "Rights Report on Nicaragua Cites Recent Rebel Atrocities," *New York Times,* 6 March 1985, A10.

13. Tim Weiner, "U.S. Judge Orders Ex-Guatemala General to Pay $47.5 Million," *New York Times,* 13 April 1995. The presidential panel, the Intelligence Oversight Board, issued a sixty-seven-page report on CIA funding for Guatemalan military officers linked to assassinations and torture. See also Tim Weiner, "Panel Faults C.I.A. on Hiring Violent Agents in Guatemala," *New York Times,* 29 June 1996, A1.

14. Commission on Integrated Long-Term Strategy. *Discriminate Deterrence* (Washington, D.C.: Department of Defense, 1988).

15. *Discriminate Deterrence* sought a bipartisan context to establish a metaparadigm for U.S. foreign (and domestic) policies, providing continuity between Republican and Democratic administrations. Former secretaries of state in the Nixon, Ford, and Carter administrations, Henry Kissinger and Cyrus Vance, advocated a political centrism of continuities and urged a closing of ranks between parties and branches of government to achieve "common policy objectives" and "domestic consensus." Calls for domestic downsizing of social benefits and programs accompanied the call to minimize distinctions between the two parties in foreign-policy initiatives, as Kissinger and Vance argued that "weaknesses of the U.S. economy may be among the most serious and urgent foreign policy challenges. . . . equitable budget reductions, must be applied quickly if we are to halt the erosion of our international position." (Henry Kissinger and Cyrus Vance, "Bipartisan Objectives for American Foreign Policy," *Foreign Affairs* (Summer 1988), 910. See also Commission on Integrated Long-Term Strategy, *Discriminate Deterrence.*)

Following this line of political thought, George Bush's inaugural address called for increased bipartisanship in a nation with more "will than wallet."

16. Michael Klare, "Low-Intensity Conflict: The War of the 'Haves' against the 'Have-nots,'" *Christianity and Crisis,* 1 February 1988, 12.

17. George J. Church, "Lying Down with Dogs," *Time,* 17 October 1994, 26–29.

18. Hannah Arendt, *The Human Condition* (Chicago: University of Chicago Press, 1958), 234.

2 / Radicalizing Language and Law: Genocide, Discrimination, and Human Rights

An earlier version of this essay appeared in *Marxism in the Postmodern Age,* ed. Antonio Callari, Stephen Cullenberg, and Carole Biewener (New York: Guilford Press, 1995), 115–25.

1. Delmo Della-Dora, *What Curriculum Leaders Can Do about Racism* (pamphlet), 1970.

2. National Education Association, *Education and Racism* (pamphlet), 1973.

3. William Patterson, ed., *We Charge Genocide: The Crime of Government against the Negro People, a Petition to the United Nations* (New York: Civil Rights Congress, 1951), xi.

4. Francis Boyle, "The Hypocrisy and Racism behind the Formulation of U.S. Human Rights Foreign Policy," *Social Justice* 16, no. 1 (Spring 1989): 71–87.

5. Ward Churchill, "Crimes against Humanity," *Z Magazine,* March 1993, 24.

6. Statistics of white and nonwhite life expectancy come from National Urban League, *State of Black America* (New York: National Urban League, 1988). Figures on Native American life expectancy are cited in Churchill, "Crimes against Humanity," 46.

7. Manning Marable, *How Capitalism Underdeveloped Black America* (Boston: South End Press, 1983), 253.

8. Carl Freedman, "Louisiana Duce: Notes toward a Systematic Analysis of Postmodern Fascism in America," *Rethinking Marxism* 5 (Spring 1992): 26.

9. Slavoj Žižek, "The 'Theft of Enjoyment,'" *Village Voice,* 18 May 1993, 30–31.

10. Michael Lerner, "Jews Are Not White," *Village Voice,* 18 May 1993, 33–34.

11. The extent to which black rage preoccupies white America was evident in discourse surrounding the O. J. Simpson case. On October 3, 1995, on the eve of the verdict announcement, National Public Radio aired an interview with a resident of Los Angeles who stated that if Simpson were convicted, "members of the black race" angry with the government would "want to get back" at the government or police, but because neither "would be around," blacks would take out their aggression on whites.

12. Anti-Semitism has historically inspired state pogroms and genocide as well as individual criminality in racist killings. For example, Richard Snell, who was allegedly avenged in the Oklahoma City bombing, killed a black highway patrolman and a white man whom he misidentified as Jewish. Today, white supremacist killings occur sporadically in the United States, whereas in the unified Germany Jewish cemeteries and dark-skinned foreigners are the targets of violent assaults. Anti-Semitism is still part of American culture. Take, for instance, the "good intentions" of the Mormon Church, whose members believed that non-Mormons should have the chance to become Mormons in the afterlife. According to an April 28, 1995, report aired on National Public Radio, following protests Mormon leaders gave up performing posthumous baptisms of Jews killed in German concentration camps, after having baptized some 350,000 people who, as one Jewish leader noted, likely died with the words of the Torah on their lips.

13. There are a number of unanswered questions concerning the relationship of black antipathy for Jews to anti-Semitism in the general U.S. culture: to what degree does this antipathy express antiwhite sentiment as a backlash to Jewish antiblack racism? to what extent do opportunistic black demagogues fuel anti-Jewish bigotry among African Americans? and what permits black anti-Semitism to be depicted as more pervasive and virulent than white anti-Semitism?

14. Cited in David Barsamian, "Information Control and the State: An Interview with Noam Chomsky," *Radical America* 22, no. 2–3 (1988): 32.

15. Peter Fitzpatrick, "Racism and the Innocence of Law," in *Anatomy of Racism,* ed. David Theo Goldberg (Minneapolis: University of Minnesota Press, 1990), 249.

16. Alisa Solomon, "An American Tragedy? The Holocaust Museum Shapes Up for Domestic Consumption," *Village Voice,* 11 May 1993, 35–36.

17. Fitzpatrick, "Racism and the Innocence of Law," 250–51.

18. Boyle, "The Hypocrisy and Racism behind the Formulation of U.S. Human Rights Foreign Policy," 76–78.

19. Ibid., 82.

3 / Hunting Prey: The U.S. Invasion of Panama

1. An earlier version of this article appeared in *Race and Class* 32, no. 1 (1990): 17–32. I gathered information in part through a visit to Panama in November 1989. The Center for International Political Studies, a research organization affiliated with the University of Panama, sponsored the International Conference against Aggression in Central America: The Case of Panama, November 26–28, 1989, Panama City. Topics included low-intensity conflicts; narcotrafficking and money laundering; political and economic effects of U.S. sanctions against Panama; human rights; and violations of the Torrijos-Carter treaties. Over a hundred U.S. citizens including elected state and city representatives, university professors, trade unionists, clergy, and activists participated.

Stopped in New York City's La Guardia Airport on reentry from Panama some weeks before the invasion, I was interrogated by a plainclothed agent and experienced one of my first political hassles due to foreign travel. This was mild compared to the grilling experienced by activists and educators returning from El Salvador, Guatemala, Cuba, and Nicaragua. For example, in 1994 a Chicana academic colleague was strip-searched by officials from the Immigration and Naturalization Service in Dallas's international airport upon her return from Cuba via Mexico.

2. Isabel de Del Resonio, interview by author, Panama City, Panama, 26–28 November 1989.

3. Ibid.

4. "Lawyers for Noriega Say He Was Paid $10 Million to Spy for U.S.," *New York Times*, 27 October 1994, A12.

5. Senate Subcommittee on Foreign Relations, *Drugs, Law Enforcement and Foreign Policy*, 100th Cong., 2nd Sess., 1988.

6. More than $250 million was approved for 1990 drug-control programs in Colombia ($90 million), Peru ($70 million), and Bolivia ($97 million). The *Los Angeles Times* reported in 1990 that at least six U.S. agencies are involved in drug enforcement in the Andean countries, including the CIA, DEA, and the State Department. So-called U.S. advisers led Peruvian troops in a "frontal assault" military operation in Peru in raids on supposed jungle cocaine labs, using nine U.S.-piloted Huey UH-I helicopters, armed with twin M-60 machine guns on the doors, and ferry units of six Peruvian police officers and two DEA agents. The *Washington Post* ran articles describing how DEA-fortified military bases are located in the heart of Shining Path territories, while U.S. troops are deployed to secure areas to train the Peruvian military in its war against the Sendero Luminoso guerrillas.

7. Allen R. Myerson, "American Express Bank Unit Settles U.S. Laundering Case," *New York Times*, 21 November 1994, A1.

8. According to Waltraud Queiser Morales, of the DEA's 1987 estimated retail value of illegal drugs, $150 billion, most profits accrued to U.S. or Western European banks, while source countries in Latin America received only 10 percent of the drug profits. Colombia, for instance, which refined 75 percent of the cocaine distributed on U.S. streets, received $1 to $2 billion in foreign exchange from drug profits in 1987. Waltraud Queiser Morales, "The War on Drugs: A New U.S. National Security Doctrine?" *Third World Quarterly* 3 (July 1989): 147–64.

9. Senate Subcommittee, *Drugs, Law Enforcement and Foreign Policy*.

10. Vince Bielski and Dennis Bernstein, "NSC, CIA and Drugs: The Cocaine Connection," *Covert Action Information Bulletin*, 28 (Summer 1987).

11. See Bielski and Bernstein, "NSC, CIA and Drugs"; Christic Institute, "Inside the Shadow Government," declaration of plaintiffs' counsel, filed by Christic Institute, U.S. District Court, Miami, 31 March 1987.

12. See 1986 executive session of the Iran-Contra hearings; Bielski and Bernstein, "NSC, CIA and Drugs."

13. Ministerio de Planificación Política Económica, *Lo Que Ha Hecho El Proceso Revolucionario por Nuestro País* (Panama City: MPPE, 1989).

14. Peter H. Herlihy, "Panama's Quiet Revolution: Comarca Homelands and Indian Rights," *Cultural Survival Quarterly* 13, no. 3 (1989): 17–24.

15. "In Panama, a New Day Arouses Old Soldiers," *New York Times,* 9 October 1994, Y5.

16. Interview by author, Panama City, Panama, 26–28 November, 1989.

17. Herlihy, "Panama's Quiet Revolution."

18. Ibid.

19. Del Resonio, interview.

20. Ibid.

21. John Weeks and Andrew Zimbalist, "The Failure of Intervention in Panama: Humiliation in the Backyard," *Third World Quarterly* (January 1989).

22. Interview by author, Panama City.

23. Weeks and Zimbalist, "The Failure of Intervention in Panama."

24. Letter from Assistant Secretary J. E. Fox of the State Department to Senator Jesse Helms, 26 March 1987, in author's papers.

25. Those temporary detention camps proved problematic: on December 8, 1994, approximately one thousand Cuban refugees injured 120 U.S. soldiers in fighting at a camp. Several hundred commandeered a civilian food truck, broke through the camp gates, and damaged military vehicles. Those hospitalized included eighteen U.S. soldiers and twelve Cubans. The United States detained about 8,600 Cubans in Panama and 22,000 at the U.S. naval base in Guantánamo Bay, Cuba. Suicide attempts were reported early in 1995 as the American agreement with Panama to house detainees neared its expiration date and plans were made to ship the remaining 7,600 refugees to Guantánamo Bay in February.

26. R. Harris, "Out of the Clouds: Secret Stealth Fighter Used in Panama Raid Gets More Exposure," *Wall Street Journal,* 27 December 1989, A1, A8.

27. "Military Lessons of the Invasion," *U.S. News and World Report,* 8 January 1990, 22.

28. Harris, "Out of the Clouds."

29. Ibid.

30. David E. Pitt, "US Is Releasing Invasion Captives," *New York Times,* 19 January 1990, A14.

31. Ibid.

32. Center for Constitutional Rights, "On Anniversary of U.S. Invasion: Five Years Later," *CCR News,* 5 (Fall 1994).

33. "In Panama, a New Day Arouses Old Soldiers."

34. Even venerable media spokespersons were appalled by state restrictions and control of the media during the Gulf bombings. Walter Cronkite described the government and military censorship of the press during the Gulf War as "an absolute abomination and miscarriage of democracy," in a National Public Radio interview aired on May 22, 1995.

35. Frederick Kempe, "The Noriega Files," *Newsweek,* 15 January 1990, 19–24.

36. Center for Constitutional Rights, "On Anniversary of U.S. Invasion."

37. FUMCA, *Porque Las Mujeres Somos Parte de Esta Lucha* (pamphlet).

38. International Conference against Aggression in Central America. See note 1 above.

4 / The Color(s) of Eros: Cuba as American Obsession

1. Gabriel García Márquez, *CUBA Update* 3 (Summer 1994).

2. Interracial Foundation for Community Organizing—Pastors for Peace newsletter.

3. For additional information on the U.S. embargo and the debate surrounding Harlem congressman Rangel's bill for free trade with Cuba, see *CUBA Update,* 3 (Summer 1994).

4. Sandra Levinson, letter to readers, *CUBA Update,* 3 (Summer 1994).

5. Alonso Casanova, "The Cuban Economy," keynote address presented at sixth confer-

ence of North American and Cuban Philosophers and Social Scientists, University of Havana, June 13, 1994.

6. Quoted in Carole Brightman, "Cuba on My Mind: Island against the Stream," *The Nation*, 7 March 1994, 298–301.

7. Ibid., 300.

8. The legal and civil rights that Americans are entitled to do not currently include economic rights such as employment at adequate wages, comprehensive health care, affordable housing and food, all of which are entitlements in Cuba.

9. Ricardo Alarcón, conversation with author, Havana, June 1994.

10. Casanova, "The Cuban Economy."

11. Isel Rivero y Méndez, "Cuban Women: Back to the Future?" *Ms.*, 3, no. 6 (1993): 15–17.

12. In the 1980s, the Reagan administration began a systematic policy of accusing Cuba of gross human-rights violations. For reports on human-rights abuses of political prisoners during the mid-1980s until the Guantánamo Bay detention of Cuban boat people, see Amnesty International reports.

13. "Gender, Race, and Class," 5th Encuentro de Filósofos Norte Americanos y Cubanos, University of Havana, June 1993.

14. Argiris Malapanis and Aaron Ruby, "Cuban National Assembly Debate Measures to Deal with Formidable Economic Crisis" (in three parts), *The Militant*, 4, 11, 18 April 1994.

15. Casanova, "The Cuban Economy."

16. Malapanis and Ruby, "Cuban National Assembly Debate Measures."

17. Elsa Agramonte, conversation with author, Havana, June 1994.

18. Casanova, "The Cuban Economy."

19. Federación de las Mujeres Cubanas, personal communication.

20. Agramonte, June 1994.

21. Osvaldo Cárdenas, conversation with author, Havana, June 1993.

22. Pedro Pérez Sarduy and Jean Stubbs, "Introduction: The Rite of Social Communion," in Sarduy and Stubbs, eds., AFROCUBA: *An Anthology of Cuban Writing on Race, Politics, and Culture* (Melbourne, Australia: Ocean Press, 1993).

23. Cárdenas, June 1993.

24. Peter Passell, "Sun and Sin in Cuba," *New York Times Magazine*, 2 November 1993, 66–67.

25. CUBA *Update* 3 (Summer 1994), back cover.

26. Pablo Rodríguez, Paula Izquierdo, Ana J. García Lazara Carrazana, and Lourdes Serrano, discussions at 1993 session on "Gender, Race, and Class." See note 13 above.

27. Alarcón, June 1994.

28. Edwin Hoffman and Jo Ann Hoffman, "Race Relating in Cuba," CROSSROADS (October 1993).

29. Lisa Brock, "Back to the Future: African-Americans and Cuba in the Time(s) of the Race," *Contributions in Black Studies* 12 (1993–94):9.

30. Rosemari Mealy, *Fidel and Malcolm X: Memories of a Meeting* (Melbourne, Australia: Ocean Press, 1993).

31. Ricardo Alarcón, address to the National Press Club, Washington, D.C., 18 November 1994.

5 / Border-Crossing Alliances: Japanese and African American Women in the State's Household

1. "Snapshots," *Ms.*, November/December 1993, 83.

2. Carole Marks, "Limits to the Decline of White Supremacy," paper presented at the Uni-

versity of California's conference on Japan's Challenge to U.S. Economic Hegemony, Santa Barbara, Calif., April 1990.

3. Ronald Takaki, "The Harmful Myth of Asian Superiority," *New York Times,* 16 June 1990, 21.

4. Jessica Hagedorn, "Asian Women in Film: No Joy, No Luck," *Ms.,* January/February 1994, 78–79.

5. See Marks, "Limits to the Decline," 19.

6. See Ernest Allen Jr., "Waiting for Tojo: The Pro-Japan Vigil of Black Missourians, 1923–43, *Gateway Heritage* 16, no. 2 (1995): 38–55. The latter position was critiqued at the April 1990 conference on Japan's Challenge to U.S. Economic Hegemony.

7. Nicholas D. Kristof, "Japan Confronting Gruesome War Atrocity," *New York Times,* 17 March 1995, A1.

8. Tim Weiner, "C.I.A. Spent Millions to Support Japanese Right in 50's and 60's," *New York Times,* 9 October 1994, A1.

9. A significant number of Japan's 700,000 ethnic Koreans resided in the Kobe and Osaka regions devastated by the recent earthquake.

10. George A. DeVos and William O. Wetherall, "Japan's Minorities: Burakumin, Koreans, Ainu and Okinawans" (London: Minority Rights Group, 1983).

11. James Sterngold, "Minorities Suffer Heavy Loss in Quake-Ruined Japan City," *New York Times,* 24 January 1995, A1, A6.

12. Akio Morita, *The Japan That Can Say "No": The New United States-Japan Relations Card* (Washington, D.C.: U.S.G.P.O. Supt. of Docs., 1989, 1990); Shintaro Ishihara, *The Japan That Can Say "No": Why Japan Will Be First among Equals* (New York: Simon and Schuster, 1991).

13. Edson W. Spencer, "Japan as Competitor," *Foreign Policy* (Spring 1990).

14. Kan Ito, "Trans-Pacific Anger," *Foreign Policy* (Spring 1990).

15. Muto Ichiyo, "Class Struggle and Technological Innovation in Japan since 1945," *International Institute for Research and Education* 5 (1987).

16. *Femintern: A Japanese Feminist Quarterly* 2 (1974). Reprinted in *International Feminism: Networking against Female Sexual Slavery,* ed. Kathleen Barry, Charlotte Bunch, and Shirley Castley (New York: International Women's Tribune Centre, 1984).

17. Mary I. Buckley, "Encounter with Asian Poverty and Women's Invisible Work, UPDATE 11 (Winter 1990). (Publication of RENEW [Religious Network for Equality for Women].)

18. UNICEF's *1989 State of the World's Children* (New York: United Nations, 1989).

19. Annette Fuentes and Barbara Ehrenreich, *Women in the Global Factory* (Boston: South End Press, 1987), 41.

20. Marks, "Limits to the Decline."

21. Evelyn Nakano Glenn, "The Dialectics of Wage Work: Japanese-American Women and Domestic Work, 1905–1940," *Feminist Studies* 6, no. 3 (1980).

22. For every one hundred hours of household labor that American women perform and every one hundred hours of leisure time they acquire, American men perform fifty-one hours of household labor and acquire one hundred and forty-one hours of leisure time (*Women in the World Atlas*). As Mary Buckley explains, "women and the subsistence work of neocolonial peoples are treated as if they were invisible as far as the economy of the world is concerned. It is as if they were a part of nature, like water, air and land." Buckley, "Encounter with Asian Poverty."

23. Sam Roberts, "Black Women Graduates Outpace Male Counterparts," *New York Times,* 31 October 1994, A12.

24. Marks, "Limits to the Decline."

25. Morrison G. Wong and Charles Hirschman, "Labor Force Participation and Socioeconomic Attainment of Asian-American Women," *Sociological Perspectives* 26, no. 4 (1983).

26. Fuentes and Ehrenreich, *Women in the Global Factory,* 48.

27. Nina Lassen, "United Nations Efforts to Eradicate Slavery and Slavery-Like Practices," in *Peoples for Human Rights: Special Issue on International Efforts to Eliminate Discrimination* (Tokyo: International Movement against All Forms of Discrimination and Racism, 1989).

28. *Femintern;* see note 17 above.

29. Jacqui Hunt, "Japan Hasn't Stopped Exploiting Asian Women," *New York Times,* 22 September 1994, A26.

30. Yayori Matsui, "Why I Oppose Kisaeng Tours," in *International Feminism: Networking against Female Sexual Slavery.*

31. Ibid.

32. Hunt, "Japan Hasn't Stopped Exploiting Asian Women."

33. Bernice Johnson Reagon, "Coalition Politics: Turning the Century," in *Home Girls: A Black Feminist Anthology,* ed. Barbara Smith (New York: Kitchen Table Women of Color Press, 1983), 359.

6 / Anita Hill, Clarence Thomas, and Gender Abstractions

1. An earlier version of this chapter appeared in Robert Allen and Robert Chrisman, eds., *Court of Appeal: The Black Community Speaks Out on the Racial-Sexual Politics of Thomas vs. Hill* (New York: Ballantine, 1992).

2. Allen and Chrisman, *Court of Appeal;* Toni Morrison, ed., *Racing Gender and Engendering Justice* (New York: Pantheon, 1993).

3. Lisa Jones, "The Invisible Ones: The Emma Mae Martin Story, the One Thomas Didn't Tell," *Village Voice,* 12 November 1991, 27.

4. Editorial, *City Sun,* 16–22 October 1991, 1.

5. One of the more interesting accounts is *Strange Justice: The Selling of Clarence Thomas,* written by *Wall Street Journal* reporters Jane Mayer and Jill Abramson (New York: Houghton Mifflin, 1994). They argue that Republican leaders crafted and financed a campaign for marketing Thomas, which included galvanizing support among African American leaders. Ironically, however, as an anti-affirmative-action and anti-civil-rights Reagan supporter, Thomas himself had no ties to black progressive organizations or civil-rights groups.

6. Even among white women, there is no monolithic woman's voice or vote. Senator Nancy Kassebaum (Rep., Kans.) voted for Thomas's confirmation while Barbara Mikulski (Dem., Md.) voted against it.

7. Margaret A. Burnham, "Thomas with Valor Can Get Us Out of This Impasse," *Boston Globe,* 12 October 1991, 23.

8. bell hooks, "Must We Call All Women 'Sister'?" *Z Magazine,* February 1992, 19–22. Critiques such as hooks's were sometimes censored in mainstream feminism. For instance, Emily Bass, in "Doubting Thomas" (*Women's Review of Books,* 10, no. 3 [December 1992]: 1, 3–4), reviewed three books on the Hill-Thomas hearings but failed to mention Allen and Chrisman's *Court of Appeal,* which included essays by prominent black women and men who supported Thomas, as well as essays by black feminists who believed Hill but were critical of her conservative politics.

9. Jones, "The Invisible Ones."

10. "African American Women in Defense of Ourselves" (paid advertisement), *New York Times,* 17 November 1991, 53.

7 / Symbolic Rage: Prosecutorial Performances and Racialized Representations of Sexual Violence

1. Ida B. Wells, *A Red Record: Lynchings in the United States* (Chicago: Donohue & Henneberry, 1895). Reprinted in Ida B. Wells Barnett, *On Lynchings* (Salem, N.H.: Ayer, 1990).

2. Ida B. Wells, *Crusade for Justice: The Autobiography of Ida B. Wells* (Chicago: University of Chicago Press, 1970).

3. Maya Angelou, *I Know Why the Caged Bird Sings* (New York: Random House, 1969); Wells, *Crusade for Justice.*

4. Having read my mother's story, I now partly understand her oft-repeated admonitions about people who "hide in the bushes" and the reason why, after her children left home, she chopped the great shrubs in the front of the house down to spindly, carrot-like stalks.

5. Walter Van Tilburg Clark, *The Ox-bow Incident* (New York: Random House, 1940).

6. Hortense Spillers, "Mama's Baby, Papa's Maybe: An American Grammar Book," *Diacritics* 17 (Summer 1987): 65–81.

7. Zillah Eisenstein, discussion at the annual meeting of the American Political Science Association, September 4, 1994, New York.

8. In this section, both Tikki and Norma are pseudonyms.

9. Paula Giddings, *Where and When I Enter: The Impact of Black Women on Race and Sex in America* (New York: William Morrow, 1984), 37.

10. Ibid., 38.

11. Suzanne Ross, conversation with author.

12. Toni Morrison, *Playing in the Dark: Whiteness and the Literary Imagination* (New York: Vintage, 1993), 17.

13. John D'Emilio and Estelle B. Freedman, *Intimate Matters: A History of Sexuality in America* (New York: Harper & Row, 1988), 297–98.

14. Sander Gilman, *Difference and Pathology: Stereotypes of Sexuality, Race, and Madness* (Ithaca, N.Y.: Cornell University Press, 1985), 25.

15. Frantz Fanon, *Black Skins, White Masks,* trans. Charles Lam Markmann (New York: Grove Press, 1967), 166.

8 / Coalition Cross Fire: Antiviolence Organizing and Interracial Rape

1. An earlier version of this chapter appeared in "Media Convictions, Fair-Trial Activism and the Central Park Case," *Z Magazine,* February 1992, 33–37.

2. Cited in *Black Women in White America: A Documentary History,* ed. Gerda Lerner (New York: Pantheon, 1972), 205.

3. Rick Hornung, "The Case against the Prosecution," *Village Voice,* 20 February 1990, 32.

4. Craig Wolff, "Youths Rape and Beat Central Park Jogger," *New York Times,* 21 April 1989, B1.

5. Michelle Hammer, "Memory, Myth and the Jogger," *Newsday,* 21 June 1990, 72, 74.

6. "Crime and Punishment: Was the Jogger Defendants' Sentence Fair?" *Phil Donahue Show,* 14 September 1990 (transcript # 3034).

7. Timothy Sullivan, "Jogger Juror Threatened to Block Verdict," *Manhattan Lawyer,* 3, no. 21 (October 1990): 1, 25–27.

8. Elombe Brath, "The Media, Rape and Race: The Central Park Jogger Case," NOBO: *A Journal of African American Dialogue* 1 (Winter 1991): 1–3.

9. Carole Agus, "Salaam's Mom Also Waits for Evidence," *Newsday,* 18 July 1990, 3, 25.

10. "Group of Blacks Sees Hiring Bias by Morgenthau," *New York Times,* 2 August 1990, B3.

11. Hornung, "The Case against the Prosecution," 32.

12. During police interrogations before his trial, George Whitmore reportedly signed a sixty-one-page false confession.

13. Erica Munk, "Body Politics at Its Worst," *Village Voice,* 31 July 1990, 11, 15.

14. Joy James, "The Myth of the Black Rapists," *Village Voice,* 14 August 1990, 14 (letter).

15. Angela Davis, "Rape, Racism and the Myth of the Black Rapist," in her *Women, Race and Class* (New York: Random House, 1981), 172–201.

16. For a discussion of Smith's reconstruction of Wells as a counterfeminist and Alice Walker's portrayal of her as a somewhat paranoid race woman, see Joy James, "Sexual Politics: An Anti-lynching Crusader in Revisionist Feminism," in my *Transcending the Talented Tenth: Black Leaders and American Intellectuals* (New York: Routledge, 1996).

17. For an incisive critique of the antiblack backlash following Simpson's acquittal, see Alexander Cockburn's column "Beat the Devil," *Nation*, 30 October 1995, 491–92.

9 / "Discredited Knowledge" in the Nonfiction of Toni Morrison

1. An earlier version of this chapter appeared in "Politicizing the Spirit: 'American Africanisms' and African Ancestors in the Essays of Toni Morrison," *Cultural Studies* 9, no. 2 (May 1995): 210–25.

2. Toni Morrison, "Rootedness: The Ancestor as Foundation," in *Black Women Writers*, ed. Mari Evans (New York: Doubleday, 1984), 342.

3. Tsenay Serequeberhan, *African Philosophy* (New York: Paragon House, 1991), xxii.

4. bell hooks, *Yearning: Race, Gender and Cultural Politics* (Boston: South End, 1990), 131.

5. Toni Morrison, "Unspeakable Things Unspoken: The Afro-American Presence in American Literature," *Michigan Quarterly Review* (Winter 1988): 18.

6. John Mbiti, *Traditional African Religions and Philosophies* (London: Heineman, 1969), 79.

7. K. Kia Bunseki Fu-Kiau, *The African Book without Title* (Cambridge: Fu-Kiau, 1980), 62–63.

8. Morrison, "Unspeakable Things," 33.

9. Ibid., 32.

10. The Garner story appears in Angela Davis (*Women, Race and Class*, 21), who is quoting from Herbert Aptheker, "The Negro Woman," *Masses and Mainstream* 11, no. 2 (February 1948): 11–12.

11. Morrison, *Playing in the Dark*, xi.

12. Morrison, "Rootedness," 343.

13. Ibid.

14. Ibid.

15. Fu-Kiau, *The African Book*, 62.

16. Sweet Honey in the Rock, "Ella's Song," on *B'lieve I'll Run On. . . , See What the End's Gonna Be* (Ukiah, Calif.: Redwood Records, 1977).

17. Sweet Honey in the Rock, "Fannie Lou Hamer," *B'lieve I'll Run On*.

18. Angela Davis, *The Autobiography of Angela Davis* (New York: Random House, 1974); Davis, *Women, Race and Class*.

19. Vincent Harding, *There Is a River: The Black Struggle for Freedom in America* (New York: Random House, 1983).

20. Morrison, *Playing in the Dark*, 17.

21. Morrison, "Unspeakable Things Unspoken," 18.

22. Morrison, *Playing in the Dark*, 12.

23. Bernice Johnson Reagon, "'Nobody Knows the Trouble I See'; or, 'By and By I'm Gonna Lay Down My Heavy Load,'" *Journal of American History* 78, no. 1 (June 1991): 111–19.

24. Morrison, "Rootedness," 339.

10 / Teaching, Intersections, and the Integration of Multiculturalism

1. Sections of an earlier version of this chapter appeared in *Feminist Teacher* (5, no. 3 [Spring 1991]) and *The Black Scholar* (23, no. 2 [Fall 1993]).

2. Patricia Hill Collins, "The Social Construction of Black Feminist Thought," *Signs: Journal of Women in Culture and Society* 14, no. 4 (Summer 1989): 754.

3. Peter L. Berger and Thomas Luckmann, *Social Construction of Reality: A Treatise on the Sociology of Knowledge* (Garden City, N.Y.: Anchor Books, 1967).

4. Mbiti, *Traditional African Religions and Philosophies;* Paula Gunn Allen, *The Sacred Hoop: Recovering the Feminine in American Indian Traditions* (Boston: Beacon, 1986).

5. Bernard Lonergan, INSIGHT: *An Understanding of Human Knowing* (New York: Philosophical Library, 1970).

6. Thomas S. Kuhn, *The Structure of Scientific Revolutions* (Chicago: University of Chicago Press, 1962).

7. Antonio Gramsci, *The Prison Notebooks,* ed. and trans. Quintin Hoare and Geoffrey Nowell Smith (New York: International Publishers, 1971).

8. Arendt, *The Human Condition.*

9. bell hooks, *Ain't I a Woman?* (Boston: South End, 1981), 194–95.

10. Rutledge M. Dennis, "Socialization and Racism: The White Experience," in *Impacts of Racism on White Americans,* ed. Benjamin P. Bowser and Raymond G. Hunt (Beverly Hills, Calif.: Sage, 1981).

11. Jon Michael Spencer, "Trends of Opposition to Multiculturalism," *The Black Scholar* 23, no. 2 (1993): 2–5.

12. Ahmad, *In Theory;* Lewis Gordon, *Her Majesty's Other Children: Philosophical Sketches from a Neocolonial Age* (Landham, Md.: Rowman and Littlefield, forthcoming).

13. Samir Amin, *Eurocentrism* (New York: Monthly Review Press, 1989), vii.

14. Sara Diamond, "Endowing the Right-wing Academic Agenda," *Covert Action Information Bulletin* 38 (1992–93).

15. Phillip Harper, Margaret Cerullo, and E. Frances White, "Multi/Queer/Culture," *Radical America* 24, no. 4 (1993).

16. Ibid.

17. Ibid.

18. bell hooks, "Culture to Culture: Ethnography and Cultural Studies as Critical Intervention," in her *Yearning,* 131.

11 / Gender, Race, and Radicalism: Reading the Autobiographies of Native and African American Women Activists

1. An earlier version of this chapter first appeared in *Feminist Teacher* 8 no. 3 (1995): 129–39.

2. I thank Rebecca Gould, Joanne Lehrer, and Jenna Magruder (hereafter identified as RG, JL, and JM, respectively) for permission to quote from their course papers.

3. Patterson, *We Charge Genocide,* xi.

4. Allen, *The Sacred Hoop,* 190.

5. Annette Jaimes, ed., *The State of Native America* (Boston: South End, 1992).

6. Kuhn, *The Structure of Scientific Revolutions.*

7. Marable, *How Capitalism Underdeveloped Black America;* Jaimes, *The State of Native America.*

8. Marlon Riggs, *Ethnic Notions* (California Newsreel, 1987; video); *In the Image of the White Man,* Public Broadcasting Service documentary.

9. Mary Crow Dog, with Richard Erdoes, *Lakota Woman* (New York: HarperCollins, 1990); Anne Moody, *Coming of Age in Mississippi* (New York: Dell, 1968); *Bravehearted Woman:*

Annie Mae (Brown Bird Productions, 1980; video); *Eyes on the Prize II: Nation of Law?* (Blackside Productions, 1989; video); Angela Davis, *Autobiography of Angela Davis* (New York: Random House, 1974); Rigoberta Menchú, *I, Rigoberta Menchú: An Indian Woman in Guatemala* (London: Verso, 1984); *When the Mountains Tremble* (New Yorker Films, 1983; video); Assata Shakur, *Assata: An Autobiography* (London: Zed, 1987); Domitila Chungara, *Let Me Speak!* (New York: Monthly Review Press, 1978); *Interview with Assata* (Gil Noble, *Like It Is*, 1988; video).

10. Marable, "Groundings with My Sisters," in his *How Capitalism Underdeveloped Black America*, 100.

11. Annette Jaimes with Theresa Halsey, "American Indian Women: At the Center of Indigenous Resistance in North America," in *The State of Native America*, 311.

Conclusion: United Nations Conventions, Antiracist Feminisms, and Coalition Politics

1. Manfred Nowak, Jacqueline Smith, and Leo Zwaak, "Editorial," *Netherlands Quarterly of Human Rights: Rights of Women* 6, no. 4 (1988): 3.

2. Ibid.

3. Environmental Defense Fund, pamphlet/poster, 1994.

4. UNICEF, *Report on the State of the World's Children*.

5. Barbara Wein, "Defusing the Bomb," *The Mobilizer* (Spring 1986): 12.

6. Henry Kissinger and Cyrus Vance, "Bipartisan Objectives," 911.

7. Women's Coalition for Nairobi, *Petition to the U.S. Delegation*, in author's papers.

8. Although the *New York Times* ran an article on the petition, its most prominent coverage featured articles by and about Betty Friedan, who described herself sitting under a baobab tree with "Third-world revolutionaries" and other women at her feet, listening attentively as she held court "like an African elder" or "tribal chief." African, Latin American, Asian, and Arab women at the Nairobi conference, however, received minimal coverage. Betty Friedan, "How to Get the Women's Movement Moving Again," *New York Times Magazine*, 3 November 1985, 85; and Elaine Sciolino, "As Their 'Decade' Ends, Women Take Stock," *New York Times*, 10 July 1985, A1.

9. "Black Women in the Academy: Defending Our Name, 1894–1994," January 1994 petition, in author's papers.

10. Justices O'Connor's and Marshall's excerpted opinions were reprinted in Linda Greenhouse, "Court Bars a Plan Set Up to Provide Jobs to 'Minorities,'" *New York Times*, 24 January 1989, A1, A19.

11. In the 1989 interview, Norton, then also an adviser to presidential candidate Jesse Jackson, advocated a "wait-and-see" attitude toward the civil-rights practices of president-elect George Bush. Bush had recently attended a black church service in honor of Martin Luther King Jr. Day, a holiday that his predecessor had vehemently opposed. Others besides Norton took a less sanguine position to the new president; the Christic Institute, for example, called for Bush's impeachment before his inauguration, citing his role in the Iran-Contra hearings, CIA gun-running, drug smuggling, and assassination plans as just grounds to impeach.

12. Francis Boyle, "The Hypocrisy and Racism behind the Formulation of U.S. Human Rights Foreign Policy," 86–87.

13. Women for Racial and Economic Equality and Women's International Democratic Foundation, testimony to the UN Commission on Human Rights, Geneva, January 1989, in author's papers.

14. Freedom Now testimony, in author's papers.

15. Ibid.

16. Margaret Wadstein, "Implementation of the UN Convention on the Elimination of All Forms of Discrimination Against Women," General Recommendations 5 and 6, UN Doc. A/43/38.

Index

Joy James teaches courses on politics, feminism, and critical race theory in the Department of Ethnic Studies, University of Colorado at Boulder. She is coeditor (with Ruth Farmer) of *Spirit, Space, and Survival: African American Women in (White) Academe* (1993); author of *Transcending the Talented Tenth: Black Leaders and American Intellectuals* (1996); and editor of *The Angela Davis Reader* (London: Blackwell, forthcoming).

Angela Y. Davis is professor at the University of California at Santa Cruz. She is the author of *Women, Race, and Class* and *Women, Culture, and Politics.*